THE WESTERN INVASIONS
OF THE PACIFIC
AND ITS CONTINENTS

THE
WESTERN INVASIONS
OF THE
PACIFIC AND
ITS CONTINENTS

A STUDY OF MOVING FRONTIERS
AND CHANGING LANDSCAPES
1513–1958

BY

A. GRENFELL PRICE
C.M.G., D.LITT. (ADELAIDE)
M.A. (OXON.), F.R.G.S.

OXFORD
AT THE CLARENDON PRESS
1963

Oxford University Press, Amen House, London E.C.4

GLASGOW NEW YORK TORONTO MELBOURNE WELLINGTON
BOMBAY CALCUTTA MADRAS KARACHI LAHORE DACCA
CAPE TOWN SALISBURY NAIROBI IBADAN ACCRA
KUALA LUMPUR HONG KONG

PRINTED IN GREAT BRITAIN
AT THE UNIVERSITY PRESS, OXFORD
BY VIVIAN RIDLER
PRINTER TO THE UNIVERSITY

PREFACE

THE use which scholars are making of *White Settlers in the Tropics* and *White Settlers and Native Peoples* has encouraged me to complete the trilogy by publishing this study of the invasion of the Pacific territories by the Western whites, who, with their accompanying diseases, animals, plants, institutions, and ideologies, created a vast panorama of moving frontiers which produced some of the greatest changes of physical and cultural landscape that mankind has witnessed. As in the previous books, the scope of the inquiry is wide, but I have used the researches of leading authorities on the various topics, and have tried to guard against sweeping generalizations. Even so, any conclusions must be regarded as tentative, and as bases for future research.

In spite of these difficulties it seems necessary that in an age of intense specialization, historical geographers should sometimes scan the whole picture that is evolving with the growth of information on the invasions of the Pacific by the Western whites, and the immense and revolutionary consequences of these movements. Many details of the picture must remain crude, and even unpainted, pending further study, but research, particularly recent research, has produced sufficient knowledge to justify an attempt to outline certain aspects of the subject. It is, however, difficult and even dangerous for an historical geographer to try to correlate the results obtained by experts in fields as widely separated as history, geomedicine, geobiology, and geopolitics, so I am deeply grateful to those who have read this book in manuscript in order to guard me against technical mistakes.

Nearly forty years of travel and research in many Pacific territories have created obligations to governments, institutions, and fellow workers which cannot possibly be acknowledged in detail. I would, however, thank those who afforded the assistance needed to complete the present book.

The French Government provided in 1955 very generous

facilities in their Caribbean and Pacific islands, while the Rockefeller Foundation, the American Geographical Society, the Royal
Geographical Society, the Royal Institute of International Affairs,
the Royal Tropical Institute, Amsterdam, the New Zealand
Government Archives, and the Bishop Museum, Honolulu, all
aided my research.

Turning to the assistance afforded by experts, I am particularly
grateful to Professor James Prescott, F.R.S., formerly Director of
the Waite Agricultural Research Institute, University of Adelaide,
to Professor C. E. Carrington of the Royal Institute of International Affairs, who read the whole manuscript, and to Dr.
Stuart K. Hetzel, Dean of the Faculty of Medicine in the University of Adelaide, and the late Mr. D. C. Swan, Department
of Entomology, the Waite Institute, who checked the chapters
on geomedicine and geobiology. In or of the United States, Professor Carl O. Sauer of Berkeley and his colleagues, Professor
J. J. Parsons and Mr. W. Borah, Professor Karl J. Pelzer of Yale,
Professor D. W. Meinig of Utah, and Mrs. Wilma B. Fairchild
of the American Geographical Society, were very helpful, as
were in England Professor R. O. Buchanan of the London School
of Economics, Dr. B. G. Maegraith, Director of the Liverpool
School of Tropical Medicine, and Mr. C. F. W. R. Gullick of
Oxford. In Australia I am indebted to the anthropologists, demographers, and geographers of the Australian National University,
and to the geographers of the University of Adelaide. In these
universities I owe particular thanks to Professors O. K. H. Spate
and G. H. Lawton, to Mrs. Ann Marshall, and to my son, Dr.
Charles A. Price.

As always, however, the chief acknowledgement must go to
my wife, Kitty Pauline Price, whose companionship, encourage-
ment, and generosity have been leading factors in my travel and
research.

                                          A. GRENFELL PRICE

University of Adelaide
1 February 1962

CONTENTS

List of Plates   viii

Introduction   I

I. The Pacific and its People before the Invasions   6

II. The Invaders and their Resources   24

III. Conquest and Colonization   43

IV. The Human Invasions—Settler Colonization   62

V. The Human Invasions—Sojourner Colonization   103
    A. East and South-east Asia   103
    B. The Pacific Islands   120

VI. The Moving Frontiers of Disease   143

VII. The Moving Frontiers of Animals and Plants   176

VIII. Geopolitics and Security in the Pacific   202

Summary and Conclusion—The Results of the Invasions   215

Notes   222

Index   229

LIST OF PLATES

I. Indian recovery and acculturation in the United
States: Navajo Indians' motor-cars outside their
Meeting House, Window Rock, Arizona   *facing page* 52

II. Indian survival in Peru: Indian population as a percentage of total population (1940)   ,,   74

III. Map illustrating population increase in eastern
Siberia   ,,   88

IV. Major populations of the world, 1750–1940   ,,   101

V. Effects of British sojourner colonization in Fiji. The
geographical distribution of Fijians and Indians
(1946)   ,,   132

VI. Disease amongst the American Indians in the sixteenth century   ,,   144

VII. Pacific: Malarious areas   ,,   148

VIII. Hospital admissions for malaria, Australia and New
Guinea, 1942–3   ,,   166

IX. Advance of exotic flora. Pasture map of south
Australia   ,,   194

X. Defeat of an exotic pest by an exotic control. Destruction of prickly pear by *Cactoblastis*, Queensland, 1928–9   ,,   196

XI. New Zealand: Exotic animals and birds, including
pests   ,,   197

INTRODUCTION

THE Western invasions of the Pacific, which occupied the four and a half centuries from about 1513 to 1958, rank with the most important events in the history of mankind, for although human beings, particularly the peoples of Asia, have wandered, fought, and plundered throughout the seven seas and all six habitable continents, their movements were on a comparatively small and slow scale until recent times. In later years, however, the scientific and industrial revolutions and the advances in technological science enabled human populations to move in vast numbers, carrying with them their diseases, plants, animals, institutions, and other cultural possessions, some of which were transported deliberately, while others accompanied their hosts as uninvited guests and frequently became unmitigated pests. By extending F. J. Turner's magnificent conception of moving frontiers of the invaders flowing across the United States, we can picture how other moving frontiers of Western peoples and cultures swept across the lands and waters of the Pacific, leaving in their wake changes which were in many cases vast and permanent. Amongst these changes none were more striking than the changed landscapes which the Westerners effected by their purposeful or accidental movements of animals and plants. It is true that authorities such as Carl Sauer have rightly emphasized the immense alterations which primitive man effected by means of fire, by the grazing of domestic animals, and by soil erosion.[1] In all probability, however, these alterations did not occur with the almost unbelievable speed with which modern man changed the landscapes of many regions by the use of his scientific implements and techniques—processes of destruction and creation that have received more and more recognition since the pioneering work of George P. Marsh.[2]

[1] Carl O. Sauer in W. L. Thomas, ed., *Man's Role in Changing the Face of the Earth*, Chicago University Press, 1956, pp. 54–56.

[2] G. P. Marsh, *Man and Nature*, republished as *The Earth as Modified by Human Action*, New York and Florence, various editions from 1864 to 1885.

Equally striking were the advances of Western cultures or ways of life. Western diseases were in many lands leading factors in the early conquests, but when Western medical science gained control, its virtues led to an immense and, in many regions, a perilous increase in the numbers of both the indigenous peoples and the exotics. Not least important were the moving frontiers of Western ideology, for in spite of the strong and sometimes unconquered resistance of religions, customs, and traditions, these frontiers created, transported, and changed landscapes of human thought, while the practices, which followed the development of scientific knowledge, revolutionized, or are revolutionizing, the numbers and cultures of mankind in almost every region of importance.

This thesis will not recount the often told story of how and why the Western invaders swarmed in their European homelands, nor retell the well-known history of their conquest of almost all the territories which surround the Pacific. It will, however, touch on certain aspects of the invasions which have perhaps received insufficient emphasis. These include the adoption by the Europeans of the lateen sail from the Arabs, the compass and gunpowder from the Chinese, and Christianity from the Jews—Asian cultural features without which the invasions might never have taken place. The thesis will also explain the important part played by the advance of various types of geographical knowledge—knowledge of the general system of winds and currents, of historic and new diseases, and of the results of exchanging mammals, insects, and plants between the Old World and the New World discovered by the whites.

From the regional viewpoint the book divides the Pacific and its territories into six immense areas over each of which the invasions presented important similarities, even while differing in many respects. These divisions are: Latin America, English-speaking America, Australasia, Siberia, eastern Asia with South-east Asia as a sub-type, and the minor islands of the Pacific.

In Latin America, English-speaking America, Australasia, and Siberia the Westerners found vast territories which, although they showed geographical differences, provided in considerable measure climates suitable for white settlement, immense industrial resources, and indigenous peoples who were comparatively few in numbers, politically divided, and militarily weak. In these lands the invaders were able to build up vigorous communities of permanent settlers who, with the outstanding exception of the Siberians, became in many cases independent political units and in some instances great and powerful nations which, in instances such as the United States, Australia, and New Zealand, acquired for reasons of security, commerce, or philanthropy, their own empires in the Pacific.

As the book may seem unbalanced, I must stress that I have not retraced the growth of these new Western peoples in well-known cultural aspects, such as the development of rural and urban civilizations, of industries, of institutions, and of ideologies. These have been efficiently portrayed by historical geographers in excellent works, many of which are cited later in the book. I have, however, dealt in some detail with a number of interesting, but less emphasized, regions, such as Alaska, Siberia, and tropical north Australia, particularly as these are of considerable geopolitical importance owing to their situation on the borders of an awakened and aggressive Asia, egged on by semi-Asiatic Russia.

In contrast to these regions of Western settlement were the lands which possessed tropical climates unsuitable for the whites, or dense indigenous populations, or, in many cases, combinations of both. Here in East and South-east Asia, and in certain Pacific islands, the Westerners could become no more than exotic sojourners, engaged for the most part as military conquerors, administrators, traders, planters, miners, or Christian missionaries, but inculcating, particularly during the last century, Western ideologies and techniques which were of fundamental importance. In a number of cases the white influence transformed small and often warring states, such as those of India or Indonesia, into great political units, in which national feeling developed strongly, while their medical science prolonged the length of life, and helped certain Asian peoples to become the most numerous groups on earth. At the same time the introduction of exotic plants and animals, capitalism, plantation systems, Christianity, democracy, communism, law, education, the emancipation of women, and, above all, the technological results of scientific knowledge, effected changes in the culture—the way of life—of many communities. So great and rapid were the advances that, when the peoples of Japan, China, and other Asian nations acquired modern weapons by manufacture or by purchase from the divided whites, they had little difficulty in securing the retreat of the Western peoples who, enervated or enlightened by fear or philanthropy, had in many cases been preparing to hand over the white man's burden to races whom, in some instances, they had trained for the task.[1]

Later chapters will examine that Western colonialism which is now bitterly criticized, and an effort will be made to reach an impartial judgement. It can be emphasized, however, that colonialism was an historic system practised by the peoples of Europe, Asia, and northern Africa, and not a Western invention to oppress Asiatics. Then again the period of Western colonialism was but a brief interlude in the Asian attacks on other peoples. From the fall of Constantinople to Pearl Harbour was less than five centuries, and even in those centuries the age of strong Western pressure on countries such as China, Japan, India, and Burma did not exceed the period 1850–1950. Finally, while in some aspects colonialism was humiliating and detestable, in others it wrought much good, and this brings to the forefront the most important point of all—the fact that while the political supremacy of the West has ended, or will probably end throughout Asia and the Pacific Islands, certain features of Western culture remain and are likely to increase. Whether or not the new ways of life will be free and democratic or tyrannic and communistic is undecided, particularly as the Asian peoples have long been accustomed to despotism, so that authoritarian governments, enforcing planned and scientific economies, may give them rapidly and effectively those higher living standards which perhaps loom larger than individual freedom or religious belief. Meanwhile, the whites seem well entrenched in the Americas, and less well rooted in

[1] I do not know of any general work which attempts to examine advancing and retreating frontiers of various types, together with certain changes of landscape. For relevant works see p. 222, note A. J. H. G. Lebon's *An Introduction to Human Geography*, London, 1952, includes important information on the extension of various types of human settlement, and of flora, fauna, and parasites.

Siberia and Australasia, towards which Asian expansion may again take place. The effects of atomic warfare between the Russian and North American heartlands, which are repeating the disunity of the early white invaders, are unpredictable, but Lord Russell and other authorities believe that man has reached such heights of scientific knowledge and technical efficiency that he can commit self-destruction by the misuse of powers which could produce inestimable benefits. Meanwhile the invasions have opened wide vistas to the geographer. Man needs further knowledge of the historic peoples and cultures of the Pacific, but even more important is knowledge of the new races and cultures which are coming into being, and which offer the student many virgin fields of research. Information is needed in all these fields. As yet we have little scientific data on the new races which are evolving in many parts of the Americas and in many Pacific islands. Ecologists have made some studies of the plants, mammals, and insects which moved with the invaders, and anthropologists have done much research on ancient cultures, but as yet there has been little study of the mixtures that are now coming to pass. The way lies clear for further vast extensions of knowledge. One can, indeed, envy those who will go farther and see the fuller light.

I

THE PACIFIC AND ITS PEOPLE
BEFORE THE INVASIONS

Definitions

As indicated in the introduction, this study of Western expansion draws most of its material from the Pacific and its surrounding continents, which contain geographical regions so vast and so numerous that little excuse is needed for the fact that comparatively few references are made to the invasions and their impacts on Africa and on the Asiatic regions outside the Pacific hinterlands. Various writers have offered various definitions of the Pacific. Some have confined the area to the ocean, together with arbitrary selections from its islands. Others have gone farther and included most of the continental territories which surround the ocean.[1] A book which deals with Western expansion, particularly in the Pacific, must define the area in its widest sense, for it is difficult to separate the historical geography of human groups which adjoin one another across continental watersheds, and it is equally difficult to discount the racial, economic, and other ties which, both during and after the invasions, bound the exotic migrants to their motherlands outside the area. Thus it is impossible to examine the

[1] Many authorities have dealt with various aspects of the Western advance and retreat and with the culture status of invaded peoples when the movement began. Useful for reference where relevant is *Man's Role in Changing the Face of the Earth*, edited by W. L. Thomas, Jr., Carl O. Sauer, Marston Bates, and Lewis Mumford (with bibliographies). There are many works on the invaded peoples in detail. For general reference to these, particularly to the Asians and the American Indians, see A. L. Kroeber, *Anthropology*, New York, 1923 and 1948. His research is well known and reliable. Some of the many publications which cover the American Indians are set out in A. Grenfell Price, *White Settlers and Native Peoples*, C.U.P., 1949. C. R. H. Taylor, *Bibliography*, Polynesian Society, Wellington, N.Z., 1951, includes the principal research on Polynesians, Melanesians, and Micronesians. For recent views on the Australoids and Tasmanoids see J. B. Birdsell, p. 11, n. 2 below.

story of California, British Columbia, or Siberia without considering the links between these territories and their distant 'Heartlands' within the continents, and, similarly, one cannot discuss Burma, Indonesia, or Indo-China without giving due weight to their historical connexions with Britain, France, and Holland. Similarly, no study of Pacific islands such as the Philippines, Tahiti, Samoa, or New Guinea, can neglect the ties which connect them, not merely with Western peoples outside the Pacific, but in some cases with new empires, or shall we tactfully say 'commonwealths'—the United States, Australia, and New Zealand—that the Western peoples established in or around the Pacific itself.

Topography and climate

The Pacific presents an immense canvas of land and water. It contains the largest and deepest of oceans, an ocean dotted with innumerable islands in the west and south, and surrounded by a vast horseshoe of lands which extend from Australia north, east, and south, to the tip of the South American continent. The ocean itself covers some 10,000 miles from east to west, and 9,000 from the Arctic to the Antarctic—a total area of some 69 million square miles, or about a third of the surface of the earth. The land masses, including Asia, occupy some 36 million out of a world land surface of 57 million square miles. Yet, prior to the invasions, the whole area, save for parts of Asia, was completely unknown to Europe. Such an immense expanse naturally embraces the majority of types of topography, soils, and climates, with their various biological effects, while the vast distances have, and still have, even in an air age, profound influence upon human communications and economics. No attempt will be made to analyse the geographical phenomena which have been discussed in many texts, but frequent references will be given to the geographical background of the invasions when these are examined later in the book.

The great size, the horseshoe rim of continents, and other geographical features of the Pacific have had, and still have, a profound influence on human life and its concomitants. First, the larger land masses and the larger areas of temperate climate lie in the Northern Hemisphere which, in consequence, offers greater potentialities for Western settlement than the lands in the south. Second, the topography of the region is peculiar in that the drainage area around the ocean embraces only 7·5 million square miles, or about a quarter of the territory draining into the Atlantic. In other words, the mountains of eastern Asia, of eastern Australia, and of western America are very often close to the coast, a fact which has produced difficulties in land communication, and has increased the isolation of some of these regions. In the west of the Americas the location of the Rockies and Andes produces very narrow coastlands which carry relatively small populations, but on the Asian side of the ocean the mountains in many areas lie farther from the shoreline and are disrupted by immense rivers whose valleys, together with alluvial coastal plains, support some of the largest human agglomerations on earth. For these, and for other reasons which will be discussed later, East and South-east Asia with their islands such as Japan, the Philippines, and Indonesia contain some 800 million people, or approximately one-third of mankind.

A third feature of the Pacific is the fact that the ocean itself contains innumerable islands, some rising from the depths, others lying on the continental shelves. A highly important factor in the historical geography of the white invasions and of the Asian invasions which preceded them was that most of the important island groups are situated on the wide Asian and Australasian continental shelves, whereas the eastern or American side of the ocean, which descends rapidly into deep waters, is almost bare of island groups. It has even been said that the important Hawaiian Islands, although nearer to America than to Asia, are in reality a frontier of the latter continent. Fortunately for the Western world, the course of historical geography ran otherwise, and the American United States, rather than Eurasian Russia, controls the islands—a matter of fundamental importance in present-day geopolitics (Chapter IV).

In contrast to the almost empty eastern Pacific, the central region is studded with islands which, though generally small in size, have some economic value and are of great importance for sea and air transport. A small-scale map gives the impression that these groups, and the individual islands within them, are in close proximity, but when one traverses the region one realizes that the intervening distances are often very great. Farther west, the shores of Asia and Australia are fringed with volcanic arcs containing islands of considerable human importance. These include Japan, the Philippines, and Indonesia, and, to the south, the very large island of New Guinea, which has been a barrier rather than a link between Asia and Australia owing to its mountainous terrain, its tropical climate, and its savage inhabitants. The most southerly of these arcs terminates in the partly volcanic islands of New Zealand, situated on the edge of the South Pacific deeps.

At this point one is tempted to turn aside to the realms of geology, biology, and other sciences and discuss problems such as the criticized Wallace and Weber boundaries between Asia and Australia—boundaries which denote phenomena that possibly did much to determine the distribution of men, animals, and plants in the remote past, with the result that the invaders faced different biological conditions in various regions; for example, the wealth of Asian flora in food potentiality can be contrasted with the scarcity of Australian economic plants.[1] Interesting as are these phenomena, they are highly complex and can best be examined from a more regional and detailed aspect.

The climate picture, too, can be referred to only in brief. The vast area contains almost every variety of climate, save that of the Polar regions, and these variations have had immense effects on the number and distribution of the indigenous inhabitants and hence on the invading exotics. Standard texts and maps explain the climatic zones which succeed one another from the Equator to the Poles on both sides of the ocean, but it must be remembered that although climate has an outstanding influence on human life and activities, many other factors—location, topography, soils, mineral resources, and non-environmental diseases—are of great importance.[2] We must also remember that there is a converse to

[1] E. D. Merrill, 'The Correlation of Biological Distribution with the Geological History of Malaysia', *Pan Pacific Science Congress* (Australia), 1923, Melbourne, vol. ii, pp. 1148 seq.
[2] A. Grenfell Price, *White Settlers in the Tropics*, New York, 1939, ch. i.

the influence of the environment on man—the influence of man on his environment. This fact, which George P. Marsh was, perhaps, the first to stress prominently in his famous book *The Earth as Modified by Human Action*, is becoming more and more evident as civilization and technological strength advance. The Panama Canal zone presents a fundamental lesson of the way in which Western peoples can defeat a tropical climate and the diseases of a tropical environment if their economic resources are sufficiently great.[1] This growing human strength is not, however, limited to the tropics. In many other zones where, in the past, man had no important servant save fire, he has recently been using technological power to force forward his frontiers and to change, in many places completely, the natural landscape.[2]

The peoples of the Pacific—Asia, Australasia, and the Islands

This book will not attempt to discuss in any detail the origin or racial characteristics of the Pacific peoples when the white invasions began, although recent research in geology and in dating by lead, flourine, or carbon-14 has greatly increased our knowledge of sub-man or of *Homo sapiens* in various areas.[3] Setting aside such questions as the age and character of the famous discoveries in Java and China, we can note the opinions of very recent authorities like A. D. Krieger in North America and E. D. Gill in Australia, that men have lived in these continents for periods of, perhaps, 12,000 to 18,000 years, during which there were considerable changes both in glaciation and in ocean levels. Thus Carl Sauer quotes authoritative information as to the presence of pleistocene man in the United States up to 12,000 years back, when, owing to greater glaciation, the seas were about a hundred feet lower than at present, and he also notes the views of Dr. Sellards that even prior to the days of these bison hunters, there were in North America elephant hunters who lived upon extinct

[1] *W.S.T.*, ch. xi.
[2] Omer C. Stewart, 'Fire as the First Great Force Employed by Man', in W. L. Thomas, op. cit., p. 115.
[3] P. T. de Chardin, 'The Antiquity and World Expansion of Human Culture', in W. L. Thomas, op. cit., pp. 103 seq.; R. Moore, *Man, Time and Fossils*, London, 1954, ch. 18.

game of the remote past. Further carbon-14 tests are throwing increasing light on this subject. Thus A. D. Krieger writes:

My conclusions are: in the overall picture of man in the New World, nothing has been established as to the time of initial entry; that this could have occurred at almost any time during the Wisconsin glaciation if not earlier (suitable game being present at all times and the crossing of the Bering Straits being no problem whenever the sea lowered enough to provide a land bridge or froze over); that cultural material is already on hand which is older than any of the projectile points popularly thought to mark the oldest American occupation; and that, beginning with the oldest known projectile points (Clovis fluted and Sandia), a general cultural sequence can be established. This began at least 12,000 years ago, possibly as much as 18,000.[1]

Similar developments have occurred in Australia, a continent which man may have entered at least 15,000 to 20,000 years ago. Carbon tests from a deposit at Lake Colongulae in Western Australia give an age of 13,700 B.P., but the immense human deposits in Tasmania may far precede the age of any mainland deposit. When the Westerners arrived, the island was inhabited by a Murrayian-negroid people, now unfortunately extinct, and although there are theories that these people arrived by canoe from Melanesia and lost their culture, it is now practically certain that they occupied Australia before the later Australoid peoples, the Barrineans and Carpentarians, and crossed Bass Strait by canoe or raft at a time, perhaps some 8,000 years ago, when the ocean level was lower and the distances between the various islands in the strait less great.[2]

It is a striking fact that on the eve of the white invasions, the Pacific was largely inhabited by Mongoloid groups, who were the predominant peoples in the coastlands from Indonesia to the Bering Strait, and possibly the only type on the American side,

[1] Carl O. Sauer, 'Early Relations of Man to Plants', *Amer. Geog. Review*, Jan. 1947, and 'The End of the Ice Age and its Witnesses', ibid., Jan. 1957; A. D. Krieger in A. L. Kroeber, ed., *Anthropology Today*, Chicago University Press, 1953, p. 241.

[2] The most recent authoritative work on the prehistory of the aboriginal peoples of Australia and Tasmania is that of J. B. Birdsell, *The Racial Origin of the Extinct Tasmanians*, Records of the Queen Victoria Museum, Launceston, Tasmania, 1948.

although authorities are not in complete agreement on this point. A. L. Kroeber, whose work is cautious and reliable (he refused to accept the Piltdown man), set out the classifications of various anthropologists, and has expressed the opinion that the Mongoloids can be divided into the Mongolians proper of East Asia, the Malaysians of the East Indies, and the American Indians, including the Eskimos, there being no great difference between the types. Furthermore, he considers that the Mongoloid proper, with his oblique Mongolian eye, is the most extreme and latest type.[1]

Various parts of the great continental horseshoe contained small groups of different and possibly earlier peoples who had drifted or had been driven to geographically sheltered regions or to the edge of the periphery. Thus Tasmania, New Guinea, the Philippines, and the Malay peninsula all contained groups of Negritos or of oceanic Negroes, while Australia, the Celebes, and the Malay peninsula harboured Australoids, who, like the hairy Ainus of Japan, appeared to have Caucasian affinities.

Kroeber, Keesing, and other scientists have sought to explain the bewildering miscellany of peoples who followed one another and fought or inter-bred in South-east Asia, and in the lands which stretch southwards to Tasmania and eastwards in the Pacific. Negritos, Ocean Negroes, Melanesians, Tasmanoids, Australoids, and Indonesians, some with Caucasoid affinities, were followed into the area by Malayan stocks such as the Protero and Deutero Malay, who mingled with the earlier peoples or drove them to remote areas and to the islands of the Pacific. Hence Indonesia became primarily Malay though subject to Indian and Chinese influences. Remote Australia retained its Australoid peoples, and even more remote Tasmania guarded a few Tasmanoid folk, who, Birdsell believes, were possibly a Murrayian-negroid mixture. The Black Islanders, or Melanesians, occupied wild New Guinea and the islands south of the Equator to Fiji, while the Micronesians or Tiny Islanders, a wide mixture of Indonesian, Malayan, Australoid, and negroid stocks, spread out into the island groups to the north. The most interesting people of all, the Polynesians, or Many Islanders, pushed out in remarkable voyages to occupy the

[1] A. L. Kroeber, *Anthropology*, New York, 1923, p. 44.

islands within the immense ocean triangle whose apexes lie in New Zealand, Hawaii, and Easter Island. While authorities such as Keesing consider that these mysterious and fascinating people came from the Malayan islands about the opening of the Christian era, Heyerdahl, of *Kon-tiki* fame, has tried to prove that some came from America. Kroeber, with his customary caution, concedes that the Polynesians may have spread out in two waves of migration during, perhaps, the fifth and tenth centuries B.C., but he believes that, although the land of their origin may have been Java, its location is uncertain and concludes as follows: 'Something of the mysteriousness, which the discoverers felt, continues to attach to the origin and history of this people and is deepened by the fact that the affiliations of their racial type remain ambiguous.'[1]

Amongst the most important works on the diffusion of the Pacific islanders are: Peter Buck, *Vikings of the Sunrise*; T. Heyerdahl, *American Indians in the Pacific*; and A. Sharp, *Ancient Voyagers on the Pacific*. Buck, a distinguished anthropologist, himself part Maori, puts forward the general anthropological view that the diffusion was eastwards across the ocean and that canoe-voyagers reached America and brought back the sweet potato to the islands. Heyerdahl contends that the diffusion was westwards from America, basing his opinions on evidence which includes his own *Kon-tiki* voyage. Sharp's contribution is to emphasize the possibly accidental nature of the canoe voyages. We will show later that botanists, such as E. D. Merrill (see Chapter VII of this book), stress the Asian character of the Pacific vegetation at the time of the invasions.[2]

The East Asian peoples

In 1500 China represented the highest degree of development throughout the Pacific. Here, in cool or warm temperate environments, long-established Mongoloid groups had developed cultures which were in some ways more advanced than were those of the invading peoples. There were, however, substantial differences

[1] Ibid., pp. 491-2. C. Barrett, ed., *The Pacific—Ocean of Islands*, Melbourne, about 1950. This includes interesting miscellaneous information on topics such as Pacific ethnography, cartography, discovery, whaling, missions, art, and literature.

[2] For biographical detail see p. 222, note B.

in the cultures of the north and south although in both regions civilization was mainly based on agriculture. With a cooler climate and ancient trade routes to the west, northern China had developed an economic system which approached the European type—a system based on wheat, barley, millet, and horses, cattle, sheep, swine, and goats. In a warmer climate and with greater isolation, southern China, on the contrary, evolved an economic system which, like that of South-east Asia, depended primarily upon the water buffalo and rice.[1]

Disregarding legends, we find that as early as the ninth century B.C. the Chinese were a populous and stable people, settled in the lower valley of the Ho hang ho, which they had probably occupied for a long period.[2] Under the Chou, Han, and Tang dynasties they pushed out their frontiers to reach the present limits about A.D. 200. Although the country was invaded by the Mongols in the thirteenth and the Manchus in the seventeenth centuries, these conquests merely substituted one ruling dynasty for another and had little demographic effect on the composition of a fairly dense population, based on agriculture aided by irrigation works.

Chinese census returns must be regarded with grave suspicion, but they were possibly right in recording the growth of a substantial population. In the first century and a half after Christ this was recorded at an average of 63 million, or about the same figure as the Roman Empire, and under the Manchus it was alleged to have increased from 125 million in 1736 to 380 million in 1881.[3] These people adopted the Taoist, Confucian, and Buddhist philosophies. They evolved picture-writing and printing; a magnificent art in textiles, jade, and metals; and a highly organized system of imperial and bureaucratic government which constructed immense public works, such as widespread canals, and the Great Wall to protect an agricultural folk from the invasion of nomad peoples to the north-west. Nevertheless, the Chinese were an inward- rather than an outward-gazing people, and hence they failed to become a great exploring or commercial sea-power, although they evolved huge junks which navigated the south

[1] G. B. Cressey, *China's Geographic Foundations*, New York, 1934, ch. 1.
[2] Kroeber, *Anthropology*, pp. 460 seq.   [3] Ibid., p. 466.

Asian coasts and carried Chinese trade to and beyond India.[1] The excavation of a Tang period jade image at Darwin in 1879 indicates a possibility that one of the famous voyages of the Eunuchs reached the north Australian coast.[2]

Latourette summarizes the characteristics of the culture which faced the Western advances, although he describes a China of a rather later date. He writes:

Here was one of the major civilizations of mankind. It was the creation and possession of what at the dawn of the nineteenth century was the largest fairly homogeneous group of mankind. While indebted to some other cultures, notably to that of India, it was quite distinct both from the other cultures of Asia and from that of the Occident. It could not be grouped glibly, as many from other areas, notably the Occident, were prone to do, under the classification of 'Oriental'. It was as unlike the cultures of India and of Central and Western Asia as it was to that of the Occident. From it several of its neighbours had appropriated large elements. This was notably true of the Tibetans, Annamese, Koreans, and, especially, the Japanese. Yet in many ways it was a world by itself, almost as different as though it had been on another planet.[3]

North and south of this great cradle of civilization the Mongoloid peoples were less advanced. To the south, Siam, Indo-China, Burma, Malaya, Indonesia, and the Philippines consisted very largely of highly broken country, containing rugged mountains which abutted on long, deep areas of the sea, and kept the peoples of the numerous river valleys apart. As the climate was monsoonal, the rainfall was heavy, floods were frequent, swamps were common, and the forests and tropical jungles were dense. These factors perpetuated fragmentation and the isolation of the peoples in small political groups. Where, however, coastal plains or really wide river valleys supported denser populations, there was a growth of somewhat larger states. Here in Malaya, Sumatra, Java, Burma, Thailand, Cambodia, and Annam, religion, administration,

[1] F. B. Eldridge, *The Background of Eastern Seapower*, Melbourne, 1945, section 1, chs. 5 and 6.
[2] C. P. Fitzgerald, 'A Chinese Discovery of Australia', in T. Inglis Moore, ed., *Australia Writes*, Melbourne, 1953.
[3] K. S. Latourette, *A History of Modern China*, London, 1954, p. 57.

and military or even naval power gained strength. Between the fifth and the fifteenth centuries, Hindu colonists, often possessing the sea-power so necessary to a broken environment, founded empires such as that of Majaphit in eastern Java, of the Shailendras in Malaya and Sumatra, and of Cambodia in Indo-China. Here, remote from the great Asian rulers such as the Chinese and Manchu emperors, the shoguns of Japan, the Indian moguls, or the Arab caliphs, the local lords developed a species of feudal system, carried out important public or religious works, such as Angkor Wat in Cambodia or Borobudur in Java, and patronized literature and art. Hinduism, Buddhism, and later Islam entered the region, the last two developing great strength. Nevertheless, the organization of the people in tribes or villages remained the basis of a society, indestructible, yet easily cowed by small exhibitions of warlike power.

To the north of China, Korea and Japan were in a state of decadence, for although these were lands of temperate climates and Chinese cultural influences, their central governments had at this time lost control, with the result that local territorial lords exercised a cruel tyranny over populations stricken with misery and want. Farther to the north again the vast cold territory of Siberia suffered from an extremely severe climate, and large sections of the country were too cold in winter, too swampy in summer, or, in general, too dry or too rugged for close settlement. Here a sparse population of Mongoloid or Palaeo-Asiatic peoples engaged in hunting, fishing, or reindeer-breeding with some pasturing or agriculture in the south.[1] Thus, looking at the western side of the Pacific as a whole, we see that it contained in the central regions of Chinese settlement substantial populations whose culture, apart from material strength, in some ways surpassed that of the whites. To the north and south of China lay less advanced Mongoloid peoples with lower population densities and poorer cultural development. To the north and south again in remote Siberia, New Guinea, and Australia the people were few and the cultural development slight. In the extreme south-east, New Zealand was an outlier of Polynesian civilization, but although its

[1] G. B. Cressey, *Asia's Lands and Peoples*, New York, 1944, ch. 21.

soils were fertile and its climate temperate, the inhabitants were still in the Neolithic stage of development.

The American peoples

The American or eastern side of the Pacific presented in 1500 some remarkable similarities to and contrasts with the Asiatic. In the first place the two American land masses were smaller than Eurasia, and were not only separated from the Old World, but were themselves connected merely by a narrow and rugged isthmus which, even in 1958, lacked complete rail or road communication between the continents. Then again, in both North and South America the western coastal plains were very narrow and were separated by vast mountain barriers from the eastern regions where the St. Lawrence, the Mississippi, the Amazon, and other rivers provided some of the finest inland waterways on earth. Again, unfortunately for man, the economic animals of the Old World, with the exception of the dog, had either failed to reach the Americas, or, like the elephant and horse, had become extinct. The llama, alpaca, vicuna, and the untameable buffalo were poor substitutes for horses, cattle, water-buffalo, and sheep. The American Mongoloids were, however, amply provided with foodstuffs, for, although the continent lacked grains such as wheat and rice, maize was so widely distributed that Indian civilization has been somewhat misleadingly called a 'maize civilization', while many of the foodstuffs which Europe imported and valued most highly—potatoes, sweet potatoes, beans, tomatoes, squash, cocoa, and the narcotic tobacco—were in use.[1] Nevertheless, the cultures of the Ameroid peoples were less advanced than those of the Chinese or Europeans. They had reached the Bronze Age and were evolving some interesting art and architecture, but they failed to produce the wheel, or the use of iron or steel, and in general are regarded as having been about 3,000 years behind Europe.[2]

The influence of the environment on man is particularly clear in the four regions in which the American Indians achieved what

[1] Kroeber, *Anthropology*, ch. 13; W. L. Schurz, *This New World*, New York, 1954, ch. ii; *W.S.N.P.*, ch. i.
[2] *W.S.N.P.*, pp. 6–8.

was probably their most advanced cultures. Mexico (the Aztecs), Peru, Ecuador, Bolivia, and Chile (the Incas), and Colombia (the Chibchas), all possess hot climates which are modified by the presence of high plateaux. Only the Mayas, an exceptionally talented people, were forced to demonstrate that, as in Java or Indo-China, civilization could evolve and flourish in tropical lowlands. Their 'Old Empire' reached its zenith between A.D. 400 and 600, and their 'New Empire' had declined when the whites arrived. The causes of this dissolution of Maya culture are one of the greatest of historical mysteries, and various authorities have attributed them to climatic changes; the impoverishment of the soil by maize-eating peoples, soil erosion, yellow fever; or the creation of antonomous and warring cities of 30,000 to 40,000 people, supporting themselves in the nearby fields whose produce had to be transported by human labour.[1] Nevertheless, before their decline, these tropical people discovered the use of the zero, evolved a system of writing and a vigesimal system of counting, devised a far more accurate calendar than that of the Spanish invaders, and were skilled architects.[2] Of the plateaux peoples, the Toltecs, and after them the cruel and aggressive Aztecs, moved from arid regions in the North American south-west, and developed the wet and productive Mexican plateau from about the time of Christ. The Incas and Chibchas evolved somewhat similar agricultural civilizations on the plateaux of western South America, and these cultures have been described as practical and material, whereas those in Mexico were more intellectual and spiritual in type.[3]

The Chibchas, the intermediate link in the middle American chain of civilizations, were isolated people engaged in sedentary agriculture in the remote high cordilleras. They possessed the political organization, priesthood, temples, and agriculture of Mexico and Peru, but had no striking individual traits. The Incas conducted an amazing achievement, for they built an extensive civilization in a territory which would seem to be as unsuited to

[1] H. H. Bartlett in W. L. Thomas, op. cit., pp. 694–5; H. R. Carter, *Yellow Fever*, Baltimore, 1931, Part III, ch. 5.

[2] Kroeber, *Anthropology*, pp. 370 seq.   [3] Ibid., p. 380.

economic prosperity and political unity as any that could be imagined. In their long and narrow mountain empire which extended north and south for 2,000 miles, they developed a fine system of roads, irrigation ditches, suspension bridges, and massive buildings. At the same time they acquired skill in the working of non-ferrous metals, in modelling colourful pottery, and in weaving textiles from cotton and from the wool of the alpaca, which they domesticated. When the Western invaders arrived, however, the Inca, like the Aztec Empire, had passed its zenith.[1]

To the north and south of these four zones of fairly advanced culture the standards of civilization declined, as they did to the north and south of the Chinese agglomeration. South of the Quechua and Aymaras linguistic families, which comprised the Inca Empire, lay the fierce and virile Araucanians of southern Chile, a forest-dwelling people who practised agriculture to a limited extent. South again lay the peripheral region of Patagonia into which, as on the south-west of the continental horseshoe, marginal groups had been forced. Here, in a cold, bleak, and forbidding environment, peoples such as the tribes of Tierra del Fuego remained highly primitive hunters and fishers. Darwin, in his scathing description, stated that he believed this people to be intellectually superior to the Australoids, but inferior in their acquirements.[2]

Northwards of Mexico the North American continent spreads out fanwise to form the southern regions of the United States with their warm, temperate, or even arid climates. This was the gateway through which the more advanced Mexican influences pushed north. Here a comparatively small area of arid lands supported the interesting Pueblo peoples, cliff- or city-dwelling folk, engaged in agriculture and skilled in the production of pottery and textiles.[3] North again, in spite of the good temperate climate and natural resources, the cultural levels were lower, although there were wide variations, for example between the

---

[1] Ibid.

[2] Charles Darwin, *A Naturalist's Voyage*, London, 1889, ch. 10, p. 280.

[3] E. L. Hewett, *Ancient Life in the American South West*, Indianapolis, 1930; E. E. Dale, *The Indians of the Southwest*, University of Oklahoma Press, 1951.

backward Californians, who seem to have become lodged in an isolated pocket, and the Iroquois of the eastern hinterlands, who carried maize culture far to the north-east and evolved a quite advanced system of government.[1]

In general, however, the American Indians, throughout most of the two continents, were nomadic hunters and fishers, who in many places practised some agriculture, and, when the invaders arrived, were still grouped in hundreds of small tribes which spoke about 150 different languages.[2] Kroeber points out that there were curious resemblances between the northerly and southerly tribes of the continents, as could be expected from the fact that they inhabited similar and hard environments. The peoples of Patagonia, northern Canada, and California were all backward, and were little influenced by the advanced cultures of Central America. The Esquimos alone showed notable originality in conquering their hard environment, and Kroeber hazards the opinion that they may have moved from Asia later than the other Ameroid groups.[3] He also believes that other northern cultures show Asiatic influences. The composite bow, first found in Asia 3,000 or 4,000 years ago, the skin boat, the conical skin tent, the body-armour of slats sewn into garments, are all restricted to the north of the continent, and may all prove to represent cultural importations from Asia. Nevertheless, Kroeber, like many other American anthropologists, takes the view that Old World influences were slight and that the bulk of American culture evolved on the spot.[4]

Many important estimates have been made as to the probable number of American Indians when the invaders arrived, and although the wide variation in such estimates indicates the difficulty of the problem, the question is discussed in Chapter IV because it is highly important owing to the effects of varying aboriginal population densities on the course of the conquest in the creation of the new groups of mixed peoples which evolved. Of the highly conservative estimates at the lower end of the scale we can reject that of Kroeber, who considered that there were

[1] *W.S.N.P.*, ch. i.   [2] Kroeber, *Anthropology*, pp. 98–101.
[3] Ibid., p. 390.   [4] Ibid., p. 392.

about 3 million Indians in Mexico and Central America, about 3 million in the Inca Empire, and some 2·5 million in the rest of the continent, a total of some 8·5 million.[1] At the higher end of the scale, H. J. Spinden and other authorities greatly multiply these figures. Spinden, for example, believes that there are now fewer Indians in the New World today than there were at the coming of the Europeans, and that about A.D. 1200, the halcyon epoch of far-flung trade during the maximum expansion of wet-land cultures, the number of the red race may have been from 50 to 75 million. Of the 'midway' authorities, Rosenblat states that there were 5·6 million Indians from the Rio Grande to Panama, and 6,785,000 in South America. If to these figures we add Mooney's careful estimate of 1 million north of the Rio Grande, we get a total of 13,385,000. This, however, seems rather too conservative, for S. F. Cook and L. B. Simpson, using Spanish military, clerical, and other estimates, gave the population for 'all Central Mexico' alone as 11 million.[2] We shall see that although many early observers in many parts of the world tended to exaggerate aboriginal numbers, it is possible that too little emphasis has been placed on the destructive factors of the invasions such as disease. It is quite clear, however, that while the aboriginal peoples were too few to defeat the invaders as did the people of China, their numbers were sufficient in the central parts of the Americas to create substantial mixed populations. Very different was the case in the more northerly and southerly lands where in regions of low native population and densities, and temperate climates, the exotics destroyed or absorbed most of the aboriginals, as happened in other regions of temperate climate and small population density—Siberia, Australia, and New Zealand.

As noted above, the circumstances are such that in most cases we are dealing with guesses rather than estimates, but authorities

[1] For references to estimates of Indian population numbers, see *W.S.N.P.*, pp. 211 seq.: H. J. Spinden's estimate is in *Amer. Geog. Review*, Oct. 1928.

[2] Estimate of Indian population numbers by recent authorities include A. Rosenblat, *La Población indígena de América desde 1492 hasta la actualidad*, Buenos Aires, 1945, p. 21, quoted in International Labour Office, *Indigenous Peoples*, Geneva, 1953, pp. 617 seq.; S. F. Cook and L. B. Simpson, *The Population of Central America in the Sixteenth Century*, University of California Press, 1948, p. 38.

have held that when the Western peoples arrived in the various Pacific regions, there may have been 63 million people in China; at least 18 million Indians in the Americas; 2·2 million Melanesians; 1·1 million Polynesians; 300,000 aboriginals in Australia; and 100,000–200,000 Maoris in New Zealand. I cannot find any estimates for Siberia, nor would the character of the early Russian invasions make estimates either easy or reliable.[1]

It is also important to realize that even when authorities quote population figures for countries such as Japan or Java at a much later date than 1500, their figures will be very low in comparison with present-day totals because the great increase in certain Pacific populations was comparatively recent. Thus the Rockefeller Report of 1950 gives the population of Japan about 1639 at only 18 million, the population of Java in 1816 as only 5 million, and the population of the Philippines as late as 1903 at only 7·6 million.[2] We must remember, however, that in considering the period of A.D. 1500 we are in general dealing, even in Europe, with small groups, for by comparison with modern times the populations of the invading countries, such as the Spain of the Catholic monarchs, or of Elizabethan England, were also small.[3]

One must give warning against an overemphasis of population densities or any other one factor in a consideration of the pre-invasion period. Distance, climate, resources, the state of political, cultural, and economic development, and, not least, religious, psychological, and other non-material phenomena, all enter the field and create almost bewildering complications. Nevertheless, a number of facts are certain, and one can draw a fairly clear picture of the general distribution and condition of the aboriginal Pacific peoples on the eve of the Western invasions.

One wishes that there was sufficient space to extend this survey to lands outside the Pacific—to southern Asia where the whites encountered advanced but divided civilizations, and to Africa,

[1] S. B. Okun, *The Russian American Company*, Harvard University Press, 1951, gives details of the Russian destruction of aboriginal peoples in their North American colonies.
[2] *Public Health and Demography in the Far East*, Rockefeller Foundation, 1950. pp. 14, 90, 100.
[3] H. Heaton, *Economic History of Europe*, New York, 1936, ch. 13.

where the Portuguese invaders and their successors found retarded and politically divided groups. The Pacific areas give, however, sufficient examples to establish the conclusions presented in this thesis, and the expert can readily apply those conclusions to lands such as South Africa or India himself.

II

THE INVADERS AND THEIR RESOURCES

WHAT historical geographer can hope to describe the Western invasions—the soul of Castilian Spain; the spirit of Elizabethan England; the courage and tenacity of Holland? The scientist can demonstrate the environmental advantages of the powers of western Europe. He can discuss their material resources such as timber and iron; he can note the inventive genius which produced the portolan chart, the astrolabe, or the comparatively long-range muzzle-loading cannon, but can he catch or explain the spirit of the age? Can he say why men and women would voluntarily leave Lisbon or Seville or London knowing that during weeks of travel in small, heaving vessels, in cramped space, on diets of stinking water and maggoty food, many would leave their bones in the Atlantic or Pacific oceans?

Did the Europeans face these things from a firm belief of an eternity in a Christian heaven? Did they face them for gospel, glory, or gold? Were they driven overseas by the fierceness of press gangs and criminal codes? All that the environmentalist can do is to quote the vivid writings of authorities such as de Madariaga or Schurz, and warn the student that the causes and course of the invasions must be examined on both the material and psychological planes. In such an examination the role of material factors must not be minimized, for even the most heroic stories, such as the rise and fall of Portugal, depend in great measure on material factors, often very simple factors, such as in the above case the meagre size of the country and its demographic weakness with a population of only 2 million people. It is from such aspects in particular that I will now discuss the invasions.

With the waning of the Middle Ages, five small countries of western Europe—Portugal, Spain, Holland, Britain, and France— became vigorous and aggressive nation states with similar foundations—the Roman law and some type of Christian faith—while in eastern Europe 'Holy Russia' developed some Western tendencies. The evolution was due to many factors. The Crusades, the journeys of the Polos to East Asia, the Renaissance, the Reformation, and the discovery of printing, all spread knowledge. Capitalism emerged, trade expanded, and the peoples of the European states bordering the Atlantic and the Urals pushed out to become explorers, traders, and empire-builders, for European civilization was passing from the epoch of the thalassic or inland seas to the oceanic age.

In the early stages, however, Europe was 'cribbed, coffined, and confined'—to the west by the boundless Atlantic—to the north by the Arctic, where the stepping-stones to America lay unused since the days of the Norsemen—to the south by the Sahara and Moslem Africa—and to the east by the usual groups of Asian aggressors who were making their customary attacks on the territory of their neighbours, the culprits in this case being the Turks, who broke up the Eastern Christian Empire and captured Constantinople in 1453. These Turks were by no means as 'unspeakable' as our forefathers believed, nor did their advance destroy the overland trade between Europe and the East which, in reality, was ruined by the Portuguese discovery of the sea routes to India.[1] Nevertheless, the Mediterranean city-states were declining powers, which on their death-beds handed much of their invaluable seacraft to their successors in the West. By 1500 the Tartars had made grave inroads on the Black Sea colonies of the Venetians. The Turks had already taken many of the Venetian and Genoese possessions, and, when they captured Egypt in 1517, they seized the colonies and *fondachi* which were the last hope.[2] Nevertheless, Portugal and Spain had the good sense to lean heavily, both for men and knowledge, on the Mediterranean powers. The

[1] There is a substantial bibliography covering the European powers and their resources, including delightful works on ships, navigation, and weapons, some of which are listed in notes below. Heaton, op. cit., pp. 231 seq., quoting A. H. Lybyer, 'The Influence of the Rise of the Ottoman Turks upon the Routes of Oriental Trade', in *Amer. Historical Association Report*, 1914, pp. 125–35, and *English Historical Review*, Oct. 1915.

[2] A. G. Keller, *Colonization*, New York, 1908, pp. 68 seq.

Italian brothers Vivaldi discovered the Azores and Madeira. The Polos conducted their famous journeys to China with some slight and temporary development of trade. High in the ranks of the great discoverers are Columbus, the Cabots, Pigafetta, Toscanelli, and Amerigo Vespucci, after whom undeservedly the Americas were named. Truly the rulers of the inland sea played no mean part in the transition to ocean navigation.[1]

The invading peoples

At the outset the lead was taken by Portugal, the most westerly of European powers, in an outstanding and oft-repeated story which is an epic in human history. It is sufficient to say that, although the Portuguese were a tiny community of only 2 million people, they had already evolved more consciousness of nationality than any other people in Europe. As early as the fourteenth century, King Diniz (1279-1325) repaired the damage of the Moorish wars, developed economic resources, checked the ever-growing power of the Church, laid the foundations of a supreme monarchy, and both employed Genoese shipbuilders and made an Italian the admiral of his fleet. Ferdinand IV and John I the Great followed Diniz in fostering commercial development, but it remained for Don Henriques (Henry the Navigator), 1394-1460, the son of an English Queen of Portugal, to organize the exploration of the West African coast in order to further his main interests—the defeat of Islam and the fostering of Christianity. Withdrawing from military life, he founded at Sagres, on the south-west tip of Portugal, the equivalent of a modern research institute which included an observatory, a school for the study of chart-making, and a shipyard. Seeking 'gospel, glory, gold'—one believes in that order—he combined the role of medieval knight and crusader, who sought the salvation of souls, with that of a scientific seeker of knowledge. To these he added the practical astuteness to realize that whether or not he turned the flank of Islam, a Portuguese discovery of a sea route to India would neutralize the excessive advantages held by the Italian cities, and above all, by Venice.[2]

[1] A. G. Keller, op. cit., pp. 73-74.   [2] Ibid., pp. 85 seq., with references.

Spain, the second country to enter the field, established a virile geographical and political unity on the verge of the Atlantic. When Ferdinand of Aragon married Isabella of Castile in 1469, he united his strong but small agricultural and commercial region in the east with a large central pastoral area, and when the Catholic monarchs captured Moorish Granada, they were able to control the whole of the Peninsula, excepting Portugal, which, however, was temporarily absorbed in 1580. When the Emperor Charles V succeeded Ferdinand, he brought by previous marriages to a Spain of about 7 million people the Netherlands, with their vast commerce, the Burgundian lands of the Rhine, and Milan, Naples, and Sicily, with their agriculture, secondary industries, and banking.[1]

In unity and spirit the Spaniards closely resembled their Portuguese neighbours. Centuries of warfare with alien invaders of their native soil had given them a national cohesion, a military spirit, endurance, courage, skill in arms, the love of adventurous life, and contempt for the arts of peace. With this spirit was mingled a religious fervour so fanatic that the Spanish conquests took on the pattern of crusades.[2] Also by 1580 the Peninsula had developed important industries in wool, silk, cattle, textiles, and hardware, and, blessed as she was by forests and deposits of iron ore, Spain had developed by 1580 the largest European merchant marine.

In one respect the origin of the Portuguese and Spanish invasions differed greatly. The Portuguese reached the East Indies, East Asia, and the Pacific by a far-sighted, firm, and long-enduring policy, of which men such as Diaz and da Gama were the agents. In the case of Spain, however, the Catholic monarchs, particularly Isabella, gambled on the novel ideas of the way-finding Columbus. In both cases the royal families sought 'gospel, glory, gold,' but it is fair to say that in neither case was the gospel the weakest of the three motives.[2]

There is no room here to consider the ideas and theories that underlay the search for unknown lands, which were ultimately

---

[1] Heaton, op. cit., pp. 261 seq.
[2] W. L. Schurz, op. cit., chs. iii, iv, and Salvador de Madariaga, *The Rise of the Spanish American Empire*, New York, 1947, Part I.

disclosed as southern Africa, the continents of North America, South America, Australasia, and the Antarctic, and the Pacific Islands. The theories have been discussed in many works, such as J. C. Beaglehole's brilliant introduction to the Hakluyt Society's *Journals of Captain Cook*, and, as will be shown below, the actuality was exposed, explored, and for the most part conquered and colonized with the development of European and scientific knowledge.

Portugal and Spain were followed to the Pacific by Holland, England, and France. The rise of the Low Countries from a region of water and sandy wastes to the chief shipping, trading, manufacturing, and financial area of Europe, was due to the geographical environment, to biological factors, and to inventive genius, courage, and perseverance. Situated where the Rhine and other great rivers reach the North Sea arm of the Atlantic, and in the vicinity of the Baltic, the Dutch developed both as traders and fishermen, and began exploiting the herring which had moved in their direction to the detriment of the Hanse. To conduct this fishing, the Netherlanders used large boats, called *busses*, and improved methods of salting, packing, and grading their fish, until, with a high reputation in foreign markets, they had by 1620 2,000 vessels afloat, and deserved the praise of a contemporary Dutch *bon mot* 'the herring keeps the Dutch trade going, the Dutch trade sets the world afloat'. Contemporarily with this development the new burgher class in the Netherlands expanded their commercial centres such as Antwerp, and pushed their trade northwards into the Baltic and to the ports of France, Britain, the Iberian peninsula, and the Mediterranean in the west and south.[1]

The Emperor Charles V, who ruled the Netherlands from 1515 to 1555, was at heart a Burgundian. He loved the Low Countries, and he was prepared to rule them with a light hand, but his son Philip II was a 'Spaniard of the Spaniards' who, although perhaps less a religious fanatic than as pictured by his enemies, carried out a policy of centralization, persecution, economic follies, and disastrous taxation which ruined the great commercial centre of Antwerp in Flanders and drove the more northern provinces into

[1] Heaton, op. cit., pp. 272 seq.

successful revolt. When in 1580 Philip II became King of Portugal, he recklessly attacked Dutch trade, and in 1595 seized some two-fifths of the Dutch Merchant Navy, 400 Dutch ships with 6,000 Dutch sailors, then in Portuguese harbours. In the same year Cornelius Houtman took the first Dutch fleet of four vessels to the East Indies, and, although he lost two-thirds of his men and brought back comparatively little cargo, the Dutch saw that the trade would be lucrative, dispatched other and larger fleets, and in 1602 founded the celebrated East India Company to assail and destroy the Portuguese monopoly which had existed in Malacca and the islands for almost a century.[1]

The years which followed saw England and France bring larger populations and greater resources into the field. France, with a population which possibly numbered 15 million in the seventeenth and 20 million in the eighteenth century, had expelled the English, absorbed the 'dukedoms', and expanded to her geographical boundaries. The French might well have become the leading European exotics overseas if their monarchs, like Louis XIV, had refrained from wasting their resources in European strife such as the Thirty Years War. As it was, the French encountered a stronger expanding sea-people in the English islanders, who, in the Seven Years War of 1756–63, robbed them of their principal possessions in North America and Asia.[2]

By 1500 England, like France, had seen a great advance towards material unity following on the loss of her continental possessions and feudal nobility. A new monarchy, sympathetic to trade and industry, was on the bridge, and a new nobility, largely recruited from the wealthy *bourgeoisie*, manned the ship. Although the country remained primarily agricultural and a European granary, her wool and other industries were expanding, and her forests and her copper, lead, tin, and zinc became the basis of important manufactures, such as shipbuilding and the casting of guns, which were in demand throughout Europe and other continents. In the south-east, near France and the Netherlands, London grew from a town of about 180,000 inhabitants in 1550 to one of 700,000 in 1700, when it was estimated to contain about a tenth of the

[1] Keller, op. cit., pp. 386 seq. [2] Heaton, op. cit., pp. 285 seq.

population.[1] These hardy islanders attempted to discover north-west and north-east passages to the Pacific, and fought with the Spaniards in the Americas, with the Dutch in the Indies, and with the French almost everywhere, for none of the small European nations was sufficiently powerful to conquer and police the entire New World. The English were, however, strong enough to found many important colonies for settlers which, as we shall see, became, with Latin America and Russian Siberia, the most important regions of white settlement in the Pacific areas.

Sea-power

The white invasions of the Pacific and other areas began, of necessity, as sea invasions, conducted in the main by seafaring peoples who combined the resources needed for shipbuilding and ocean navigation with the genius to convert the medieval trading crafts of the Baltic, North Sea, and Mediterranean into ocean-going sailing vessels. As noted above, the peoples who effected this were those of the European borderlands—Portugal, Spain, the Netherlands, Russia, England, and France, and the lands which they discovered and conquered were parts of Africa, east, south-east, and southern Asia, Siberia, Australasia, the two Americas, the Pacific Islands, and uninhabited Antarctica. The pattern was, however, not entirely uniform, as the Russians pushed eastwards by land and river to occupy Siberia, and their invasions did not become seaborne until they attacked the western coast of North America. Similarly, when the Western invaders had established bridgeheads on the east and west coasts of the two Americas and Australia, they became land invaders whose advances were largely determined by such environmental factors as rivers, mountain passes, and valleys, and hot and cold deserts. Nevertheless, the sea remained of fundamental importance. Its products, such as fish, furs, and whales, were for many decades a leading objective and support of the invaders. Its waters carried them to make assaults on regions such as western North America or western and northern Australia, which were remote from the main settlement zones. Ocean transport actually grew in importance in many

[1] Heaton, op. cit., ch. 14.

areas as population, migration, and commerce increased, both within and outside the Pacific, and sails gave way to the immensely greater power of steam. Even when rail and motor transport improved land communications, and later when air power and air transport created an air age which threw world security and world transport into the melting-pot, a large part of the Pacific and the borderlands remained, and still remains, dependent upon sea communications.

European sea culture

On the whole it is safe to assert that the European whites could never have invaded the Pacific and its borderlands, with the exception of north-eastern Asia, had they not developed a sea culture which included the building of ocean-going vessels, propulsion by new types of sails, cannon of low, but improved, efficiency, and instruments of navigation that enabled them to calculate direction (latitude, and later longitude) which they depicted on increasingly accurate maps. Nor might the invaders have settled so numerously in remote regions, such as Australia, if they had failed to remove the menace of sea diseases, such as scurvy, a menace which developed with the long ocean voyages. To effect these achievements the Western Europeans required racial aptitude for, and experience in, seamanship, the cultural and material incentives of religion, colonization, and trade, together with an increasing knowledge of the oceans, their winds, currents, and other physical phenomena that made the voyages possible. Finally, the invaders would have been immediately defeated in several regions, such as East Asia and parts of the Pacific, had they failed to evolve a sea culture which was superior to that of the indigenous inhabitants—the Chinese, Japanese, Koreans, Arabs, and some of the island folk. The Arabs in particular had created over many centuries a fairly advanced sea culture, which enabled them to trade westwards along the eastern shores of Africa and eastwards to South-east Asia, where they successfully exchanged Mohammedanism for spices and other oriental products.[1] In point

[1] Eldridge, op. cit., section 1, ch. 4, with references to Beazley and other authorities; G. F. Hourani, *Arab Seafaring*, Princeton University Press, 1951.

of fact, the European successes were largely due to the adoption and improvement of certain Asian inventions including the compass, lateen sails, and gunpowder.

Ships

J. H. Parry has pointed out that at the beginning of the fifteenth century European ships were 'markedly inferior in design and workmanship to the vessels used in many parts of the East; but at the close of the sixteenth century the best European ships were the best in the world'.[1] Throughout the Middle Ages the seafaring peoples of the Mediterranean had elaborated the open galley, which was primarily propelled by oars. This galley, which the Romans developed into a vessel of perhaps 500 tons, was efficient for inland sea navigation but was unsuitable for long ocean voyages. It may even be suggested that England defeated the Spanish Armada in 1588 partly because the Spaniards continued to build galleys after their victory over the Turks at Lepanto in 1571, and hence were forced to rely to some extent on merchant ships for their ocean venture against England. It is true, of course, that the Vikings crossed the Atlantic to Greenland and North America in open vessels. The Gokstad ship found near Oslo in Norway is a fine-looking vessel, but she is only 79 feet in length, 16 feet 8 inches in beam, and 6 feet 8 inches in depth. Such ships were clinker built with side planks overlapping one another. Propulsion was by a single mast carrying a single square sail, and by a number of comparatively light oars. Steering was effected by a paddle set on the starboard quarter and controlled by an athwart ship tiller. Even if we admit the contention of R. J. Russell that the Greenland voyages followed routes which would be impossible today, across seas now regularly blocked by ice, the achievements of the Vikings were too perilous to be followed by regular trade.[2]

As the age of great European discoveries approached, the Western sea peoples made revolutionary improvements in the

---

[1] J. H. Parry, *Europe and a Wider World, 1415–1715*, London, 1955, pp. 21 seq.; Boies Penrose, *Travel and Discovery in the Renaissance*, Cambridge, Mass., 1955, pp. 268 seq.

[2] R. J. Russell in W. L. Thomas, op. cit., p. 456. For Viking ships see G. S. Laird Clowes, *Sailing Ships*, London, 1952, Part I, pp. 41–44, Part II, pp. 12–13.

hulls, sailing qualities, and offensive strength of their vessels. They largely replaced the clinker with carvel construction, a method by which each plank is butted against those above and below, thus providing greater strength for the carrying of heavy guns, and they built hulls which could be pierced more safely for numerous gun ports. Another essential improvement was the introduction of a heavy rudder at the stern in place of the former side-paddle tiller, an invention which has been accredited to the Dutch.[1] Laird Clowes stated that 'the earliest seal in which the rudder is shown definitely to be hung on the stern post instead of being lashed to the quarter, is the seal of Ipswich, which has been traced back to 1200'.[2] In their hulls, however, the medieval ships remained heavy, broad, and clumsy, the warships carrying high fore and aft castles for the use of light artillery, boarding parties, and cross-bowmen. The proportion of length to breadth decreased from the days of the galleys, and sailing ships became only three times as long as they were broad. It is, however, hard to dogmatize on this subject as few pictures of ships survive, at any rate in Britain, and drawings on seaport seals, the main sources of information until the middle of the fifteenth century, were not shown in proportion owing to limitations of space. It is also very difficult to calculate the tonnage of these ships by modern standards. In the fifteenth century, warships, some 120 feet long from stem to stern post, were probably about 600 tons. The normal large fighting vessel was of 400 to 600 tons, while sea-going and ocean-going vessels of about 200 tons carried the bulk of the trade.[3]

Parry notes that, even by the fifteenth century, the Portuguese and Spanish caravels, which conducted the great explorations, were stout, handy, seaworthy, and fully decked vessels, not the tubs or cockle-shells of popular history. Nevertheless, the long voyages—in some cases of two years duration—must have been hideously uncomfortable, for the usually crowded ships were wet throughout in bad weather, and there were no adequate sleeping facilities until in later years the use of hammocks was copied from

[1] Laird Clowes, op. cit., Part I, pp. 45 seq.; Parry, op. cit., pp. 21 seq.
[2] Laird Clowes, op. cit., Part I, p. 48.
[3] Ibid., p. 59; Parry, op. cit., and Penrose, op. cit.

the American Indians. Governments and other employers seem to have made no provision of warm or adequate clothing, or for cleanliness and bathing. Indeed, in the English Navy, a man who undressed by day or night while at sea could be ducked three times from the yard arm. As a supposed precaution against fire, vessels carried on deck open tubs full of urine, while the provisions for sanitation were probably as bad as those in the ships which carried migrants to Australia as late as the early nineteenth century. A recent student of the migration to South Australia about 1840 states: 'As the only enclosed space in the steerage of most ships was a single privy for women, the Board thoughtfully issued dressing gowns to female emigrants in lieu of privacy.' Ventilation and adequate headspace were conspicuous by their absence, and over-crowding, both in warships and passenger vessels, had calamitous results.[1] Indeed, when Cook was able to work the *Endeavour* of 368 tons with only 94 people, including eleven scientists, on the voyage of 1768–71, the allowance of some 4 tons of ship capacity per person was regarded as a creditable achievement.

Sails

No less important than the improvements in shipbuilding were those made in sails, an essential advance, for, as noted above, the Western invasions were for three and a half centuries sailing-ship invasions. The revolution was amazingly rapid. In 1400 the European ship was a small single-masted vessel, limited in her voyaging by the fact that she could move ahead only if the wind was wholly or almost astern. Yet in the short space of the fifteenth century, that is by 1500, the Portuguese and Spaniards had evolved the famous *caravela latina* or *caravela redonda*, comparatively large, long, narrow, and speedy ocean-going ships equipped with three masts which carried square, lateen, or, more generally, a combination of both types of sail. The lateen rig, which enabled vessels to sail close to the wind and avoid the danger of lee shores, was vital to the invaders. In the words of Hourani, 'without the lateen, the

---

[1] Douglas Pike, *Paradise of Dissent*, London, 1957, p. 157. For general conditions in the British Navy during the seventeenth and eighteenth centuries see R. S. Allison, *Sea Diseases*, London, 1943.

European mizzen on the three-masters would have been impossible, and the ocean voyages of the great explorers could never have taken place'.[1] There were, of course, some exceptions, as when Columbus used *caravela redonda*, or square-rigged caravels, on his first voyage, but by 1500 it was the three-masted caravel with her complete rig that had developed the sea routes to India and America.

Authorities such as Laird Clowes, Hourani, Penrose, and Parry have given details of this amazing transition. The Europeans realized that, in spite of its disadvantages, the square rig enabled them to divide the total sail area into a number of small and easily handled units, and hence equipped their increasingly large ships with three masts that carried a number of comparatively small square sails. The Arabs had, however, brought from India the fore-and-aft, or lateen, rig, under which small vessels were equipped with a single mast carrying a large fore-and-aft sail suspended from a long spar whose size was limited by the size of the vessel. Realizing that this fore-and-aft rig enabled Arab vessels to sail comparatively close to the wind, the Europeans adopted it, using the area abaft the mast as a fore-and-aft mainsail.

The Portuguese and Spaniards, first in the field of ocean navigation, usually equipped their caravels with square sails on the foremast, square or lateen sails on the mainmast, and lateen sails on the mizzen, the mast nearest the stern. Penrose traces the evolution of the comparatively small caravel of 50–200 tons into the larger merchant vessel—the *naos* or ship of perhaps 400 tons—and finally into the galleon or carrack, sometimes a very large ship of 1,000 or more tons capable of carrying 1,000 people on her seven or eight decks. Thus in a single century the Westerners evolved the means to carry their conquerors and colonists throughout the seven seas. In the words of Holland Rose, 'the age long toil of designers, builders and workers of all kinds had put together that greatest of all human triumphs hitherto, the ocean-going ship'.[2]

---

[1] For the evolution of the three-masted sailing ship see Laird Clowes, op. cit., Parry, op. cit., and Penrose, op. cit. For Arab vessels see Hourani, op. cit.

[2] Holland Rose, *Man and the Sea*, Cambridge, 1935, p. 75. Rose's treatment of the evolution of the ocean-going ship is excellent.

Weapons

It was essential for the Europeans to possess a superiority in weapons if they were to conquer the Pacific, and this was particularly the case in regard to Asia. Factors such as armour were not negligible; for example it was said that the only way to kill a Portuguese soldier in his impenetrable armour was to smother him, but the all-important factor in sea warfare was the offensive weapon, and the all-important weapon was the cannon. Like the lateen sails, Europe gained fire-arms and gunpowder from the Arabs who employed them in Spain in the thirteenth century. By the fifteenth century the Westerners were using primitive cannon, as at the battle of Crécy in 1346, although it has been said that the English made their French conquests by the use of the long-bow in the fourteenth, and were driven from France by fire-arms in the fifteenth century. Parry considers that it is difficult to say who first introduced ship-borne artillery, but thinks it was the Venetians during their quarrels with the Genoese in the fourteenth century.[1] By the middle of the fifteenth century, however, most of the European fighting ships were carrying guns, and by the end of the century, when the Westerners were penetrating eastern Asia and the Americas, their vessels were armed with heavy cannon and fired broadsides through portholes. The Portuguese, the leaders of all Europe in nautical matters in the fifteenth century, seem to have been the first people to recognize the gun rather than the soldier as the main weapon in naval warfare, and to use cannon against the enemy's ships rather than against his men. Significantly, the first battles fought on the principle of sinking ships by gunfire were fought in the Indian Ocean, not in the Atlantic or the Mediterranean.[2] Yet in the end it was the English under leaders such as Drake who gained most by the conversion of the old troop-carrying warship to a mobile battery. As Trevelyan says, 'it was not the boarder but the broadside that made England mistress at sea'.[3]

In reviewing the astonishing development in the north, Clowes

[1] Parry, op. cit., p. 27; A. Manucy, *Artillery through the Ages*, Washington, 1949, for evolution of cannon and gunpowder.   [2] Parry, op. cit., p. 28.
[3] G. M. Trevelyan, *History of England*, London, 1926, p. 343.

points out that the very early cannon both on sea and land were constructed of wrought-iron bars welded longitudinally to form tubes, which were strengthened by shrinking iron hoops around them. It is a remarkable fact that many of these guns were breach-loaders, often provided with a number of barrels so that they were really the quick-firers of the period. Amongst the most interesting survivals of the times are breach-loading guns which one sees in the Doge's Palace in Venice. They are attributed to Leonardo da Vinci, and are said to have been used at Lepanto in 1571. Very interesting too are the early English breach-loaders that sank with the *Mary Rose* in the mouth of Portsmouth Harbour in 1545 and are now in the Tower of London.[1] Unfortunately for their owners, the breach-loading arrangements of these weapons were so primitive that they were almost as dangerous to their gun crews as to the enemy, against whom they had little striking power. For this reason the breach-loader was abandoned for the muzzle-loading cannon cast from a single block of brass, bronze, or iron and then provided with a bored barrel and a touch-hole for the firing of the charge. These were much more powerful weapons, and their comparatively long range with ball or grape-shot had a terrifying effect on primitive peoples in the Pacific, as Wallis proved when on discovering Tahiti he dispersed native attacks at the range of a mile.[2]

By 1509 the English were fitting this type of cannon in their larger warships. The *Sovereign*, rebuilt in that year, carried three brass culverines, a new and much heavier gun which weighed up to 4,850 lb. and threw a cannon-ball of 18 lb. Before the death of Henry VIII in 1547, a complete sequence of brass guns had been introduced and embellished with delightful names such as demi-cannon, cannon-perier, culverine, culverine-bastard, demi-culverine, saker, and minion. They were in effect the 32, 24, 18, 12, 9, 6, and 3 pounders, which attained, in brass or bronze, such a standard of excellence that they remained substantially unaltered for 150 years.[3] Even then, muzzle-loading cast-iron guns, mainly

[1] Laird Clowes, op. cit., Part I, p. 64, and Part II, p. 20.
[2] G. Robertson, *The Discovery of Tahiti*, Hakluyt, London, 1948, pp. 155-6.
[3] Laird Clowes, op. cit., Part I, pp. 62 seq., Part II, p. 20.

32, 24, 18, and 12 pounders, remained the chief offensive weapons until the nineteenth century saw the arrival of iron and steel ships, of steam, and of breach-loading guns of entirely new types, materials, construction, and size. It must be remembered, however, that although such weapons, together with steam, and later technological advances, account for the immense progress of the Western peoples during the last century of their invasions, these same inventions carried with them the seeds of white retreat when they passed into the efficient hands of Pacific peoples such as the Chinese and Japanese.

Instruments and maps

It is doubtful if the Europeans could have conquered the Pacific had they not invented, or borrowed from the Asians, several essential navigating instruments, and steadily improved the efficiency of their navigation by the construction of more and more accurate maps. The first problem, that of direction, was solved by the use and improvement of the compass which the Westerners obtained from the Chinese, probably by the twelfth century. This instrument advanced from a needle thrust through a piece of wood which floated in a bowl of water, to a pivoted needle swinging above a compass card marked with the four winds and thirty-two points. The variation of the compass was observed, but the invaders had no idea of the extent of the variation in different latitudes.[1]

Knowing the direction in which he was steering, the navigator had to make frequent estimates of his position by calculating his latitude and longitude. By the fifteenth century the Europeans were using astrolabes and quadrants which enabled them to calculate their latitude or distance north or south, from the height of the pole-star in the Northern Hemisphere, and the height of the sun at noon in the south. As the motion of small vessels made it extremely difficult to take accurate readings, the Portuguese explorers landed whenever possible. Columbus carried with him on his first voyage both an astrolabe and a quadrant which he used regularly to take pole-star sights.[2] The sixteenth century

[1] G. R. Crone, *Maps and their Makers*, London, 1953, p. 35; Parry, op. cit., p. 19; Penrose, op. cit., p. 267.   [2] Parry, op. cit., p. 20.

saw the introduction of cross-staffs and back-staffs—improved instruments.

The problem of calculating longitude, the distance east and west, was far more difficult, and until comparatively late in the eighteenth century the unfortunate navigator had no method save to reach the parallel of latitude of his desired destination and follow that parallel east or west until his goal was sighted, or, as frequently happened in the case of small islands, passed. Attempts were made to calculate distance by means of the almost wholly unreliable log which consisted of a piece of wood fastened to a long line that was divided into equal sections by knots. To calculate speed, and hence distance, the log was cast overboard, or streamed, and the speed with which the knots ran out timed with a sand-glass.[1] Needless to say, the device proved most unsatisfactory on ocean voyages, and ignorance of position frequently had disastrous consequences. In 1711, for example, when Sir Hovenden Walker lost eight ships at the mouth of the St. Lawrence through an error of 45° in the calculation of the position of the fleet, the British conquest of French Canada was probably delayed for a further fifty years. Again, a similar mistake cost Sir Cloudsley Shovel four ships and 2,000 men on the shores of the Scilly Islands.

In an effort to solve this grave problem, the English Parliament appointed a Commission, which was soon known as the Board of Longitude. This Board offered the then very large prize of £20,000 for a solution, and from 1714 to 1828 dispensed £100,000.[2] There were two means of overcoming the difficulty—astronomy and the 'lyttle clocke'. Of the first, Crone writes: 'In the eighteenth century the fundamental advances in mathematics and astronomy, initiated by Sir Isaac Newton, gradually bore fruit. The motions of the heavenly bodies were marked out so that they could be accurately predicted for long periods, and eventually published annually in the Nautical Almanac from about 1767.'[3] James Cook, and the astronomer Green, made during

[1] Parry, op. cit., p. 19.
[2] J. A. Williamson, Cook and the opening up of the Pacific, London, 1946, p. 112.
[3] Crone, op. cit., p. 142.

Cook's famous first voyage of 1768–71 frequent calculations of lunar distances with the aid of tables apparently prepared by the Astronomer Royal, Nevil Maskelyne. 'By these tables', wrote Cook in 1773, 'the Calculations are rendered short beyond conception and easy to the meanest capacity.'[1]

In spite of Cook's opinion, it was still necessary for mariners to seek some surer and more rapid method of calculating longitude than by observing the heavenly bodies from the heaving decks of small ships, when climatic conditions happened to be favourable, and then securing a result from elaborate mathematical calculations. As early as 1530 a German astronomer and mathematician had suggested the method of the 'lyttle clocke' to calculate distance east and west, but for 200 years watchmakers struggled vainly to produce a watch which, regardless of climatic changes, would retain with complete accuracy the time at the primary meridian, so that when this was compared with the time at the given position, the mariner would know his longitude. After years of labour by a number of clockmakers, an Englishman, John Harrison, devised a chronometer that was successfully tested by voyages to the West Indies. Cook used on his second voyage of 1773–6, which circumnavigated the Antarctic continent, a chronometer made by Kendall from Harrison's designs. The accuracy of this instrument was so remarkable that by the end of the three years it was only seven minutes slow. The problem of calculating longitude had been solved and, with the aid of George III, Harrison wrung from a mean and reluctant Board the greater part of their prize.[2]

A further aid to the European conquerors was the construction of improved maps. Unhappily few of these survive, but those which remain afford a valuable picture of the steady growth of knowledge which the invasions produced.[3]

Equipped with these technological advances the Western exotics

[1] R. A. Skelton, 'James Cook as a Hydrographer', *The Mariner's Mirror*, Nov. 1954, pp. 109 seq.

[2] Hugh Carrington, *Life of Captain Cook*, London, 1939, pp. 188 seq. For technical details of chronometers, including Harrison's, see F. A. B. Ward, 'Time Measurement, Part I', *Historical Review*, Science Museum, London, 1952, ch. vi.

[3] Crone, op. cit., ch. vi.

began to discover and utilize the great sea routes for sojourner and settler colonization. Also, because the invaders depended so much upon sail, they needed and secured an ever-increasing knowledge and use of environmental factors such as winds and ocean currents, a knowledge which grew steadily from the times of Columbus to those of M. F. Maury, who systematized our knowledge of ocean phenomena.[1] H. M. Wallis,[2] in a brilliant thesis on this subject, has shown that, in his first voyage, Columbus had the accidental good fortune to cross to the West Indies with the Trades and to return farther north with the Westerlies, and that Magellan was delayed so long in his Strait that he crossed the Pacific in a season when the winds, both north and south of the Equator, were favourable.[3] The growing knowledge and use of the world system of winds and currents can be traced through Diaz, Tasman, and Cook to Maury and the romantic days of the famous 'clippers'.[4] We must remember, however, that with the discovery of Siberia, the Americas, and Australasia, the invaders began to advance by land, river, and lake. Then evolved the use of exotic transport animals such as the horse, and of technological inventions, the river steamer, railway, motor, and aircraft. In Australia the invaders discovered desert Lake Eyre with horses in 1840; they examined its northern shores with camels in 1874–5, but it was not until 1951 that they solved (by the use of motor trucks, motor boats, and aircraft) the extent of its filling and evaporation.[5]

This chapter has emphasized the importance in the invasions of European sea culture—ships, sails, weapons, charts, and instruments

[1] M. F. Maury, *Physical Geography of the Sea*, London, 1870 (various editions).
[2] Helen M. Wallis, 'The Exploration of the South Sea 1519–1644,' MS. British Museum and Mitchell Library, Sydney.
[3] For Columbus and winds see Wallis, op. cit., pp. 22, 23, noting S. E. Morison, *Admiral of the Ocean Sea*, Boston, 1942. For Magellan see Wallis MS., pp. 36 seq. G. E. Nunn published his theory that Magellan crossed the Pacific by a secret route as set out in *Amer. Geog. Review*, New York, Oct. 1934. H. J. Wood in *Exploration and Discovery*, London, 1951, is inclined to support Nunn.
[4] For James Cook see definitive edition of the journals now being published by the Hakluyt Society (ed. J. C. Beaglehole), and A. Grenfell Price, *Captain James Cook in the Pacific*, New York, 1958.
[5] A. Grenfell Price in *Lake Eyre, South Australia—The Great Flooding of 1949–50*, Report of Lake Eyre Committee, Royal Geographical Society, South Australian Branch, 1955.

of navigation—and has, perhaps, underestimated that gallant, ruthless, and yet religious spirit which characterized more or less strongly all the invading nations. A. P. Newton believed that the emphasis which the medieval peoples placed upon negation and unhappiness produced in the age of discovery a reaction, during which men created a world of beautiful and marvellous dreams. Hence Columbus sought a terrestrial paradise, and believed that the Orinoco was one of its outflowing rivers. The Spaniards named California after an Indian island of romance, which lay near this earthly paradise and was very rich in gold and jewels. Quiros attempted to turn the savage New Hebrides into a 'New Jerusalem', and in spite of his failure and 'timely death', achieved a spiritual exploit that recalls the crusading era.[1] Trained by an apprenticeship of European wars, hardened by experiences at sea, equipped with new scientific knowledge, and yet still inspired by religious and missionary zeal, the Western peoples brought to their tasks of conquest and colonization the greatest forces man had so far seen.

[1] A. P. Newton, *The Great Age of Discovery*, London University Press, 1932, ch. ii, and G. A. Wood, *Discovery of Australia*, London, 1922, chs. ix–xii.

III

CONQUEST AND COLONIZATION

Definition of colonization

BEFORE I turn to the human and other biological aspects of the invasions it seems advisable to discuss briefly the forms of Western conquest and control as affected by the environmental influences which were at that time operating in the various lands. This is a matter of fundamental importance because different Western peoples, in different environments, were forced to spend different periods of time in their conquests and colonizations, which also varied greatly in character, range, and strength. These factors affected in turn the speed with which the moving frontier advanced in each particular region and the changes in the physical, human, and cultural landscapes which followed each advance.

After exploration came conquest, and after conquest colonization, but in many cases two and even three of these processes were simultaneous. For example, on his first voyage of exploration in 1492, Columbus built a fort in Haiti, and left behind him a colony of thirty-nine men whom the Indians very properly murdered, as the invaders did much evil to the inhabitants, taking, according to Oviedo, 'their wives and daughters and all that they had, at their own pleasure'.[1]

Authorities have given very many definitions of colonization and of the various types of colony, the word 'colony' always connoting an area occupied by migrants from a metropolitan power which maintains political and usually other links with the migrants. Thus A. G. Keller considers that the fundamental ideas are a movement of population and an extension of political power, and for these reasons colonization must be distinguished from both migration and conquest.[2] Harrison Church believes that the

[1] F. A. Kirkpatrick, *The Spanish Conquistadores*, London, 1946, ch. 2, p. 25.
[2] A. G. Keller, op. cit., ch. 1, p. 1.

outstanding feature of the phenomenon is the mass movement of peoples. He quotes Robequain's opinion that 'the originality of the geography of colonization lies in its study of the geographical aspects of colonial contact between the colonizers and indigenous peoples'.[1] We will see how forcibly this dictum applies to colonization in the Pacific.

It is considerably easier to define the word 'colonization' than to discover a definition which covers the very many types of colony that resulted from the process. Leroy-Beaulieu, Keller, and others have, for example, made a leading distinction between what they term 'farm colonies', which are usually conducted by migrants in zones of temperate climates, and 'plantation colonies' in which the migrants employ and exploit under plantation economies indigenous peoples in most cases in the tropics.[2] To my mind this definition, which takes its name from a main economic feature, is unsatisfactory from the geographic, the demographic, and even the economic viewpoints; for example, migrants in farm colonies have usually engaged in a wide variety of primary and secondary industries including important sea pursuits, while plantation colonies have by no means been confined to the tropics. Then again notice must be taken of innumerable colonies or posts which have been founded purely for trade or strategic purposes. As McMahon Ball has pointed out: 'The Western political control of East Asia rested mainly on sea power . . . the string of British fueling and naval bases from Aden to Hong Kong was a prominent reminder of Western military power.'[3] This dictum can be applied far and wide throughout the areas of white conquest. No brief definition of colonization can be completely satisfactory, but perhaps the least unsatisfactory is a clear-cut definition which treats the process from a demographic viewpoint and divides the types of colony into those occupied by migrant sojourners and those occupied by migrant settlers.

[1] R. J. Harrison Church, *Modern Colonization*, London, 1951, p. 13.
[2] Keller, op. cit., ch. 1.
[3] W. MacMahon Ball, *Nationalism and Communism in East Asia*, Melbourne University Press, and Institute of Pacific Relations, 1952, pp. 1, 2.

Sojourner colonization

Under the first heading come all those colonies, trading posts, and strategic points which are occupied by migrant peoples purely as sojourners—missionaries, traders, soldiers, plantation owners, and miners—temporary dwellers bent upon fulfilling religious or military duties or acquiring wealth before returning to their homelands. Those of us who have visited British, French, Dutch, and American colonial possessions in Asia, the Pacific, and the Caribbean have often been amazed by what can be termed the rapidity of the sojourner turnover—the speed with which the exotic population changes as military or trading folk come out to a colony for a term and then return home; and this applies not only in the tropics but in the temperate lands, if they are too densely inhabited by indigenous peoples for the exotics to take root. Sometimes, in the more primitive regions, the sojourner males have taken temporary wives from the natives and have left half-caste children behind them. In a few cases, such as in Java, a minority of white migrants became settlers in spite of the tropical climate and the numerous indigenous inhabitants, but such cases are uncommon and sometimes even unfortunate.[1] As Meredith Townsend wrote of India:

not only is there no white race in India, not only is there no white colony, but there is no white man who purposes to remain. . . . No ruler stays there to help or criticize or moderate his successor. No successful white soldier founds a family. No white man who makes a fortune builds a house or buys an estate for his descendants. The very planter, the very engine driver, the very foreman of works, departs before he is sixty, leaving no child, or house, or trace of himself behind. No white man takes root in India.[2]

Even where the Western exotics mingled with the indigenous inhabitants, the production of mixed bloods, at any rate in the larger and more important countries, was infinitesimal compared with the numerical strength of the native populations. Thus, on the verge of the Pacific, India contained in 1921 319 million

[1] Paul W. Van der Veur, 'The Eurasians of Indonesia—Castaways of Colonialism', *Pacific Affairs*, June 1954.   [2] *W.S.T.*, p. 14.

Asians, 113,000 Eurasians, and 156,637 whites of whom only 45,000 were women. Nor was the position of the mixed bloods satisfactory. An Indian Statutory Commission wrote in 1930 as follows: 'The [Eurasian] community has played an honourable part in developing the country and in supporting the forces of order. . . . But it is, generally speaking, a poor community. . . . It is domiciled in India and must make India its home, and it now finds itself, largely as a result of . . . the process of Indianization, exposed to the danger of falling between two stools.'[1]

I have taken these examples from India because they are striking and because they represent what has happened in almost all the main regions of white sojourner colonization both within and outside the Pacific. In 1931 the British in Malaya numbered only 17,768, or 0·4 per cent. of the population, while according to the census of 1930 the Netherlands East Indies then contained 60,727,233 people of whom only 240,417 were white.[1]

Paul W. Van der Veur of Yale set out in 1954, under the striking title of *Castaways of Colonization*, the pathetic plight of the Eurasians of Indonesia after the withdrawal of the Dutch. He stated that these people had increased in numbers from 14,000 in 1854 to 134,000 in 1930, or 56 per cent. of the total population classified as European. After Indonesia gained her independence about 100,000 Eurasians made their way from the unfriendly Indonesian environment to Holland, although the Dutch Government did not favour wholesale transplanting, as the lower strata in particular might become an undigested lump. It was evident that Holland and Indonesia were facing one of those difficult minority problems which the invasions so often produced.[2]

The main causes of the Western failure to form permanent settlements under these conditions are clear. In spite of the arguments as to the all-importance of climatic considerations, the most weighty factor was often the numbers and strength of the indigenous inhabitants. China and Japan, for example, had very large areas with excellent climates for Western settlement, yet no permanent settlement evolved. It is true that in many lands

---

[1] *W.S.T.*, p. 15.   [2] Van der Veur, op. cit.

tropical climates assisted greatly in the defeat of the whites; for example the Westerners found it difficult to establish settlements of permanent white workers in the low wet tropics excepting in a few cases such as Panama which had unusual advantages. Nevertheless, the Western exotics did succeed in establishing permanent white working settlements in the marginal tropics of Queensland and Florida, with the result that the climatologists were forced to admit that, with the development of science and its application to transport, housing, and medicine, unfavourable climates were no longer a complete barrier.[1] In reality each region must be examined from the viewpoint of local conditions, for isolation, altitude, natural resources, markets, and so forth can modify the general rule. Nevertheless, it can be said that the Western invaders failed to establish settler colonies in many regions where the indigenous peoples were numerically strong, and, as we shall see, this same strength of the indigenous peoples and other factors prevented the white sojourner colonies from becoming permanent, even where they were established.

In this field of sojourner colonization one finds that the population changes and numerical increases were most important, not only amongst the exotics but amongst indigenous peoples where the introduction of Western civilization increased the food supply and raised standards of health, more particularly by reducing the death rates and increasing the length of life. Under such conditions the population of Japan advanced from perhaps 35 million at the Meiji Restoration in 1868, to 73·1 million in 1940, and 88 million in 1954. The influence of the Dutch increased the population of Java and Madura from about 5 million in 1816 to 41 million in 1930.[2]

[1] *W.S.T.*, chs. v, vi, xi. Marston Bates comes to the same conclusions in his authoritative book on the tropics *Where Winter never Comes*, Gollancz, London, 1953.

[2] The United Nations estimated the population of Asia, without the U.S.S.R., at 1,317 million in 1953. Recent statistics throughout this book are usually taken from the United Nations *Population and Vital Statistics Reports*, Statistical Papers, Series A, vol. vii, no. 1, New York, Jan. 1955. Earlier Asian statistics are from authorities such as the Rockefeller Report, 1950; G. B. Cressey and G. T. Trewartha.

One must admit that many population statistics are unreliable and that some increases, as in China, were due less to technology and social economic organization than to the extension of land uses on traditional lines. Nevertheless, the fact that the population of Asia increased from 500 million in 1750 to about 1,300 million in 1950 was due largely to Western influences. Whether or not this increase, like the European increase of an earlier era, contributed, and will contribute, to the good of mankind as a whole is a question which lies outside the scope of this work.

Before concluding these brief comments on the human side of Western sojourner colonization, one must mention the important changes in the distribution of population which resulted from the movements of non-Western exotics such as the Negroes, and non-Western indigenous peoples such as the Chinese or Filipinos, to or within the zones of conquest. Like many examples of colonization throughout the ages, Western sojourner colonization was frequently based on various types of slavery, serfdom, and indentured or plantation labour, while free non-Western peoples, such as the Chinese or Indians, frequently migrated under the lures of gold-mining, tin-mining, or other employment in the new colonies, together with the added advantages of speedy transport, particularly with the coming of steam.[1]

Leaving the fields of population types and numbers and turning to Western commensals, one finds that a second aspect of the sojourner invasions was the introduction of Western diseases which was, of course, closely linked with population decline or increase, both indigenous and exotic. As we shall see, the whites not only spread indigenous diseases, but they introduced to non-immune peoples the diseases which afflicted the Westerners, and the diseases of the Asians and other peoples who moved, or were

---

[1] It is impossible to include the titles of the many books on this subject. Bibliographies will, however, be found in works such as Gunnar Myrdal's *An American Dilemma—The Negro Problem and Modern Democracy*, New York, 1944; W. D. Borrie, *Italians and Germans in Australia*, Canberra, 1954; V. Thompson and R. Adloff, *Minority Problems in Southeast Asia*, Stanford, 1955; D. L. Oliver, *The Pacific Islands*, Harvard University Press, 1951; H. Conroy, *The Japanese Frontiers in Hawaii—1868–1898*, University of California Press, 1953. New research is, however, constantly being published.

moved by the whites, about the Pacific. In general it may be said that, where in the zones of sojourner colonization, as in East and South-east Asia, the indigenous populations were vast and partly immune to diseases such as smallpox, the effects on these groups were slight. Indeed, it was the invading peoples, like the Portuguese, who suffered most until the advent of modern science. On the contrary, where the aboriginal peoples were few in numbers and not immune to European and Asian diseases such as smallpox, measles, tuberculosis, or leprosy, the destruction was great until the appearance of modern medicine and the establishment of some degree of immunity led to recovery and population growth. Here, as we shall see, lie important and almost virgin fields for historical research (Chapter VI).

A third feature of the sojourner colonization in the Pacific was the introduction of exotic animals, plants, weeds, and pests, a subject on which I can find no adequate general treatise, probably because I am not a zoologist or botanist. Nevertheless, Merrill, Gressitt, and others have carried out important research on various aspects of the problem such as in the Philippines and Micronesia, and it is clear that this aspect of the sojourner invasions has been of great if of varied importance. In some instances, as in the plantation areas, important plants such as sugar or rubber, and exotic animals such as cattle or pigs, have taken basic places in the economy, but it must be remembered that this fact applies more to regions of plantation type rather than to lands such as China or Japan which were already stocked with historic and basic animals and plants such as pigs and rice (Chapter VII).

Finally, it may be said that perhaps the most important aspect of Western sojourner colonization was the inflow of exotic cultures of many types; for example, ships, cannon and Christianity, in the early stages of the invasions, and later, after the scientific, industrial, and democratic revolutions, democratic or communist government, law, scientific medicine, and the application of technological science to many types of industry and transport. As a result the world saw a revolutionary transformation of countries such as Japan or Hawaii, and great alterations in life and thought, not only in lands such as Indonesia and the Philippines, which experienced conquest and plantation economies, but also in China and Thailand which maintained their independence. Some of these cultural features disappeared, or will disappear, with the departure of the Western peoples; others are undoubtedly permanent and their frontiers will spread under the guidance of Asian or even of Pacific Island folk. Indeed, it is no exaggeration to say that the cultural effects of the invasions are likely to prove the most outstanding and permanent results of Western sojourner colonization in the Pacific.

Settler colonization

Very different was the evolution of settler colonies, which were established in climates suitable to the Western peoples and in areas not already thronged by indigenous folk. In such regions the exotic could settle permanently, bring out a European wife, and rear a white family which succeeded him in the task of developing the new habitat. Here, although he utilized the native flora and fauna, he introduced from Europe and other areas suitable (or sometimes unsuitable) Old World cultures, animals, and plants. To these regions, too, he brought Western diseases which played an outstanding part in decimating the unfortunate natives, thus giving the migrants further room in which to expand their settlements, until in some cases the regions occupied grew into nations of Western type, occasionally larger and stronger than the metropolitan powers from which they sprang.

This settler colonization of the Western peoples had in general certain common characteristics. First, the incoming Europeans usually sought zones of cool or warm temperate climate with the result that their occupation was to some extent controlled by latitude and altitude; for example, even the Spanish conquerors, many with a Mediterranean background, sought regions of moderate elevation and moderate temperatures in the Central and South American tropics.[1] Second, apart altogether from conquest, the course and vigour of the occupation varied greatly with the numbers, strength, and attitudes of the indigenous peoples. Sooner or later the Westerners, with their exotic diseases and superior

[1] W. L. Schurz, op. cit., chs. i, iv.

technological equipment, defeated the American Indians who were never as numerically strong or even as politically united in their defence as were the great Asian peoples of Japan and China.[1] Nevertheless, in many regions, such as large parts of Latin America, the conquered majority largely absorbed the conquering minority, while in others, such as Mexico or Peru, the aboriginal peoples are still by no means absorbed. To this demographic phenomenon we must add the fact that the Europeans found the Indians intractable and unsuited to become slaves in plantations or mines.[2] Hence the Western settlers, like the sojourners, imported Negro slaves of many ethnic types, and later opened the doors of the various American countries to free labour from Europe and Asia. For these reasons the Americas became the outstanding racial mixing or melting-pots of recent times, and this applies particularly to Latin America where there is, in many regions, comparatively little racial or colour feeling, and where the American Indians, the whites, the Negroes, and various immigrant peoples are producing a kaleidoscope of blends. Nevertheless, Latin America is not an unhappy region. In spite of Western sneers at the occasional political instability and frequently low living standards, its inhabitants, who in certain areas are turning to advanced industrialism, proclaim with just pride that for many years the continent has remained uncursed by major wars.[3]

Throughout the one-time colonies of settlement, the progress of civilization and economic developments has proceeded to a greater or lesser extent upon similar lines. In almost all regions the whites began by exploiting the natural resources—furs in the northern United States, Canada, and Alaska; furs in Siberia; whale and fur seal products in Australia and New Zealand; and, in Latin America, the gold and other wealth of the two advanced civilizations, the Incas and Aztecs. This was the stage of moving frontiers —the invasion of settler regions by Western peoples with their diseases, animals, plants, and cultures. It was at the outset, in most regions, a brutal age: an age in which swarms of savage invading males slew, raped, plundered, and enslaved the natives or

---

[1] *W.S.N.P.*, chs. i, ii, iv.   [2] Schurz, op. cit., ch. ii.   [3] Ibid., p. 408.

decimated them with exotic diseases, after which they replaced them in some instances by hardier and more complacent slaves. On the human side, as will be shown later, the era of the moving frontier was followed by periods of missionary and scientific care for the aboriginals of certain regions, with the result that some native peoples recovered through Church protection, as in parts of Latin America, or through national and scientific protection as in the United States and New Zealand.[1] (Pl. I.)

From the geographical and economic aspects the process of invasion showed similarities in many settler regions. After occupying the coastal areas and establishing primary production at sea or on shore, the Western peoples moved their frontiers across the continents or islands in a process which began with explorations and which took, in the cases of Canada and the United States, over 200 years.[2] As the human frontier advanced, the settlers with the steel axe and other technological equipment replaced the native vegetation with exotic economic plants and weeds, and in this and in other ways created, and are still creating, changed landscapes.[3] Similar advances occurred in the field of culture. Although in some instances the invading settlers adopted native ideas and native devices, as, for example, native means of transport such as the canoe, their European cultures moved forward with their frontiers and, behind those frontiers, crystallized into changed landscapes of Western cultural devices and Western thought as is clear in the advances of Christianity and technological science. At the same time it would be foolish to underestimate the changes in Western life and outlook which pioneering conditions in new environments and borrowed indigenous cultures frequently produced. Settler regions, as unlike and as remote from one another as Latin America and Australia, saw the evolution of native and nationalistic types; for example the Latin American creole, the

[1] W.S.N.P., chs. iii, ix, x.

[2] Of the many authorities available one notes: R. H. Brown, Historical Geography of the United States, New York, 1948; J. Russell Smith and M. O. Phillips, North America, New York, 1942.

[3] For a brief summary see Grenfell Price, Presidential Address, Section 'P', A.N.Z.A.A.S., Dunedin Meeting, 1957, with references. For greater detail see numerous articles in Man's Role in Changing the Face of the Earth.

PLATE I

Indian recovery and acculturation in the United States: Navajo Indians' motor-cars outside their Meeting House, Window Rock, Arizona

Photo—U.S. Department of the Interior, Navajo Service, 1939

colonial born Spaniard, who protested as emphatically against the indignity of being classed as inferior to his metropolitan born cousin, as did the 'Dinkum Aussie' who had become in every way a genuine Australian, with interests centred in his own Pacific country and with no thoughts of Britain as 'home'.[1]

Before concluding this section I must again emphasize the importance of what may be termed the time factor over these centuries of Western invasion and colonization. The first 300 years from 1500 to 1800 must be called a prescientific or early scientific period during which the invaders were comparatively few, their resources small, their scientific development embryonic, their pressure in many regions non-existent or slight, and their progress slow. After the democratic, industrial, and scientific revolutions, and the immense growth in European population, matters became very different, and the invaders poured forth in an ever-increasing flow and strength which culminated in entirely new human phenomena, such as the leadership in world democracy and in many aspects of science passing to a one-time settler colony—the United States which developed to such an extent that they could no longer be the asylum for all mankind and hence had to close their doors to the mass migration even of European peoples. At the end of the century and a half (1800–1950), which witnessed this acceleration, the invasions had created a number of immense new nation states with huge and increasing populations and with, in some instances, horrifying means of destruction. Thus high authorities, such as A. J. Toynbee, could claim not unjustly that chaos would follow unless some one democratic or communist power conquered and subdued the whole world, or all nations handed their authority to one supreme international government equipped with the means to enforce its will for the general good.[2]

[1] Brown, op. cit., ch. 2, for the early effects of American Indians on the economic life of the Western migrants; B. Moses, *Spain's Declining Power in South America 1730–1806*, University of California Press, 1919, pp. 318–19; A. C. Wilgus, *Readings in Latin American Civilization*, New York, 1946, pp. 167–8; W. Keith Hancock, *Australia*, London, 1930, ch. iii, 'Independent Australian Britons'.

[2] A. J. Toynbee, *Civilization on Trial*, O.U.P., 1948, chs. 2, 7.

The collapse of colonialism—the political frontier in retreat

Finally, one records the little-recognized fact that the so-called, and much and often unjustly maligned, colonialism embraced both the settler and sojourner zones of colonization, and was far more important and far wider than its present popular conception— a method of tyranny and exploitation exercised by Westerners over Asiatics. In point of fact it was the settler colonies which, often under colonial born leaders, conducted those sometimes bloody revolutions that in many cases created collapses in colonialism long before the sojourner colonies in Asia and elsewhere had reached a stage when their indigenous inhabitants could revolt. Thus the Westerners of the United States gained their freedom from Britain towards the end of the eighteenth century (1776–83), while the Latin Americans won freedom from Spain and Portugal in the early nineteenth century (1810–20), although not without the support of Britain and the United States, a fact which again demonstrates the continual disagreements of the Western powers on these colonial questions. Other settler colonies such as Canada and Australia remained for many years longer in the fold, and under the then sure shield of British sea-power, but at very early dates they made it crystal clear that they remained to some extent dependent at their own desire and primarily in their own interests. The leading sojourner colonies, on the other hand, remained in a condition which may be described as one of increasing tutelage and decreasing subjection, until the complete collapse of colonialism in almost every major area after the Second World War. Writing in 1939, on the eve of that war, I was able to foretell the inevitable, at any rate in regard to white sojourner settlement in the tropics. At that time I wrote:

The progress of science has not strengthened the political position of the sojourner in the tropics. On the contrary his status has declined. Scientific food production, medicine, and sanitation are increasing the populations of many coloured nations, and education is elevating them. Modern means of communication are enabling them to place their points of view and demands for self-determination before the citizens of such white democracies as still survive. In these circumstances the grip of the sojourner ruler is loosening. The freeing of the Philippines and the trend in India indicate that some of the coloured races of the tropics will soon secure freedom, even though such freedom may immediately expose them to the domination of a new set of races, perhaps even coloured races, from the temperate zones.[1]

In less than two decades the coloured peoples of the chief sojourner colonies were to gain their freedom, while in some cases the advance of communism had already proved that freedom to be of a delusive and temporary nature. Thus, with some striking exceptions, such as parts of Latin America and the Caribbean, together with Indonesia and the Philippines, the period of real Western supremacy, the dominion over palm and pine, was remarkably brief. The Westerners never conquered large parts of Asia, while in lands such as Burma, Malaya, and Indo-China their period of true control was about a century or even less.

The fundamental point, however, is that by the time the settler and sojourner colonies did gain their freedom, a world-wide revolution in man and his culture, and in flora, fauna, and other biological factors, had taken place. The new Western settler powers, such as the United States, Brazil, and the Argentine, became in many respects stronger and more important than their parents, while efficient and often honest and disinterested Western management, together with Western scientific benefits, grouped parts of Asia and Africa into vast and densely populated nation states whose coloured inhabitants were awakening and demanding that their living standards should be raised towards those of the West.

Areas of settler and sojourner colonization

The above brief sketch of Western sojourner and settler colonization indicates that under the influence of varying factors such as climates, natural resources, and the densities of the indigenous population, Western colonization took various forms. As an example we can divide the Pacific Ocean and its continents into six major areas, each of which represents within itself a certain degree of uniformity in spite of some differences in geographical

[1] W.S.T., p. 38.

environments, in flora, in fauna, and in human types and cultures. These divisions are:

A. Latin America from the Rio Grande to Cape Horn.
B. English-speaking America from the Rio Grande to the Arctic.
C. Russian Siberia.
D. Anglo-Australasia (Australia and New Zealand).
E. East Asia, with South-east Asia as a sub-type.
F. The minor islands of the Pacific.

It is not suggested that these divisions rest on any general uniformities of physiography, climate, resources, or race. Each exhibits, however, certain cultural and other similarities, many of which resulted from the Western advance. Thus most of Latin America (A) evolved a civilization which was due largely to Western influences of an Iberian and Catholic-Christian type. Again, although there were important exceptions such as French Canada, the civilizations of English-speaking America and Australasia (B and D) evolved largely under British Western culture, while the civilization which spread slowly over parts of vast Siberia (C) was Western in character, first of a 'Holy' Russian, and later of an unholy communist type. As previously noted, almost all these areas, with the outstanding exception of Siberia, passed from Western settlement colonies into independent Western nations, often larger and more powerful than their European parents.

Very different was the course of events in East and South-east Asia (E), where the whites encountered difficulties created by unsuitable tropical climates, by vast indigenous populations, or in some lands, such as India and Java, by both. They also experienced, if on a very minor scale, similar problems of a climatic nature in the lovely but tropical islands of the Pacific (F), although in certain aspects, such as the results of exotic diseases, the Western invasions produced results resembling those in the zones of white settlement. In these Asian and Pacific Island territories the invaders failed, even in the conquered lands, to advance beyond the stage of sojourner colonization, and they never subdued the whole of

China and Thailand, although in these cases their cultural influence, indirect as it was, proved revolutionary. Slight at the outset, the Western pressure increased greatly over the century 1850–1950, during which the whites dug their own graves by introducing Western ideas, scientific knowledge, and Western women, who in self-defence promoted those false ideas of racial superiority and colour barriers which remain today and tend to shroud completely the many good results of the white advance. Those who had experience of Western behaviour in lands such as Burma witnessed the process. In 1930, in a white club in the Shan States, I asked why I was not introduced to a poor soul who crept ungreeted into the back of the club and read the British papers in a corner by himself. The answer was that in the early days of the mines many of the white personnel had taken Burmese wives and raised mixed blood families, but that when Western women came to the frontier, this man, and a few others, who had the courage and decency to acknowledge and stand by their Burmese wives and families, were ostracized. Very different was my experience of the Dutch. In 1933 I toured the Caribbean island of St. Martin with the kindly Dutch governor, and we discussed throughout the day many aspects of the colour problem including health and race. Much of the conversation must have amused him greatly, for when we went on to Government House I found that his charming wife was a Negress.

Whatever the causes, however, the important point is that through disunity, fear, and philanthropy, the Western domination of zone E was in general very brief. Yet brief as was the interlude of white sojourner colonization in the lands of Asian peoples, who had often engaged in stormy aggression—an aggression which Japan immediately reopened—the exotics left results of immense importance, which will be examined in the remainder of this book.

For the moment the Westerners retained their hold on the minor Pacific islands (division F), partly because their inhabitants were in general too backward to conduct self-government, and partly because the islands possessed strategic, economic, or transport value owing to their situation on the sea or air routes. To many of these islands the Westerners brought exotic labour forces of several types. The resulting evolution of mixed exotic and indigenous peoples and cultures presented a joyous hunting ground for academic anthropologists, and a wealth of headaches to the geographers, demographers, medical men, and other scientists who were watching with anxiety the evolution of the new mixed peoples and their social and economic impacts.[1]

Colonization routes—by sea

A few historical geographers have conducted interesting research on the extent to which the early explorers opened up by sea and land the routes which were subsequently followed by officials, missionaries, colonists, traders, and others who carried the diseases, flora, fauna, merchandise, and ideas of the Old World to the Pacific and brought back many New World products. With growing knowledge of the world system of winds and currents, the Europeans established several routes across the Atlantic. The work of M. F. Maury, who issued in 1851 his celebrated *Winds and Currents' Charts* and *Sailing Directions*, was based on the logs of a great number of sailing ships when crossing this ocean. These vessels either tacked from Europe to North America against the variable Westerlies, and came back with these winds, or crossed farther south with the Trades, which carried them to the southern United States, whence they drifted north with the Gulf Stream. If in the earlier periods such ships reached the Americas in winter, they wintered at Charleston or in the West Indies, as it was not then realized that vessels could thaw out in the warm Gulf Stream current.[2] Farther south, the Trades carried voyagers to the Atlantic coasts of South America. Rio de Janeiro became a frequent, if not customary, calling place for vessels which then used the Westerlies to round the Cape of Good Hope to reach southern Asia, the East Indies, or Australasia by the sailing routes discovered in part by Asian seafarers and later developed by the Portuguese and Dutch.[3]

[1] Chapter V (B), p. 224, for references.
[2] L. R. Jones and P. W. Bryan, *North America*, London, 10th ed., 1954, Part 1, ch. i, for a study of the North Atlantic sailing routes.
[3] F. B. Eldridge, op. cit., deals with the evolution of the sailing routes to and in

Although in those early years the Spaniards poured across to the Americas they could reach the Pacific itself only by the passages in the south of South America, by crossing the isthmus of Panama, or by traversing Mexico to ports such as Acapulco, which in some cases could be reached only by difficult and precipitous routes. Nor was the navigation of the Pacific shores of the Americas easy, as there was arid country along the coasts of northern Mexico and Peru, and Spanish vessels, which tried to reach California, had to beat their way against the prevailing northerly winds.[1] Nevertheless, the Spaniards from the time of Balboa built ships on the American Pacific coast and developed an intercontinental and coastal trade.[2]

From Acapulco and from Lima (Callao), the chief port of Peru, Spanish expeditions crossed the Pacific to the East Indies and colonized the Philippines which became, after Legaspi's annexation of 1565, a main centre for Spanish, Asian, and American contacts. To and from the Philippines evolved the famous Acapulco–Manila galleon route by which a very limited number of Spanish galleons, built in the Philippines, sailed to Mexico by the use of the westerly winds and back from Acapulco to the Philippines with the Trades. Although the Spaniards discovered and utilized Guam, they failed to find the Hawaiian Islands and hence their losses from famine and scurvy were immense. Nevertheless, the Spanish voyages to and in the Pacific, both via Cape Horn and Acapulco, were of considerable importance, not only in colonizing the Philippines and making the islands the only strong Christian country in Asia, but in introducing valuable American plants and vigorous weeds.[3] One cannot examine here the immense revolution in diets and habits wrought in both the Old and New Worlds when the one discovered the other, but we shall see that Edgar Anderson sets out a number of highly important

the Indian Ocean and western Pacific and includes a brief but useful bibliography, pp. 367–70.

[1] Jones and Bryan, op. cit., ch. ii.

[2] For bibliographical detail see p. 223, note C.

[3] E. Anderson, *Plants, Man and Life*, Boston, 1952, ch. x, and 'Man as a Maker of New Plants and New Plant Communities', in Thomas, *Man's Role in Changing the Face of the Earth*, pp. 763–77, with bibliography.

American plants which were unknown in the Old World until the Columbian discoveries, and that these include cacao, tobacco, cassava, potatoes, maize, quinoa, peanuts, lima beans, tomatoes, avocados, guava, papaya, strawberries, and pineapples.[1]

Still more important, as previously mentioned, were the great trade routes which the invaders opened up to India, and to the Pacific countries such as China, Japan, the East Indies, Australia, and New Zealand, via the Cape of Good Hope. By these routes the peoples, plants, and animals of western Europe and the Mediterranean were transported to South America, South Africa, and the countries of the western Pacific, indigenous or exotic American and African species of plants, weeds, animals, and pests being accidentally or purposely picked up *en route*. As Merrill says:

> It is no accident that tropical American economic plants and the more numerous aggressive American weeds almost immediately began to appear in the Orient. The former were purposely introduced by the early Portuguese and Spanish colonizers, and later by the Dutch, British and French. The weeds merely came along as commensals, for they are definitely commensals, as far as man is concerned, as are rats, mice, the common cat, fleas, lice and intestinal parasites.[2]

Later came even greater exchanges between the Old World and the Pacific world with the opening up of the Suez Canal in 1869 and the Panama Canal in 1914. By 1914, however, the scientific annihilation of distance was in full flow with the introduction of the telegraph, the telephone, and the internal combustion engine which made possible the motor-car and aeroplane.

Colonization routes by land

It is impossible to discuss in any detail the land routes which the explorers of many continents opened up for the pioneer colonists. Gulfs, rivers, and canals were developed for water transport. The valleys, mountain passes, and desert oases which the explorers had found became the sites first of tracks and then of roads and

[1] Anderson, op. cit.
[2] E. D. Merrill, *The Botany of Cook's Voyages*, particularly ch. 5, for the Spanish routes.

railways, although the colonists themselves opened up many new routes. An excellent example of the process is the fact that Blaxland, Lawson, and Gregory discovered a ridge by which they could scale the almost impassable cliffs of the Blue Mountains behind Sydney, and today the railway and the Great Western Highway follow that ridge towards the magnificent pastoral country which lies to the west of the Great Australian Divide. There is, of course, no rule that the course of settlement always followed the tracks of the explorers. E. J. Eyre and Burke and Wills in their crossings of Australia paved few roads which the pioneer colonists could follow with any profit. Nevertheless, historical geographers have given us many delightful pictures, for example, of the way in which the North American pioneers, their roads, and their railways gained the interior of the continent and then reached out to a Pacific coast where colonization had already commenced, largely through the agency of the sailing ship.[1]

It is impossible to discuss in detail the routes and means by which the Westerners travelled. One can, however, enlarge in imagination, as noted above, F. J. Turner's vivid pictures of the moving frontiers at the Cumberland Gap in the Appalachians and a century later at South Pass in the Rockies, to embrace the vast throngs of peoples, diseases, plants, animals, and cultures which poured into the Pacific regions by sailing ship, wagon, canoe, and sledge in the early stages, and later by the steamship, railway, motor-car, and aircraft.[2]

[1] For select bibliography on the course of settlement in some of the regions of Western colonization see p. 223, note D.

[2] F. J. Turner, *The Frontier in American History*.

IV

THE HUMAN INVASIONS—SETTLER COLONIZATION

The sweep of Western settlement

IT may seem strange to group together the Western settlement of Latin America, Siberia, and English-speaking North America and Australasia, but in these regions the invaders encountered certain similarites in the environments and in the numerical and other weaknesses of the indigenous peoples, which produced further similarities in the courses of the invasions and in their results. To recapitulate, the whites encountered in these lands large areas which possessed suitable climates for their settlements—weak, divided, and, in most regions, sparsely settled native peoples, and adequate natural resources for future development. Hence the Westerners poured into these territories in increasing numbers, conquered and destroyed or absorbed the indigenous folk in most areas (although Latin America presents important exceptions), and built up primary, secondary, and tertiary industries with a gradual but growing concentration on great industrial cities, a development which permitted large populations to reap the advantages of scientific technology and to secure and maintain high standards of life. These advances naturally varied immensely in different areas, in the time which they occupied, in their vigour, and in their success. Perhaps it is safe to say that the earliest and greatest progress was won by the United States, that Canada, Australia, New Zealand, and Latin American countries such as the Argentine followed suit, and that the most recent advances have occurred, as we shall see, in Siberia, and in lands such as Brazil which were but are no longer wholly backward countries.

In all these regions the moving Western frontiers swept over the native peoples, cultures, plants, and animals, and the invaders created changed landscapes. Sometimes these landscapes retained high percentages of the indigenous forms of life and culture, but often, as in the case of the great cities and industrial areas, they were almost wholly exotic. Today there is little left in cities such as New York or Melbourne to remind the inhabitants of the former peoples, cultures, animals, and plants, although it must be admitted that these are advanced cases of almost completely changed landscapes. Led by the example of the English-speaking people of the United States in 1776–83, most of the descendants of the settler colonists, whether free, serf, or slave, ultimately gained complete independence, and, where they controlled the requisite territories and natural resources, became nation states or even metropolitan states with their own colonial empires. In cases such as the United States, the Argentine, or Brazil, these new nations advanced until they exceeded in population and power their European parents, although it must be emphasized again that in a number of instances the bulk of this immense growth came in the last 200 years, as it followed the political, social, industrial, and scientific revolutions of the late eighteenth and early nineteenth centuries.[1]

We will now examine a few of the innumerable aspects of this settler colonization, in general avoiding those well-known, advanced, and densely settled regions which other students have already portrayed so ably and fruitfully, and concentrating on more or less known lands, particularly on certain frontiers and population problems in Latin America, eastern Siberia, north Australia, Canada, and Alaska, which American scholars have termed their last frontier.

[1] I do not know of any work which treats on general lines the story of Western settler colonization and its effects in Latin America, English-speaking America, British Australasia, and Russian Siberia. There are, however, important publications in many particular fields, for example C. E. Carrington, *The British Overseas*, C.U.P., 1950, or the International Labour Office, *Indigenous Peoples*, Geneva, 1953. Some of the outstanding authorities in demography, disease, flora, fauna, and culture are mentioned in the notes which follow. Works on Siberia in English are comparatively few, and, indeed, almost rare during the Soviet period. The recent publications of W. Kolarz, *Russia and her Colonies*, London, 1952, and *The Peoples of the Soviet Far East*, London, 1954, are important. S. B. Okun's *The Russian American Company* is a valuable study.

Some population and frontier problems in settlement regions

(A) *The destruction of the indigenous peoples*

I tried to show in *White Settlers and Native Peoples* that the invasions subjected the aboriginals of the lands of settler colonization to initial and brutal periods of moving frontiers, which were followed first by well meant but often destructive missionary efforts, and then more recently by eras of scientific management under which some of the native groups recovered, although by this time they had in many cases travelled far along the path to assimilation. As indicated in the previous section, the brilliant work of the Berkeley Research School—Sauer, Parsons, Borah, Cook, Simpson, Schurz, Meigs, and others—has now proved beyond doubt that the Spanish invasions produced some cycles of population decline, followed in certain instances by recovery in Latin America and Arizona. Of this, Table I (p. 66) is an example.

Unfortunately, when I last visited Britain and the United States in 1955 I was unable to discover research which would explain in detail the destruction of the indigenous peoples of Siberia. It is clear, however, that a decline in many native groups took place, particularly as there was fierce fighting in Kamchatka and other areas, and it is alleged that the Cossacks exterminated groups who failed to pay the fur tribute in spite of the fact that the Russians established monasteries in conjunction with the ostrogs or forts which they built to command the all-important portages connecting the rivers and tributaries that were the leading geographical factors in their routes to the East.[1] The evidence presented by Golder, Kerner, Czaplicka, Okun, Kolarz, M. Holdsworth, and others proves the advance in Siberia and Alaska of singularly savage frontiers which effected the defeat of the native groups and left the way clear for Russian colonists to destroy or seriously impair the surviving social systems. Liquor shops were established to expedite and debase the assimilation process, while the priest

[1] R. J. Kerner, *The Urge to the Sea*, Univ. of California Press, 1946, see note D, p. 223, chs. iv–vi; W. Kolarz, op. cit., chs. iii and iv; M. A. Czaplicka, *Aboriginal Siberia*, O.U.P., 1914, pp. 21 seq. Note particularly Kerner, p. 88: 'Official graft and private brigandage on the part of the merchants and trappers brought about a fearful decline in the native population and a woeful oppression of the survivors.'

with his ikon conferred a divine benediction on the newly established order.[1] In S. B. Okun's valuable work on the Russian American Company we find further evidence of the destruction wrought by the Russians in the North Pacific as evidenced by the Company's own statistics. It is clear that this semi-official organization wantonly and foolishly decimated useful and friendly hunting peoples such as the Aleuts, dishonestly doomed its own employees to almost unbelievable privations, and recklessly destroyed the natural resources which were its own support.[2]

In 1944 B. H. Sumner made an interesting comparison between the causes and results of the frontier advances in English-speaking North America and Russian Siberia. He pointed out that the Russians, like the Americans, were adapted to the physical and climatic conditions. Although in both cases the numbers of the invaders were small, they had vastly superior weapons and indomitable courage, together with a love of adventure and a greed which was egged on by the demand for furs. Again, like the Americans, the Russians encountered sparsely settled and mutually hostile tribes on whom the impacts were as disastrous as were the American–Red Indian contacts.[3] M. Holdsworth, who kindly lent me her manuscripts, and W. Kolarz quote population figures which agree and indicate that the Russians have reduced the aboriginals of eastern Siberia and the islands to about 60,000, which might perhaps be about one-third of the pre-conquest figure, if we use Okun's statistics on the destruction of the Aleuts. While early figures can be nothing better than very wide approximations, and while recent figures undoubtedly include many mixed bloods, Table I may be accepted as giving an indication of the trends towards destruction and, in some instances, the trends towards recovery in various settler regions.

Recent developments in regard to the Maoris and Australian aboriginals are set out in the *Report of the Board of Maori Affairs*, Wellington, 1958, and *Progress towards Assimilation*, an account of

---

[1] G. Curzon, *Russia in Central Asia*, London, 1889, p. 391.
[2] Okun, op. cit., particularly chs. viii and ix.
[3] B. H. Sumner, *Survey of Russian History*, London, 1944, pp. 30 seq. Further research is needed on the effects of the moving frontiers in Siberian history.

aboriginal welfare in the Northern Territory, Australia, issued by the Commonwealth Minister of Territories in the same year. By the end of 1957 Maori numbers had reached 145,671 and were expected to be 250,000 by 1975 owing to the high birth-rate and the large proportion of young people. Unemployment threatened to become a problem and the Maoris were moving to the towns from their population reservoirs on the east coast in the Rotorua–Bay of Plenty district, and in Northland. The Government saw that one of the most important tasks facing the nation was the placing of the Maori people fully and usefully into the New Zealand social and economic structure.

TABLE I

Aboriginal population statistics (to the nearest thousandth)

Peoples	Pre-invasion numbers	Numbers during the declines (not necessarily at the lowest points)	Recent
Latin American Indians .	18,885,000	8,634,000 (1825)	16,212,000 (1940)
Central Mexican Indians .	11,000,000	1,500,000 (1650)	3,700,000 (1793)
U.S. Indians	845,000	244,000 (1880)	421,000 (1950)
Canadian Indians	220,000	93,000 (1931)	156,000 (1951)
Australian Aboriginals .	300,000	55,000 (1933)	41,266 (1957)
Tasmanoids	2,000	Exterminated by 1876	..
Maoris .	110,000–200,000	40,000 (1890)	146,000 (1957)
Eastern Siberia .	180,000	..	60,000

The Australian publication stated that there were about 16,100 aboriginals in the Northern Territory, of whom only a few hundred were nomads who lived beyond the range of the settlements or missions. As was the case with the United States Indians and the Maoris, the evil days of the moving frontiers had ended, and the period of missionary enterprise which had followed was being replaced or supplemented more and more by government welfare organizations. From 1949–50 to 1957–8 the Commonwealth had increased its direct annual expenditure on aboriginal health and education from £133,009 to £914,574, while the aboriginal share in the general health services cost, in 1957–8, £1,038,000. Aboriginal conditions varied under the state governments, which, in cases such as Western Australia, had, in the past, been extremely neglectful and mean. Leprosy was prevalent in the north-west of the continent, and a cult of despair, the Kurangara cult, had developed and spread southwards, possibly under communist influences. Important research by Dr. Fay Gale in the University of Adelaide indicated that when the aboriginals moved to the towns they were rapidly assimilated by the white population, but in the more remote areas, where the natives provided invaluable labour in the cattle industry, the whites were too few to absorb them, with the result that some groups were possibly increasing in numbers.

One gathers that a census of aboriginal numbers was taken with the general census of 1954, but that the figures were not released; for example, the *Commonwealth Year Book* of 1956 gave an estimate of 46,638 full bloods and 27,179 mixed bloods in 1947, a total of 73,817. The 1956 *Year Book* adds, p. 622, that according to the State Protectors there had been little change in numbers, but it was significant that whereas in Western Australia the total of full and mixed bloods was 24,912 in 1947, the estimate of 1952 had fallen to 21,051. More recently T. G. H. Strehlow quoted in his *Dark and White Australians*, Adelaide, 1957, the following statistics from the 1957 report of the Aboriginal Friends' Association. These figures, which, like those given for 1947, exclude the Torres Strait islanders, were: full bloods, 41,266; mixed bloods, 30,123— a total of 71,389. It seems, therefore, that, as in the past, the mixed bloods are showing a slight increase, while the full bloods continue to register a steady decline.

(B) *The growth of exotic populations*

Far more important than aboriginal and mixed blood numbers is the immense size of the exotic populations which the invasions produced. According to U.N. figures for 1954 the populations of the United States, Canada, Australia, and New Zealand number respectively 160,026,000, 15,313,000, 8,962,000, and 2,103,000 people, while it seems fairly definite that the population of East

Siberia exceeds 5 million. If to this total of 191,404,000 we add, after deducting 16 million Indians, some 142 million Latin Americans, we find that the Pacific lands of settler colonization may contain over 300 million people with exotic blood—a vast population which at the moment completely dominates the Americas, Siberia, and Australasia, lands which still offer much room for expansion, as the population densities are 50 per square mile for the United States, 19 for Brazil and New Zealand, 16 for the Argentine, 6 for Canada, 3 for Australia, 2 for the U.S.S.R. in Asia (R.S.F.S.R.), and 0·2 for Alaska.

It is a vital question as to how far these numbers are increasing, particularly in view of the fact that in Asia crowded populations are turning hungry eyes to these seemingly under-populated lands, some of which like Australia, Siberia, and Alaska are not far distant. In view of the inaccurate demographic prophecies, not only by Asians such as Chandrasekhar, but by Westerners such as Warren Thompson, on the alleged future decline of population increase such as the Australian, the following table, based on U.N. statistics 1955, contains some surprising facts.[1]

TABLE II

Natural increase—excess of births over deaths (per thousand)

Taiwan–Formosa	35·8	New Zealand	15·3
Mexico	29·0	United States	15·1
Ceylon	28·5	U.S.S.R.	15·0 (estimate)
Colombia	25·4	Australia	13·8
Alaska	23·7	Japan	12·6
Chile	22·9	Philippines	11·9
Canada	19·3	India	11·2 (1952)
Australia (tropical)	16·6 (1948–52)	S. Korea	9·3 (1944)
Argentina	15·9	Pakistan	5·7
Burma	15·7		

(From *Population and Vital Statistics*, U.N., New York, January 1955, and *Australian Commonwealth Statistics*.)

Here we find that the natural rates of increase for a number of South American countries, for Canada, for Australia, and tropical

[1] Warren S. Thompson, *Population and Peace in the Pacific*, University of Chicago Press, 1946, p. 55.

Australia, for the United States and for New Zealand are higher than those of Japan, the Philippines, India, South Korea, and Pakistan. The surprisingly high figures for north Australia were supplied by the Commonwealth Statistician, Canberra, and are published in *Northern Australia* (Angus & Robertson, Sydney, 1954), pp. 194–6. The superiority of the tropical over the temperate figures is only slightly due to people leaving the tropics to die, as the death-rates are: tropical 8·58, temperate 9·67. The main superiority lies in the birth-rate: tropical 25·22, temperate 23·03. Charles A. Price points out, however, that this difference in birth-rates may arise in part from the recent and relatively heavy migration into the Northern Territory of young adults who are still in the ages of high fertility and who have not yet reached the ages of high mortality.

(C) *The Latin-American peoples*

In Latin America, as in East and South-east Asia, the Westerners encountered in certain regions problems of warm climates and fairly dense Indian populations, facts which made some aspects of the Latin-American invasions unique. The Spanish conquest was a vast, romantic, and courageous story, and, although the romance obscures much underlying cruelty, squalor, and slavery, authorities such as Salvador de Madariaga and W. L. Schurz have shown that in some fields the Spaniards achieved even more than the British. Firstly, in spite of initial losses, the Indians recovered from the frontier days largely through the protection of the Spanish Catholic Church, which operated even the Inquisition comparatively lightly. Second, in spite of stormy beginnings, some of the young Latin-American republics have given a war-torn world examples of co-operation and peace. As Schurz infers, Latin America now largely comprises an Iberian froth overlying a mestizo shandy, peaceful and almost unruffled during the recent decades of bloodshed and strife.[1]

Latin America from the Rio Grande to Cape Horn contains some 158 million people—120 million in South and 38 million in Central America. The vast area includes a variety of physical

[1] W. L. Schurz, op. cit., pp. 408 seq.; de Madariaga, op. cit., ch. xx.

features and climates, and although much of the region is tropical, the Spaniards found in the temperate lands, and on the plateaux of the warmer zones, country to their liking. The vale of Chile, for example, seemed a promised land from which there was no return or desire to return. On the other hand, they loathed the high cold Andes, and in this region they regarded residence as 'a boarding house in a vast mining camp'.[1] The external situation also affected the conquest. The Atlantic coast was the front door to Europe and north-eastern America, but until the Americans performed their wonderful feat in constructing the Panama Canal against immense difficulties of engineering and health, Peru and Chile were remote. As previously noted, it is impossible to estimate accurately the numbers of pre-Columbian Indians, and calculations vary from 13 to 75 million. Rosenblat accepts 5·6 million for Mexico and Central America, and 6,785,000 for South America, a total of 12,385,000. He considers that the indigenous population reached a low of 8,634,000 in 1825, but in 1940 numbered 16,212,000, or more, he thinks, than in pre-Columbian days. If to these figures we add a mestizo population which has increased from 29,794,800 in 1930 to 34,362,987 in 1940, the white invasions would appear to have multiplied by four the people with Indian blood. Unfortunately, however, Rosenblat's pre-Columbian figures disagree with those of Cook and Simpson, who by three different methods set the population of central Mexico at 11 million in 1519, a figure which accords much more readily with the later effects of exotic disease. If Cook and Simpson are right we should, perhaps, add at least 6·5 million to Rosenblat's figures, making the population of Central America 12·1 million and that of the whole of Latin America 18,885,000. If this is the case the Indian population still remains lower than in pre-conquest days[2] (Table I, p. 66). Rosenblat distinguishes two zones as regards the demographic structure of indigenous America, a peripheral or extinction zone and a zone of concentration or increase. In the first zone European diseases, land robbery, and racial mixture destroyed or drove out the relatively small groups of Indian nomads, who were in part replaced by

[1] Schurz, op. cit., pp. 6–8.
[2] A. Rosenblat in *Indigenous Peoples*, pp. 28 seq. and statistical table L, p. 617.

Negroes. In the second zone of denser aboriginal population the white conquerors were a small minority with the result that the Indians maintained their languages and their culture, in a somewhat stagnant form, and registered a steady population increase. Rosenblat's peripheral or extinction zone was composed of the coastal and forest regions, while the zone of concentration and increase comprised the high mountains and plateaux of Mexico and Central and South America.[1]

Past records show that, as usual, disease amongst a non-immune people, land robbery, slavery, and war reduced the aboriginals until the growth of immunity to sickness and other factors brought recovery. W. Borah gives the following population figures which Cook and Simpson worked out for central Mexico:[2]

TABLE III

Total population of central Mexico

1519	.	.	.	11,000,000
1540	.	.	.	6,427,000
1565	.	.	.	4,407,108
1650	.	.	.	1,500,000
1793	.	.	.	3,700,000

White, mestizo, and negro elements were significant in 1650 and 1793. By 1650 they numbered perhaps 300,000, the Indian population being about 1·2 million.

The Spaniards formed settler colonies although they were based on Indian labour, and, as in Costa Rica, they brought in Spanish women. Nevertheless, they bred freely with the Indians, and as they introduced other European peoples, Asians, and Negroes, the population is now extremely and very widely mixed, and it is in this aspect that Latin America differs so greatly from the Anglo-American and Anglo-Australian regions. The outstanding authority, H. L. Shapiro, taking Rosenblat's figures for 1940, gives the whole Western Hemisphere a population of 152 million

[1] Ibid., pp. 31–32.

[2] W. Borah, *New Spain's Century of Depression*, University of California Press, 1951, p. 3, using S. F. Cook and L. B. Simpson, *The Population of Central Mexico in the Sixteenth Century*, University of California Press, 1948, section ii.

whites, 23,202,000 Negroes, 15,619,000 Indians, 30,933,000 mesti-
zoes, and 8,113,000 mulattoes, which he states is a total of
247,245,000. The mixed peoples comprise one-sixth of the total
for the Western Hemisphere, and as this is far more than the
Chinese–South-Asian mixtures (4 million), the white–negro
crosses in South Africa (1 million), the Dutch–Indonesians
(200,000), the Eurasians of India (140,000), or the Chinese–Polynesians (100,000), the Americas appear as the leading areas of
racial mixture.[1]

Although many writers believe that the Indian will be absorbed,
he remains in great numbers in Mexico and the Andes (Pl. II). It is
as yet impossible to forecast the character of the mixed races that
will evolve, but on the whole experienced observers are hopeful of
satisfactory results. Meanwhile these vast and attractive lands offer
fascinating research on many varieties of races and of economic
and social life. Conditions vary greatly. On the one hand are
nations such as Peru, where a landed aristocracy, still predominantly European, dominates the restless mestizo masses, while aloft
and aloof in the Andes live the disinherited heirs of the Incas–
Indians whose only wish is to maintain their prehistoric culture.
On the other hand, there are republics such as Chile, a
country that is under the growing ascendancy of a vital and
intelligent middle class which draws its membership both from
above and below, and offers the prospect of a peaceful evolution
of a well-balanced national society free of catastrophic stresses and
strains.[2] The industries of the immense area should show the same
type of variation, but in general the Iberian feudal society is in
process of dissolution, and urban industrialization is proceeding
apace. The vastness of the country, the great variations of every
type, the speed of development, and the unlimited future prospects
are greatly impressing visiting authorities like the British geographers L. D. Stamp and J. A. Steers who travelled in Latin
America recently. Here in South America alone is a population of

---

[1] H. L. Shapiro, *Race Mixture*, U.N., Paris, 1953; C. Wagley, *Race and Class in
Rural Brazil*, U.N.E.S.C.O., Paris, 1952, particularly pp. 142 seq.; Schurz, op. cit.,
chs. ii, v, vi, x, and epilogue; *W.S.T.*, ch. ix.
[2] Schurz, op. cit., pp. 410–12.

120 million people, who are increasing more rapidly than the population of any other continent, and yet face a land which is still largely empty. Here one can see an industrial revolution actually in operation, large modern cities which are rapidly growing in size, and busy airports which meet the needs of widespread air services. In the words of L. D. Stamp: 'Anyone who visits Brazil can scarcely fail to come away with the impression that here one of the great giants of the earth, which had been sleeping for some time past, is now awakening and developing with incredible vigour.'

Recent population figures support this opinion. From 1950 to 1954 the population of Brazil advanced from 51,976,357 to 55,772,000; that of Mexico from 25,791,017 to 28,850,000; and that of Argentina from 15,893,827 to 18,742,000 in 1947–54. It is, indeed, unjust to sneer at the Iberian achievement and to damn these evolving races for low living standards in some areas, or for occasional political instability. As noted above, it is far better for critics to join those who have been to Latin America, and who, with knowledge of the position, wish these promising mixed races even greater success in their efforts to advance.[1]

(D) *English-speaking America*

There is neither the space nor the necessity to trace in detail the history of the moving frontiers in the United States and Canada, as very able historians and geographers have explained the tongues and troughs of settler colonization which moved across the continent, the opening up of the Pacific coast by sea and land, the depletion in numbers of the aboriginal peoples, and the wars and annexations by which the citizens of the United States built up an empire of vast and varied resources, both in the continent and in

[1] P. E. James, op. cit., pp. 38–40; J. A. Steers and L. D. Stamp, 'South American Prospect', in *Geog. Journal*, London, Sept. 1957, pp. 329 seq.; C. Wagley, op. cit., pp. 142–55. Wagley is not altogether happy about the Western racial concepts which are entering Brazil with industrial and technological improvements. Schurz, op. cit., ch. ix, 'The City'; L. B. Simpson, *Many Mexicos*, University of California Press, 1952, ch. 27. The Institute of International Affairs, London, is publishing a useful series of small books which cover individual countries. U.N., *Population and Vital Statistics Reports*, New York, Jan. 1955.

the oceanic region. *White Settlers and Native Peoples* quoted authorities such as J. Mooney, Clark Wissler, P. Meigs, and Diamond Jenness to show that white diseases, alcohol, fire-arms, land robbery, removals, and slaughter reduced the number of Indians in many regions, even more sweepingly than in Latin America. It seems that in the United States bad treatment by the British and Americans reduced Indian numbers from 845,000 before the conquest to 244,000 in 1880. In Canada, however, the French, and to some extent the British, treated the Indians considerably better, partly because they were of use to the fur trade, so that numbers fell from a possible 220,000 to 93,000 in 1921. It should be noted that in both areas the more recent figures probably include large numbers of mixed bloods.[1]

Satisfactorily as the historical geography of the United States and Canada has been written, three subjects may still be given some consideration—the question of population increase, which is particularly important owing to the growth of inhabitants in communist Russia and China, and the situations on the two human frontiers, which are still in motion, northern Canada and Alaska—particularly the latter whose historical development has not attracted very much attention in the United States.

Population increase in the United States and Canada

As previously noted, the growth of population in English-speaking America is vital to the so-called Free World. Russell Smith, the distinguished American geographer, gave in his *North America* various estimates by leading demographers which indicated that the population of the United States, numbering 120 million in 1930, might advance by A.D. 2000 to an estimated total which varied from 150 to 185 million. In point of fact the population reached 160 million as early as 1954. As in 1953 there were 3,909,000 births to 1,519,000 deaths—a high natural increase—the growth in future may be both rapid and

---

[1] For bibliographies see *W.S.N.P.*, chs. i–iv. The classic study of aboriginal numbers in pre-Columbian North America is J. Mooney, *Aboriginal Population of America*, Smithsonian misc. coll., Washington, 1928, vol. lxxx, no. 7.

PLATE II

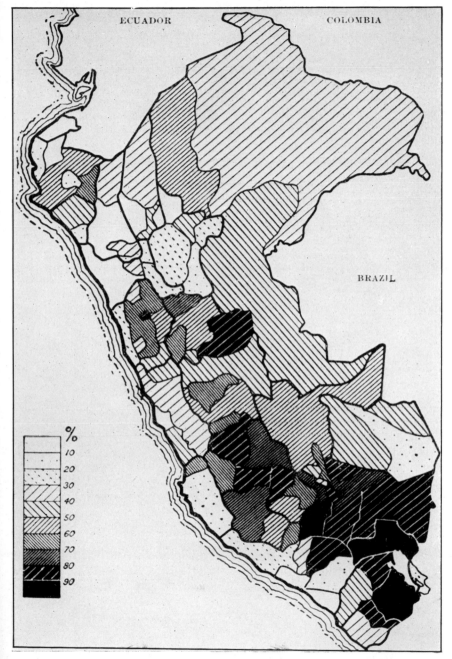

Indian survival in Peru: Indian population as a percentage of total population (1940)

From *Indigenous Peoples*, International Labour Office, Geneva, 1953

substantial. It is noteworthy that the rate of advance seems to have exceeded the most optimistic forecast quoted by Russell Smith, that of Pearl and Reed of Johns Hopkins University, made in 1921.[1]

Russell Smith was very hopeful of the future of Canada, a land he says of 'wholesome invigorating climate' and 'good resources'. This great country, one of the most united, prosperous, and promising zones of Western settlement, contained in 1955 some 15 million people, who were registering an annual increase of 1·93 per cent., or more than 2·5 million persons per decade. The distinguished Canadian authority Diamond Jenness was perhaps less optimistic than Russell Smith when he published in 1932 a cautious survey of the population potentialities of the Dominion in the light of the then known resources, and came to the conclusion that, with half of its area lying north of the 60th parallel, the country would not be able to support more than 35 million people at the existing high living standards. In 1954 B. K. Sandwell published some important demographic predictions in *Canada's Tomorrow*. He stated that the population of the country had become approximately 8·5 per cent. of that of the continent north of Mexico, and it could be expected to maintain something like that percentage in relation to the population of the United States as the population of the two countries advanced. He said that United States government statisticians and other authorities had recently estimated that by 1975 the population of the United States would rise to a figure of between 173 and 225 million, so that a Canadian total of 20 million by 1975 seemed a reasonably conservative forecast. Sandwell added the further important opinion that

the possibilities of sustaining an expanded population without any serious reductions of the standard of living are immensely greater in Canada than in the United States, where the authorities are already viewing with deep concern the inroads already made, and those which will continue to be made for some years more, upon the natural resources of the area. The very inaccessibility of vast areas of Canada has preserved until now their mineral and forest contents. . . . The new

[1] J. R. Smith and M. O. Phillips, op. cit., pp. 968–9.

means of transport and of surveying and research by air have suddenly opened the whole of Canada to exploitation.[1]

In the same year Griffith Taylor drew on his wide experience both of Canada and Australia to outline a comparison of potentialities which was more than favourable to the northern country. He considered that in Canada the areas of satisfactory temperature and rainfall were double those of Australia; that Canada possessed about 1,300,000 square miles of forest to only 120,000 square miles in the Commonwealth, and that the Canadian potential of water power was some 40 million h.p., or over eight times that of Australia. Canada also had an overwhelming superiority in her mineral resources of coal, gold, silver, lead, zinc, copper, and iron, while petroleum, nickel, and platinum had not yet been discovered in payable quantities in Australia. Canada also led in agricultural produce, cattle, dairying, and fisheries, and had an immense lead in factory production. Only in sheep and wool was Australia overwhelmingly superior.

In these circumstances Taylor repeated his estimate of 1922 that Australia could contain about 30 million people at the existing living standards, but now added his opinion that Canada could support two or three times this population, which gave her a maximum of from 60 to 90 million.[2]

(E) *The North Canadian frontier*

Authorities divide this frontier into the Canadian Arctic archipelago, the eastern north lands, and the north-west. The last two regions, which are the more important from the human viewpoint, are separated by the Hudson Bay–Mackenzie divide. When the whites arrived these vast cold lands contained only a sparse population of hunting, fishing, and collecting people—Eskimoes and Indians. Even with the protection of climate and isolation these tribes suffered from exotic diseases, particularly smallpox,

[1] D. Jenness, 'The Population Possibilities of Canada', *Univ. of Toronto Quarterly*, July 1932, p. 422; B. K. Sandwell, 'The Canadian People', in G. P. Gilmour, ed., *Canada's Tomorrow*, pp. 11–34.
[2] Griffith Taylor, *Australia and Canada, A Comparison of Resources*, Report of A.N.Z.A.A.S. Meeting, Canberra, 1954, Sydney, 1955, pp. 277–314.

from the destruction of their natural resources, from conflicts which arose from tribal movements resulting from white pressure, and even from deliberate slaughter, as when the Micmacs joined with the English and French to destroy the unhappy Boethuk Indians of Newfoundland. As elsewhere disease was probably the chief killer. Smallpox appeared amongst the Montagnais of the lower St. Lawrence in 1635, and by 1700 it had spread over half the continent, leaving a trail of death and devastation. In 1746 typhus carried off a third of the Micmacs of Acadia and in 1902–3 destroyed the entire population of Southampton Island in Hudson Bay. In 1830 the Indians of British Columbia suffered heavily from influenza. Pulmonary afflictions, particularly tuberculosis, attacked the Indians at an early date and have continued to cause a high mortality. Unscrupulous fur traders supplied alcohol to non-immune Indians and debased tribal life until the governments, with the warm approval of both the decent traders and the Indian chiefs, prohibited the traffic. It is impossible to calculate the numerical decline which resulted from these factors, but the census of 1944 recorded that there were 6,400 Indians in the sub-arctic parts of British Columbia and 7,400 in Alberta, together with 1,500 Eskimoes in the north-west. In the early days of the conquest there was much miscegenation. Indian girls, trained in the convents, made excellent wives for isolated farmers and fur traders, and the French in particular had little racial prejudice. Farther to the north the eastern tribes were assimilated less rapidly and happily, with the diminution of the fur and other natural resources, so that many groups have become almost extinct.[1]

The development of northern Canada dates from the foundation of the Hudson Bay Company in 1670, but fur trading and whaling were the only important industries until the Klondike gold rush of 1897 and 1898. Even then there was little progress until oil was struck on the Mackenzie in 1920, a discovery which led to the foundation of the North-west Territories and Yukon Branch of

[1] G. H. T. Kimble and D. Good, *Geography of the Northlands*, Amer. Geog. Society, New York, 1955, ch. xv, 'Northwestern Canada' by D. Good, and ch. xvi, 'Eastern Canada' by J. B. Bird; D. Jenness, *The Indians of Canada*, Nat. Museum of Canada, Ottawa, 1934, particularly Part I, ch. xvii, 'Interaction of Indians and Whites'.

the Federal Department of the Interior, and attempts were made to preserve natural resources. Then came the aeroplane—'the greatest single instrument introduced into the Canadian Far North to aid in the discovery of mineral resources and to facilitate their exploitation'. In 1929 came the first air-mail flight down the Mackenzie to the Arctic, and in 1930 an air-borne prospector discovered silver and pitchblende ore at Great Bear Lake—the genesis of the richest radium and uranium mine in the world.

With the advent of the Second World War, the Americans and Canadians realized the proximity of Japan and Asia and entered upon immense construction projects—airfields, the Alaska Highway, the Richardson Highway from Big Delta to Fairbanks, and the vast Canol project which was to open up oil connexions from Norman Wells, the most northerly oilfield in the continent, to Whitehorse. This project involved the building of airfields and roads to an extent which gave access to thousands of square miles of hitherto unexplored country.

Mining seems to present the chief hope of economic development, for pitchblende, oil, iron, and gold all hold potentialities. Water power also offers possibilities, and lumbering, fishing, and, on a small scale, agriculture and stock-raising are being developed. Richard Finnie suggests that as the Russians are said to be using their aboriginal tribes in the Arctic sections of their five-year plans, the Americans and Canadians should make use of their Eskimoes, a cheerful intelligent people, masters of their environment, who in the handling of motor schooners and other equipment have already shown a mechanical bent.

It is interesting to compare the numerical strength of the Canadian population of these semi-deserts with that of the Americans in Alaska, the Russians in Siberia, and the Australians in their tropics, as all these people live in or on the margin of cold or hot deserts. The census of 1951 recorded that there were 505,000 whites in the sub-arctic parts of the provinces of Alberta (390,000), British Columbia (90,000), Saskatchewan (15,000), and Manitoba (10,000). The population of north-east Canada was about 945,000, including some 25,000 Indians. This total figure of nearly 1·5 million whites can be compared with 205,000 whites in Alaska and 288,000 in tropical Australia. The number of whites in eastern Siberia is far greater if we accept the figure of 5 million for 1955 to which might perhaps be added 'the vast number of people in forced labour camps' (p. 51). Recent progress in these cold zones justifies to some extent the attention which Vilhjalmur Stefansson and others have demanded for the sub-arctic regions in books such as *The Northward Course of Empire*, and although few white men and even fewer white women would willingly live in these bleak lands, the mineral discoveries, and the strategic implications of an air age, make their occupation and exploitation a matter of necessity rather than of choice.[1]

In conclusion a word should be said on the interesting question of French Canada, for, although this book uses the general title of English-speaking America for the region north of the Rio Grande, there are large areas inhabited by peoples other than British who are undergoing or resisting acculturation. Outstanding amongst these latter are the French Canadians who number 5 of the 16 million inhabitants of the Dominion. In this case differences such as those of language and religious culture have retarded acculturation even more than race, so that the British and French remain separate people. Yet, while their views differ at times, the links between them are historic and strong, for they shared in various ways the pioneering of the moving frontier together with the development of the fur trade, facts which made them North Americans rather than British or French. Later, the remarkable liberality and foresight shown by the Motherland in the Quebec Act increased Canadian unity in the face of the anger of the southern colonies, and, when these became the United States, the Canadas retained their British connexion.

From that time onwards the peoples of Canada fought for survival against United States intrusion and domination, and at the time of the American Civil War they created their own

[1] Kimble and Good, op. cit., ch. xv, pp. 314–36; R. Finnie, 'Canada's Northward Course', in H. W. Weigert, V. Stefansson, and R. E. Harrison, *New Compass of the World*, London, 1949, pp. 25–39. For the development of air transport in northern Canada: K. R. Sealy, *The Geography of Air Transport*, London, 1957, ch. vii; V. Stefansson, 'The Soviet Union Moves North', J. W. Watson, 'Canada: Power Vacuum or Pivot Area', and other chapters in *New Compass of the World*.

Dominion. Today the British and French Canadians, closely linked by geography and economics, are opposed to certain aspects of Americanization, even though they remain unassimilated peoples. Indeed, the French claim that they are less like the Americans than are the British Canadians, and hence are more fitted to resist intrusion.[1]

(F) The Alaskan frontier

An important frontier, which has been to some extent neglected, is the Alaskan, although the country comprises 586,400 square miles (one-seventh the area of the continental United States), possesses in the south a tolerable climate, and still offers, in spite of lamentable exploitation, some of the finest primary resources in the continent. Ernest Gruening, the Governor of Alaska from 1937 to 1953, divides the period of American control into: the era of total neglect, 1867–84; the era of flagrant neglect, 1884–98; the era of mild but unenlightened interest, 1898–1912; the era of indifference and unconcern, 1912–33; and the era of growing awareness, 1933–54.[2] If we add to these American periods the era 1799–1867, and call it 'The Russian epoch of blind and bloody exploitation', we have a brief summary of what remote Alaska has suffered from the whites. Nevertheless, the future may see very great improvements, for in 1959 Alaska became the 49th American State.

Alaska possesses in some areas the main factors which are essential for white settlement qualified by the limitations which nature so frequently imposes on lands that rim cold or hot deserts. The south has a moderate climate, as Kodiak registers an annual average temperature of 40° F. and the climate compares with those of Trondhjem in Norway or St. John, Newfoundland. The interior

[1] Based on a lecture given by Professor J. M. S. Careless of Toronto in the University of Adelaide on 30 July 1958.

[2] For Alaska see Kimble and Good, op. cit.; Okun, op. cit.; C. L. Andrews, *The Story of Alaska*, Idaho, 1938; E. Gruening, *The State of Alaska*, New York, 1954; Smith and Phillips, op. cit. There are a number of official publications, e.g. *Seal and Salmon Fisheries and General Resources of Alaska*, 4 vols., Washington, 1898 (detailed reports on fur seals, &c.); *Regional Planning*, Part VII, Alaska, National Resources Committee, Washington, 1938.

—the golden heart of Alaska—has greater extremes, but in spite of frost could carry considerable expansion of agricultural and pastoral pursuits. Surviving destructive exploitation, the country still offers vast resources of timber, fish, furs, and gold, together with a scenic splendour of mountain, glacier, fjord, and forest, which is most alluring to tourists.

After Bering discovered the region and its furs in 1741, Siberian merchants sent out hunters who, by the end of the 1750's, had stripped the Aleutian Islands, and, by 1750–61, had reached Unalaska and the Alaskan peninsula. These voyages were conducted largely by ignorant captains with crews of landsmen in crazy vessels built in Okhotsk or Kamchatka. Up to 1800 at least 75 per cent. of the vessels employed in the trade were wrecked, and those which did manage to return spent, according to Petroff, up to seven years on the round trip across the Bering Sea which the schooners of a later day accomplished in about three weeks.[1]

The Russian Government now became interested owing to the fur tribute, the desire to check England and Spain, and its grandiose plans to control the North Pacific. In 1784 Shelikov, whom the Soviets are now terming 'The Russian Columbus', founded a settlement on Kodiak Island, and in 1799 the Government gave a charter to the famous Russian American Company which was to cloak an aggressive policy directed towards forcing the English trading companies from Alaska while at the same time proceeding with further expansion. Under this policy the North Pacific was to become an inland sea of the Russian Empire, California the agricultural base of the Russian American colonies, and the Hawaiian Islands the naval base controlling all trade with China.[2] In pursuance of this policy Baranov, the great governor, who from 1790 to 1818 represented first the Shelikov and later the Russian American Company, pushed the frontier from the islands to the mainland and then southwards down the American coast until in 1812 he founded the Ross Colony in California. In the

[1] I. Petroff, Report in *Seal and Salmon Fisheries and General Resources of Alaska*, p. 334. Andrews, op. cit., p. 33, recounts a shocking incident when Russian fur gatherers seized, and later murdered, some twenty-five Alaskan girls and a number of men without incurring punishment.

[2] Okun, op. cit., chs. ii, iii.

north he introduced vegetables and Siberian cattle, and in California cattle, grain, the vine, and even peach trees from Chile, but the Californian colony failed owing to the advance of the Americans and the lack of good agricultural and pastoral land, of fertilizers, and of suitable labour, although the introduction of 'patient and industrious Chinese' was suggested.[1] Even less successful, but of great historical significance, were the efforts made by Baranov from 1815 to secure the Hawaiian Islands and so complete in the North Pacific the great triangle of Russian possessions. Although the Russian agent, Dr. Scheffer, met with some initial success by supporting the sub-chief Tomari against King Kamehameha, the Russian Government refused aid owing to other commitments, and the influence of English and American traders drove Scheffer out. Had Russia permanently secured Alaska and the Hawaiian Islands in addition to eastern Siberia, the menace of communism to the democracies might have become even more serious.[2]

Up to Baranov's departure in 1818 the Company had surmounted incredible difficulties in the form of storms, scurvy, poisonous sea foods, and native attacks—the warlike Tlinkets actually storming in 1802 the Company's chief station at Sitka. The oppression and destruction of the valuable Aleut hunters, the reckless exploitation of the fur-bearing animals, particularly the sea otter and the fur seal, the poor methods of curing pelts, the collapse of the Chinese fur market, and the advance of the Hudson Bay Company with superior merchandise, all began to bear fruit. In 1824–5 the English and Americans gained conventions that granted them the free navigation of rivers which crossed Russian territory to the sea, and during the Crimean War the English actually approved of a neutrality pact between the Hudson Bay and Russian American companies for fear that the Russians might sell Alaska to the United States. Britain, however, could not avoid the inevitable. From the 1840's onward Russian attention became more and more concentrated on her vast Asiatic possessions, and the discovery of gold in Alaska aroused fears that an influx of 'diggers' would create a situation utterly beyond the control of

[1] Okun, op. cit., ch. vi.   [2] Ibid., ch. vii.

a distant metropolitan government. Under these circumstances Russia in 1867 sold Alaska for $7 million (less than 2 cents an acre) to a reluctant United States, whose Secretary of State, Seward, was one of the few leaders who saw the wisdom of the purchase.

So ended this Russian–American frontier period, which perhaps lacked the time to pass through the full cycle of frontier exploitation, missionary control, and official management, based on increasing scientific knowledge. The Russian Church and missionaries did not attempt to mitigate the brutality of the Company and claimed in 1860 that Alaska contained 10,668 Christians exclusive of Russians. The population statistics quoted by Petroff for the years 1830 to 1863 are illuminating. It appears that from 1838 to 1845 the Christian population declined from 11,022 to 7,224 owing to a smallpox epidemic which killed nearly 3,000 people in 1837 and 1838, but a recovery began in 1846 and numbers reached 10,075 by 1860. Petroff considered that if the mortality was 20 per cent. in areas accessible to medical treatment and vaccination, it would be 50 per cent. or more in densely populated but remote districts such as the Yukon, and this he thought was proved by native tradition and abandoned villages. It appears that at the time of the transfer Alaska contained 577 Russians and 1,892 creoles. The estimates of native population were quite unreliable, but Petroff gave guarded approval to Veniaminof's estimate of about 40,000 in 1835. Allowing a very moderate reduction of 25 per cent. during the smallpox epidemic of 1838–9, we have a figure of 30,000. K. H. Stone in a recent article gives a total of 28,000 for the population in 1867, including perhaps 600 whites.[1]

Congress placed Alaska first under the control of the army and then the navy, and instead of introducing taxation and other concessions to encourage migration and enterprise and providing the vessels necessary for adequate administration, all that was done was the imposition of customs duties. No adequate effort was made to conserve natural resources, and the fur-seal herds of the Pribilof Islands were reduced by the indiscriminate slaughter of females

---

[1] Petroff, op. cit., pp. 217 seq., for population. Petroff's historical sketch, pp. 316 seq., is most interesting if used to supplement Okun. K. H. Stone, 'Populating Alaska—The United States Phase', in *Geog. Review*, July 1952, p. 391.

from 2 million animals at the time of the transfer to 125,000 in 1910.[1] When at last enlightenment came, the herds grew from 125,000 in 1911 to 1,151,000 in 1935 by the limitation of the slaughter to that of bachelor seals. Up to 1880 similar neglect marked almost every aspect of the United States' management. The census of 1880 recorded a population of 33,426 of whom 31,234 were natives and 1,756 creoles, as against only 430 whites.

The progress which then followed was due to the fact that private citizens began to perceive the value of Alaskan resources and created an American moving frontier in spite of government neglect. The three most prominent features of the progress were the discovery of gold in the Silver Bow basin and the foundation of Juneau, the development of the fisheries, which included the inception of the canning of salmon at Sitka and Klawak in 1878, and the beginning of the foundation of schools and missions accomplished by the churches, all without assistance from the Government, which owned the whole domain and its resources, yet did nothing towards the development of them or even towards the preservation of the lives of the native inhabitants of the land.[2]

By 1897—thirty years after the transfer of 'Seward's icebox'— private enterprise had moved the frontier forward with considerable effect. Thirty-five fish canneries were in operation and the pack of 1897 was valued at $2,977,019, or nearly half the sum which the United States had paid for Alaska.

Sealing and whaling were bringing in such profits that even by 1890 the total return from the territory was more than $75 million, or ten times the price that the United States had paid. Nevertheless, the progress had been made at an unduly high cost owing to government neglect. The salmon were decreasing because of incessant fishing and the illegal obstruction of streams. With the displacement of whale oil by kerosene, the baleen alone was taken and the valuable carcasses jettisoned. The walrus, hunted only for their ivory tusks, were almost exterminated, and as a result the plight of the coastal Eskimo was so serious that even Congress

[1] Andrews, op. cit., pp. 147 seq., and Petroff, op. cit., pp. 238 seq. and 466 seq.
[2] Ibid., and Andrews, op. cit., pp. 156 seq.

joined private subscribers in introducing the reindeer.[1] In spite of
the fact that the United States Government was at last assisting
private enterprise in forwarding education, and that the Treasury
was making immense profits from the seal islands, the territory
completed its first thirty years under conditions which were still
deplorable in many respects. Of the thirty years 'seventeen had
been without laws, ten of them under military rule, seven under
the navy, and the remaining thirteen under a makeshift government'.[2] Then came the great gold discoveries with a rush and
boom that rivalled the thrilling days of the Californian or Victorian diggings. When news came of rich placer deposits on the
Klondike river, a tributary of the Yukon, and just across the border
in Canada, frontier seaports emerged at Dyea and Skagway, and
thousands of miners poured into the upper Yukon across the
Chilkoot and White passes. The United States made scant provision to meet the emergency. The United States' Marshal joined
the forces of the bandit gangs until he was arrested. The management of the Canadian Government presented a notable contrast.
Other routes developed, for example, from Port St. Michael up
the Yukon which was soon thronged with steamers, and a railway
project succeeded when with British capital a line was built from
Skagway to White Horse rapids on the Yukon.[3] In 1903 a sub-
committee reported that Alaska had enriched the nation by $52
million in furs, $50 million in fisheries, and $31 million in gold.
The Treasury had benefited to an extent of $1 million over its
expenses. The census of 1900 showed a population of 63,592. The
gold rush had raised the white population to over 30,000, or more
than the native.[4] Under the Organic Act of 1912 Alaska became
a territory.

In spite of some improvement Gruening could call the period
1912–33 the era of indifference and unconcern until the Second
World War produced an era of growing awareness, when the
nation became far more conscious of the great resources and

[1] Gruening, op. cit., pp. 93 seq.
[2] Andrews, op. cit., p. 180.
[3] Ibid., ch. 27; Gruening, op. cit., ch. 10.
[4] *Regional Planning, Part VII—Alaska*, p. 183, for railways. Gruening, op. cit.,
ch. 10, pp. 118–19, for report of 1903.

strategic perils of the region in spite of the seasonal character of occupations such as the fisheries, and the dangers of the frequent comparisons of the territory with Scandinavia, which had high living standards and European markets in close proximity. Thus the Resources Survey of 1937 recognized that in spite of agricultural developments in places such as the Mananuska, Tanana, and Susitna valleys, where the invaders were able to introduce cool temperate cereals, potatoes, root crops, vegetables, fruit, and livestock with some success, production extended little beyond the local Alaskan markets, and there seemed slight hope of building up a really large population based on agricultural settlement in spite of the joyful surprise which came from the discovery that the agricultural frontier could be established so far north and under such conditions.

The fisheries (salmon, halibut, herring, whale, clams, crabs, and shrimps), together with fur-catching and fur-farming, gave better returns and prospects for export. In 1936 the value of the fishing products was $50,455,272, that of mining $23 million, and that of furs shipped $1,932,894. Forestry also offered important prospects as estimates showed that the south coast had 4 million acres of spruce and hemlock forest, 'capable under proper forestry treatment of supplying the nation with 1 million tons of newsprint per year in perpetuity', while the vast interior contained 40 million acres 'of fairly dense forest of small trees that can contribute materially to the home-making needs of a large future local population'. Investigations into water resources showed that at least several hundred thousand horse-power could be developed cheaply in south-east Alaska.[1]

The Americans also realized the importance of extending the Alaskan roads, railways, and airways, not least for strategic purposes. In 1923 they completed a railroad from Seward to Fairbanks in the interior, and they and the Canadians finished in 1942, at a cost of $114 million, the great Alaskan highway which ran from Dawson Creek, British Columbia, to Fairbanks—a distance of 1,523 miles.[2] Airways also were extended to serve large areas, and

[1] *Regional Planning, Part VII—Alaska*, staff reports on resources, pp. 55–144.
[2] U.S. Dept. of Interior, *Mid-Century Alaska*, Washington, 1952, 'Transporta-

Fairbanks became an important station on the routes between North America and Asia.

A brief reference to education will indicate the way in which the Americans recently extended the cultural frontier in this pioneer region. Instead of the former complete neglect, the Territorial Government administered in 1952 some 88 schools for white and native students, while the Alaskan Native Service maintained schools in about a hundred native villages. The University of Alaska was established at Fairbanks with 2,250 acres of land, and a Geophysical Institute. In 1950 it awarded forty-three degrees.

Smith and Phillips and other American authorities have made important estimates of the potentialities of this frontier region, and have condemned the former mishandling of invaluable resources, of which the decline of the salmon fisheries was 'another of those perfect and sickening examples'.[1] Their conclusion is that Alaska needs people, capital, and long-range planning, which only the Federal Government can provide, but they end with the question which comes to the lips of so many who refuse to pioneer these rim lands of the hot and cold deserts—'But why go to the Arctic'? One answer, of course, is the danger of having an empty country within 56 miles of Asia, although Siberia has shown that cold countries are not very attractive to Asian folk. Another reason to increase the population is strategic, although in the light of atomic warfare the strategy of the past is obsolete. Whatever the reasons, however, the American frontier is moving in Alaska. From 1950 to 1955 the population increased from 128,643 to 205,000 and is now within sight of the population of tropical Queensland, which was 270,536 in 1948–52. In a recent and valuable analysis of the Alaskan population problem K. H. Stone notes that in 1930 the distribution of population 'seemed to show some signs of stability', and that after 1935 'a more rapid population growth began'. In his opinion the white population is now showing both permanence and increase, but that multiplicity of function is essential for the establishment of permanent settlements, and

tion', pp. 13 seq.; J. J. Teal and I. Skarland, 'Alaska', ch. xiv of Kimble and Good, op. cit.
    [1] Smith and Phillips, op. cit., p. 742.

research should be undertaken into this factor 'to protect the potential Alaskan settlers who are already going north'. Such research is essential if Earl Hanson is correct when he writes: 'It seems safe to say that the development of the territory, the northward flow of capital, enterprise, energies and millions of human beings, the inauguration of a new American pioneer movement into the vast, wealthy and beautiful empty empire, are now only questions of time.' One hopes that Hanson is correct. One hopes that other enthusiasts such as Stefansson are correct, but one cannot overlook the reluctance of Westerners to pioneer both very hot and cold countries unless population pressure is irresistible, or particular attractions such as those set out by G. Valentina Khetagurova in Siberia beckon invitingly. If the frontier is to go farther forward the Americans must answer the question, 'But why go to the Arctic?[1] Will the answer be more simple now that Alaska is the 49th State?

(G) *The Siberian frontier*

I have mentioned the Russian exploration of Siberia and the destruction of many of the natives. There remains a consideration of the Russian colonization and development of the country. These are important matters to all Pacific peoples, for the Soviets are forcing rapid progress in this huge land. In 1954 the whole of Siberia was estimated to contain 4,729,450 square miles and 16,577,000 people, but it was then thought that if the population had advanced at the same rate as the total Russian population, which grew from 193 to 207 million from 1939 to 1954, the Siberian population must substantially exceed 20 million. Particularly important in any consideration of the Pacific is eastern Siberia, or the Soviet Far East, of which the most important divisions are the Khabarovsk Territory on the Amur river, the Amur Province administered from Blagoveshchensk, the maritime territory with its capital Vladivostok, and the island of Sakhalin. The population in these areas forms a block of white and Western

---

[1] K. H. Stone, 'Populating Alaska—The United States Phase', particularly pp. 399–404; E. P. Hanson, *New Worlds Emerging*, New York, 1949, ch. xv, 'Alaska—America's Frontier'; *New Compass of the World*, pp. 18–24.

PLATE III

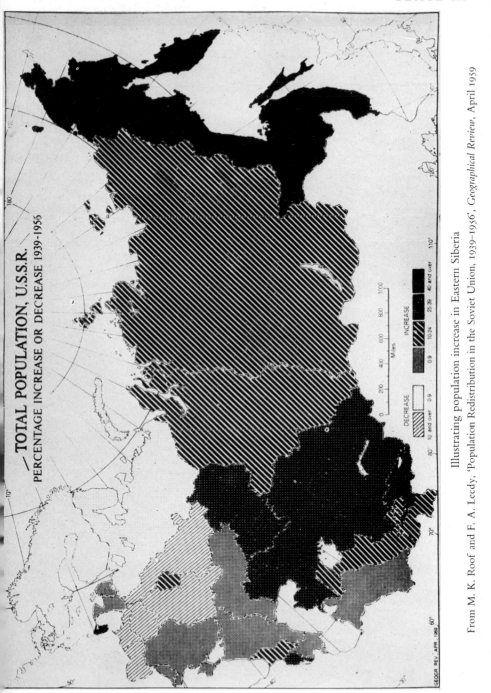

Illustrating population increase in Eastern Siberia

From M. K. Roof and F. A. Leedy, 'Population Redistribution in the Soviet Union, 1939–1956', *Geographical Review*, April 1959

peoples in the regions of the least severe climate and along the Chinese northern border. Also Vladivostok was a window on the Pacific and its people resented the rigid isolationism of the Soviets, who in 1948 closed the American Consulate in Vladivostok to indicate that that city must not become a link between Russia and the West. Nevertheless, the Soviets are developing the area with great speed and energy. Kolarz estimated that the total population of the Soviet Far East and islands could not have exceeded 3 million in 1946. In 1950 it may have reached 4·2 million and in 1955, 5 million—excluding 'the vast number of people in forced labour camps'.[1] (Pl. III.)

This book will not discuss the Cossack advance across Siberia and the checking of that great drive by the Chinese armies which forced the Russians to sign the Treaty of Nerchinsk in 1689. This gave the Russians the north and central east with their severe climates, permo-frost country, forests, and furs, but kept them out of the lower Amur and maritime areas. Kerner asserts that 'the lack of an adequate grain-producing region in Eastern Siberia was to make Russia's hold on the Pacific precarious for two centuries'.[2]

As happened so frequently in the Western invasions the real colonizing pressure was not exerted until quite recent times. W. Kolarz (1954) has given an interesting and important outline of this colonization. It seems that although the Russians established ostrogs, monasteries, and villages over much of the vast area, including the Pacific coast, there was little colonization until an advance on the Amur in 1858–60. Even then, however, the only way of reaching the Far East was by a primitive journey on horseback which occupied several years and left the migrant exhausted.

[1] *Bulletin of the Institute for the Study of the History and Culture of the U.S.S.R.*, Munich, vol. ii, no. 3, Mar. 1955, p. 22, gives the detailed estimates (apparently from *Izvestiya*, 25 Dec. 1954), which reach 5·1 million, and notes that these figures 'do not include the vast number of people in forced labour camps'. According to the Bulletin, population grew as follows:

1917	933,000	1939	2,387,000
1925	1,072,000	1947	3,450,000
1938	2,700,000	1955	5,100,000

The figure of 4·2 million in 1950 is taken from W. Kolarz, *The People of the Soviet Far East*, p. 22.   [2] Kerner, op. cit., p. 83.

As a result the numbers of new-comers to the Soviet Far East did not exceed 1,000 a year. From 1883, however, the Russians opened a sea route from Odessa to Vladivostok and established some organization to care for settlers, but although some thousands of migrants came in under the improved arrangements, it was not until the completion of the Trans-Siberian Railway in 1903, and the reduction of the far eastern journey to thirty days, that a boom in colonization began, the number of migrants reaching 76,637 in 1907. Nevertheless, by 1926 there were only about 1·6 million Europeans in the far-eastern territory. Kolarz considers that the Russians used four types of colonization: convict, military, komsomol, and normal.[1] Where most other nations had long abandoned the use of their more remote territories as human sewers, the Soviets continued this obsolete practice by using Siberia both for convicts and for free migrants exported to Siberia under 'recruitment rackets'. As Madame Khetagurova wrote, 'quite a lot of scum was sent to the Far East'.[2]

To handle the convict question, the Soviets established a powerful State enterprise called 'Dalstroy', manned largely by convicts and ex-convicts for the development of agriculture, mining, road building, and other activities, and for the establishment of towns in almost uninhabited regions such as the hinterland of the Sea of Okhotsk. The Soviets also used ex-members of the Red Army and the Red Fleet who settled with their families in regions such as the Ussuri river territory or worked at lumbering and fishing, or on the railways. Very important was the contribution of the Communist Youth League, the Komsomol, which is the backbone of the Soviet armies in the Far East, and amongst other exploits has founded the town of Komsomolsk on Amur. An outstanding achievement was that of Madame Khetagurova, the wife of a major in the Soviet Far Eastern Army. In a famous letter published in 1937 Khetagurova made a brilliant use of patriotism and sexual longings to inspire thousands of Soviet girls to secure by migration a wonderful future of wonderful work amongst wonderful people in an exotic dreamland where, above all, each was certain of securing, like Valentina Khetagurova herself, a husband; for

[1] Kolarz, op. cit., pp. 12 seq.   [2] Ibid., p. 20.

Siberia was a land of males, where from the polar tundras to Korea everyone dreamt of women.[1]

Amidst these efforts by convicts, soldiers, and man-hunting females, normal colonization continued under the urge of 'Stalin privileges'—taxation and other concessions, as in similar pioneering regions such as the Northern Territory of Australia. Under the second five-year plan many migrants established themselves in the towns, so that from 1926 to 1939 Vladivostok expanded from 108,000 to 206,000, and Khabarovsk from 52,000 to 199,000 —somewhat to the neglect of agriculture. Nevertheless, both the towns and industries of eastern Siberia are of growing importance. Amongst these are the coalfields of the Amur basin; near Vladivostok the giant metallurgical plant Amurstal; in Komsomolsk mineral deposits, including gold; and the Jewish settlement at Birobidzhan which contained in 1939 108,419 inhabitants.[2]

A recent and important development from the viewpoint of both strategy and economics has been the opening up of a northern sea route from Archangel, on the White Sea in Europe, to the Bering Strait. Up to the Second World War only one explorer, Adolf Erik Nordenskiöld of Sweden, had navigated this passage in 1878–9, but the Soviets had used ice-breakers, meteorological stations, and aircraft with such good results that in 1936 over a hundred ships operated on various sections of the route. During the war Glavsevmorput—the chief administration of the northern sea route—put into service improved American- and Soviet-built ice-breakers to reinforce the older British-built ships, a very necessary action as German submarines were sinking Russian merchant vessels. Although the Soviets have enforced secrecy since 1947, 'activities do continue on at least as big a scale as before'. Even prior to 1939, the timber centres and timber trade on Siberian

---

[1] Ibid., pp. 16 seq.

[2] Georges Jorré, *The Soviet Union*, London, 1950, pp. 84 seq.; Kolarz, op. cit., pp. 19 seq.; *Bulletin of the Institute for the Study of History and Culture of the U.S.S.R.*, pp. 22 seq. The Institute noted reports from the Khabarovsk Krai that of the hundreds of millions of hectares of land available, only 150,000 hectares were being cultivated, and expected that the near future would see a campaign to cultivate the vacant lands of the Far East, which would include mass migration from the European areas.

rivers such as the Ob and Yenisei had increased greatly, and Igarka, on the latter river, had grown from a few fishermen's huts to a town of over 20,000 people.[1]

J. P. Cole, using very recent material, came to the conclusion that Russian propaganda had exaggerated the importance of the shift of industry to Asian U.S.S.R., although the Soviets had selected for expansion certain regions east of the Urals, owing to the need of protection from the atomic weapons of the Western democracies, the establishment of communism in China, and the development of new agricultural lands in western Siberia and northern Kazakhstan. Nevertheless, Russian production, excepting perhaps that of food, is still concentrated in three great regions, Moscow, the south in Europe, and the Ural area which is partly European and partly Asiatic. Cole's statistics show that the regions east of the Urals contain less than 10 per cent. of the U.S.S.R.'s steel-producing capacity and that almost all the new iron or steel works listed in 1954 were in the Urals or in Europe. In Siberia almost the whole of the industrial development is close to the trans-Siberian railway, away from which industrial development has been very limited. Nevertheless, the sixth Soviet five-year plan includes the highly important projects of developing the comparatively safe regions of Kuzbas to the west of the Yenisei and of the Lake Baykal area, which is nearer to Peking and the Chinese industrial centres north of that capital than are the Siberian industrial centres such as Khabarovsk. Already the Sino-Russian partnership has completed a most important railway across Mongolia to connect the Lake Baykal region with Peking. This railway shortens the journey from Moscow to Peking by 1,141 kilometres.[2]

In spite of Cole's cautious appraisement of the development in the far-eastern section of Siberia, the region is important to the Pacific peoples who naturally regard such activities as the stationing of Russian submarines at Vladivostok with anxious eyes. In

[1] T. E. Armstrong, 'The Soviet Northern Sea Route', *Geog. Journal*, London, June 1955.

[2] J. P. Cole, 'A New Industrial Area in the Asiatic U.S.S.R.', ibid., Sept. 1956; V. P. Petrov, 'New Railway Links between China and the Soviet Union', ibid., Dec. 1956. See also Chapter VIII below.

spite of the harsh climate (the mouth of the Amur is frozen for 177 days a year) the area is making progress and already contains important industrial centres and fairly large and growing cities such as Khabarovsk, Vladivostok, Komsomolsk, and Birobidzhan. Birobidzhan is the capital of the Jewish autonomous province, and of its population of 106,000, 25,000 are Jews.[1]

In conclusion a word should be said on the 'White Siberian Policy' which is in direct contradiction to the Soviet recommendations on racial equality, and, in Kolarz's opinion, contains the seeds of grave trouble in the relations between Russia and China. Although the Soviet attitudes to Japan were those of a ruthless European power against an Asiatic people, Russia was friendly to the Chinese and Koreans, so much so that there may have been as many as 300,000 Koreans in the Soviet Far East where it seemed that a little Soviet Korea was being built up. About 1937, however, the position changed completely and the Koreans disappeared. The Soviets adopted the same attitude to the Chinese who numbered 22,000 in Vladivostok in 1926. In spite of the Chinese and other orientals supplying 50 per cent. of all manpower in the coal-mining and 35 per cent. in the timber industries, the Chinese were purged so drastically that between the censuses of 1926 and 1939 their numbers in the Soviets fell from 92,000 to 29,000, even on conservative Russian estimates.[2] Kolarz believes that Russia is attempting the impossible in trying 'to uphold the nationalist Russian "mystique" and the policy of the White Soviet Far East' . . . 'in other words, if Soviet Russia remains nationalistically Russian, then she is bound to be involved in a conflict with the Far Eastern nations, as a result of which she might lose her far-eastern possessions'. If, on the other hand, she swings to an international communist attitude, she must honour this change of heart by a voluntary retreat. Naturally, in a world situation where Russia and China are bound together by the common fear and hatred of the West, questions like those of Chinese migration into the Soviet Far East and the future of Mongolia are of secondary importance, but

[1] Jorré, op. cit., pp. 214–20, and M. Holdsworth, 'The Peoples of the Far North and the Far East', MS., Oxford, 1955, p. 5.
[2] Kolarz, op. cit., ch. ii.

these problems do exist and will require a solution one day.[1] In 1958 the position of the white peoples in east Siberia to the immediate north of an expanding China was certainly intriguing.

(H) *Population problems in British Australasia*

Omitting a few small islands, English-speaking Australasia consists of Australia and New Zealand. The total area of Australia is 2,974,581 square miles, with a total population of 8,307,481 in 1950, which increased to over 9 million in 1954 and reached approximately 10 million at the end of 1958. The three islands of New Zealand comprise an area of 104,000 square miles with a population of 2,037,553 in mid-1953. Of these 123,199 were Maoris. Deducting some 2 million square miles of tropical or arid Australia, the areas suitable for Western colonization, without subtracting high mountain regions, comprise in Australia 720,000 square miles of country with a temperate climate and uniform or winter rains, and the whole 104,000 square miles of temperate New Zealand. This total of 824,000 square miles contains some 10 million Australians and 2 million New Zealanders, a total of about 12 million people, over 14 to the square mile. Permissible American comparisons in areas and climates are the block of country which includes California, Washington, Oregon, Nevada, and British Columbia, an area of 793,885 square miles, with 15·8 million people (1950–1), and Argentina—1,078,769 square miles and 18,379,000 people (1953). It appears, therefore, that from the aspects of numbers and density, the Western peoples of Australasia have made rather less progress than the invaders of temperate western North America or the temperate Argentine.

The patterns of the Western invasions of the region and of their consequences resemble those in the zones of settlement colonization in English-speaking America and south-eastern Siberia, for the climates were temperate and the aboriginals few—perhaps 300,000 Australoids, 2,000 Tasmanoids, and 200,000 Maoris. The British Australians exterminated the Tasmanoids as the Canadians did the Boethics of Newfoundland, and reduced the mainland aboriginals from 300,000 to 71,389 in 1957 (p. 67). Of these

[1] Kolarz, op. cit., ch. vii.

41,266 were full bloods who are still decreasing in numbers, while there were also 30,123 mixed bloods who were showing a slight advance. The Maori, whom the white invasion of New Zealand decreased from perhaps 200,000 in 1820 to 37,500 in 1871, made such a remarkable recovery that in 1957 they numbered 145,671, as noted, although it is certain that the group now contains much white blood, perhaps up to 50 per cent.[1]

There were differences, however, the principal being that the Westerners did not make any important contacts with Australia until 1788, or with New Zealand until the early part of the nineteenth century when Europe was entering the period of the democratic, scientific, industrial, and agrarian revolutions with the swarming of peoples and the growth of liberal ideas. Hence no Spanish curtain descended over these lands for a period of centuries, nor did the Europeans cling, as in the United States, to the coastal margins for many decades. For these reasons the Western invasions of these two young countries are particularly interesting, for the advances were recent enough for various aspects of the moving frontiers and changing landscapes to be clear and understandable from the outset. Also the changes were ethnologically simpler than in most other regions, for the aboriginal types were comparatively few and the exotics outstandingly British. Again, although both Australia and New Zealand possessed fine forests and other natural resources, the shortage of economic plants and animals was so great that the invaders were forced to rely almost wholly on exotics. These importations produced great changes in the landscape, as the invaders put vast areas under pastoral grasses

---

[1] For authorities on the Australian aboriginals and Maoris, see *W.S.N.P.*, chs. vi–ix. Little new material on the history of the administration of these peoples has appeared since E. J. B. Foxcroft, *Australian Native Policy*, Melbourne University Press, 1941, and I. L. G. Sutherland, *The Maori People Today*, Auckland, 1940. In Australia, however, the Hon. Paul Hasluck, Federal Minister of Territories and author of *Black Australians*, Melbourne University Press, 1942, has been putting into practice for the benefit of the aboriginals of the Northern Territory a policy in part resembling that of John Collier's 'New Day for Indians', under Franklin D. Roosevelt's New Deal. The policy and its results are set out in publications such as *The Progress of the Australian Territories*, 1950–6, and *New Hope for Old Australians*, Dept. of Territories, Canberra, 1957; also *Indigenous Peoples*, 'Australian Aboriginals', pp. 84 seq. and 283 seq.; 'Maoris', pp. 285 seq.

and clovers, and under grains such as wheat, and effected the sweeping alterations necessary for industrial city life. In Australia, in particular, the invasions resembled those in the United States. There were similar advances from the east coast westwards, similar mineral discoveries which 'precipitated Australia into nationhood', similar conquests of arid conditions, similar development of pasturing, agriculture, and secondary industry, and the same increasing tempo which accompanied the coming of steam transport, of the internal combustion engine, and of the aeroplane.[1]

There is no room here to discuss in detail all the population problems of Australia and New Zealand, but something should be said about their migration policies and about the attempts made by the Australians to develop their frontier in the tropics. As regards migration, both countries were to a large extent populated by British peoples, both have considerable ethnic uniformity, and both wish to maintain this uniformity together with high living standards partly supported by tariffs and advanced social legislation. Nevertheless, both countries were badly frightened when the Second World War extended to their doors, and both realized that they must increase their populations for reasons of defence. H. Belshaw, writing in 1947, pointed out that to reach a population of 5 million within fifty years, New Zealand would have to absorb 70,000 persons per annum, from birth or migration, as large an increase as took place from 1936 to 1941. Recent government statements, he said, had shown a willingness to allow some increase in migration, particularly from the United Kingdom, but the nation would be nervous in regard to the admission of persons of non-British stock in large numbers and the unions would fear any competition which might affect labour standards.[2] In a later work Belshaw stated that in 1950–1 net immigration to New Zealand

---

[1] For Australian references see: *Cambridge History of the British Empire*, vol. vii, Part I—Australia, C.U.P., 1933, and *Australian Encyclopedia*, Sydney, 1958 (10 volumes), also *The Australian Junior Encyclopedia*, Melbourne, 1951 (2 volumes). For a summary of the main authorities see *A.C.A.* For New Zealand: *Cambridge History of the British Empire*, vol. vii, Part II—New Zealand, 1934; H. Belshaw, ed., *New Zealand*, University of California Press, 1947; H. Miller, *New Zealand*, London, 1950; F. R. Callaghan, ed., *Science in New Zealand*, Wellington, 1957.

[2] Belshaw, op. cit., p. 122.

was running at the rate of some 10,000 per annum, of whom about half were assisted persons. The policy of the Government was to raise the number of assisted migrants to 7,500 in 1951 and 1952, and thereafter to 10,000 per annum. In 1952 3,848 assisted migrants came from the United Kingdom and 1,099 from the Netherlands, together with 2,661 displaced persons. In 1947–50 the population was advancing at rather more than 2 per cent. a year, or more than double the rate of 1926–45. Belshaw felt that this advance to 2 per cent. per annum was as much as the country could absorb.[1]

New Zealand as a small country received comparatively little criticism for the paucity of her population. This, after all, averages 19 to the square mile, which is about the same as Brazil and considerably more dense than regions such as Borneo that are closer to the expanding populations of Asia.

Very different was the case of Australia with 10 million white people in 2·9 million square miles, or roughly 3 to the square mile, including the really arid country and the tropics, which is the way in which the outside world, and particularly the peoples of Asia, regard the problem. This may be fairly compared with Canada 6 and Russia in Asia 2 per square mile. If, however, we deduct the arid lands and tropics as in most cases unsuitable for settlers, we find, as noted above, that Australia had in 1958 some 10 million people in 720,000 square miles of country, or about 14 to the square mile, which obviously is still far below its capacities. Australians naturally estimate the potentialities of the continent at the high living standards of the Western countries—a fact that the outside world, particularly the Asian peoples, know full well.

Various authorities have made estimates of the population potentialities which for 'any race' run up to 200 million. On the basis of rainfall Barkley (1930) estimated 46 million for any people. Griffith Taylor (1940), using rainfall, temperatures, coal, and topography, placed possible numbers at 60 million at European living standards, or 30 million at double such standards. Gentilli (1949), using precipitation effectiveness and topography, with United States densities as a comparison, reached the very low totals of 13 million for white peoples and 18·7 million for any race. One

[1] H. Belshaw, *Immigration*, Wellington, 1952.

difficulty about all such estimates is the failure to allow for the inventiveness of man. Time and again in the Mediterranean region of South Australia, the settlers felt that their agricultural or pastoral or secondary industries had reached their limit, only to find that by dry farming with the use of trace elements, or by the pumping of water for quite unexpected distances, production and population density continued to increase. We have already shown that the Australian population has advanced at a rate which has made ridiculous the pessimistic guesses of authorities such as Warren S. Thompson, who wrote in 1945: 'Australia now belongs to that group of European peoples which were placed in the "stationary" category. Her total population cannot reasonably be expected to increase much beyond eight millions by the end of the present century unless there is a much larger net immigration or unless the birth rate increases.'[1] Such critics failed to foresee the possibilities of the Australian natural increase advancing from 7·95 in 1931–5 to 13·4 in 1950–4, with a consequent natural growth in numbers from 52,649 in 1931–5 to 117,293 per annum in 1950–5.[2]

Her proximity to Asia and her vast area of low population density have aroused much criticism against Australia, and this has been turned almost to fury by her so-called White Australia Policy —her famous or infamous methods of restricting migration. This she adopted because in the early days the Chinese immigrants, who in the gold-rush period numbered some 38,000, undercut the white Australians, while in Queensland the Kanakas or South Sea Islanders revenged themselves for Australian treatment (which included 'blackbirding' in the sugar industries) by developing and handing on diseases to such an extent that white male health became the worst in the continent.[3] Today medical developments could

[1] W. S. Thompson, op. cit., ch. iv, p. 55, above. For population estimates: Griffith Taylor, *Australia*, London, 1940, pp. 440 seq. The underestimate of Australian population growth seems to have come from S. H. Wolstenholme in the *Economic Record* of Dec. 1936, which has been extensively quoted by authorities such as W. D. Forsyth in his very useful *Myth of Open Spaces*, Melbourne University Press, 1942, pp. 146, 202.

[2] *Australian Commonwealth Year Book*, 1956, p. 579.

[3] For Asians in Australia: J. Lyng, *Non-Britishers in Australia*, Melbourne University Press, 1935, pp. 157 seq.; Myra Willard, *History of the White Australia Policy*, Melbourne, 1923; *H.P.N.T.* and *W.S.T.*, ch. vi.

improve coloured migrant health, although the Americans still suffer from the Negro in this respect.[1] Nevertheless, the vast bulk of historic and contemporary evidence from North America, South Africa, Fiji, and so on, supports the Australian in refusing to admit to permanent residence peoples who are in race, outlook, and experience remote from the European Australian, and who are therefore in the short term almost impossible to assimilate, although in the long term the mixture might produce a people of higher capacity than either parent race. In point of fact, the 'White Australia Policy' is no more offensive or foolish than the White American, the White Siberian, the Yellow Chinese, or the dozens of similar policies by which various ethnic groups have resisted, and still resist, the more polite forms of what in reality are invasions. The aboriginals of Fiji were credited with the habit of eating anyone 'with salt in his eyes', that is anyone arriving from the sea, and the later history of Fiji under European invasions and diseases indicates that the islanders might have been happier if they had made no exceptions to their cannibalistic diet.

Australians feel that the only fault with which they can be justly charged has been their failure to follow the United States in permitting a small token migration of coloured peoples in order to prove what is actually true—the fact that the Australian policy of restriction is economic and usually is not based on any racial distaste. Urged on by fears and criticisms, Australia made in the post-war years vigorous efforts to foster immigration, efforts which strangely enough were initiated and for some years led by Australian Labour governments, who in the past had not been over-friendly to migration. From 1950 to 1954 Australia assisted in bringing to the country a total of 469,074 migrants (the surplus of arrivals over departures), an average of 93,815 per annum, which, with an improved natural increase of 1·43 per cent., lifted the total population from 8,307,481 (1947) to 9,090,395 (1954). This post-war migration differed from the early migration which was so largely British and resembled, to some extent, the 1930's pre-war migration which Forsyth termed in 1942 'the new immigration' and in which, as for example in 1938, Italians, Greeks,

[1] G. Mydral, *An American Dilemma*, New York, 1944, particularly ch. 7.

Poles, and Germans predominated.[1] This swing away from an almost exclusive British migration continued after the recent war. For example, in 1947–51 permanent arrivals numbered 572,300, of whom 278,500 were British and 293,800 non-British, the latter including 168,200 displaced persons. Charles A. Price, however, showed in 1957 that the official statistics followed international usage and failed to indicate important points such as the number of Australians who returned after more than a year overseas. His calculations were correct in reducing substantially the figures of both total and British migration, which seem to make the natural increase even more significant.[2] Australians can claim that they are taking the majority of their migrants from some of the most crowded countries on earth. The statistics for the density of population given by the *Australian Commonwealth Year Book* of 1956 indicate that in 1953 the United Kingdom (540) had a denser population per square mile than India (293); the Netherlands (839) than Japan (610); and Italy (413) than Indonesia (139).[3]

A few words are necessary on the Australian tropics, a matter that has aroused criticism against Australia for her so-called empty north which is invitingly near the increasing millions of Asia. Australia can, however, justly defend herself on geographical grounds. She has not neglected her tropics, and the story of her successes and failures provides a lesson for all peoples who attempt to send permanent white settlers to such areas. In Australia some 1,149,320 square miles of country—the whole of the north—lies in the tropics. This can be divided into a small area of 94,000 square miles of country in or fairly near the coastlands of north Queensland which enjoys uniform rains from the monsoons and Trades. To the north and west of this region lie 470,000 square miles of country to which the monsoons bring in summer rains of from

[1] For Italians and Germans in Australia: W. D. Borrie, *Italians and Germans in Australia*, Canberra, 1954; C. A. Price, *German Settlers in South Australia*, Melbourne University Press, 1945; Forsyth, *Myth of Open Spaces; W.S.T.*, ch. vi.

[2] C. A. Price, 'The Effects of Post War Immigration on the Growth of Population, Ethnic Composition and Religious Structure of Australia', *The Australian Quarterly*, Sydney, Dec. 1957.

[3] *Commonwealth Year Book*, 1956, p. 585; A. J. Rose, 'European Immigration in Australia' ,*Geog. Review*, Oct. 1958.

PLATE IV

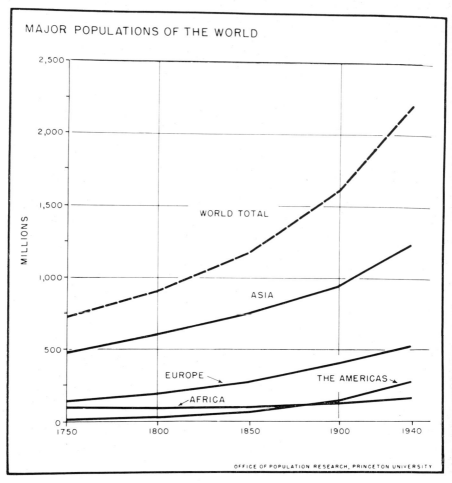

Major populations of the world, 1750–1940

From *Public Health and Democracy in the Far East*, The Rockefeller Foundation, 1950

50 to 20 inches. The rest of the Australian tropics, areas of almost 585,000 square miles, experience a low and uncertain rainfall and a high evaporation so that they can be included in the 1,660,000 square miles of country which must be classed as arid lands or deserts. The Australian experience in the small area of uniform rains was remarkable. The moving frontier entered Queensland in the 1860's, and the comparatively well and safely watered coast-lands and plateaux with some fertile soils were developed for sugar with Kanaka (South Sea Island) labour. Terrible white and coloured mortality followed, and to the fury of the Western exploiters, which nearly produced another brother's struggle like the American Civil War, the Kanakas were repatriated after the Federation of 1901, and an amazed world saw Australian sugar succeed with white labour, protected by bounties.[1] With the expatriation of the Kanakas health recovered. I found in 1936 that the white peoples showed few, if any, signs of supposed tropical degeneracy; indeed the birth, death, and marriage rates of tropical Queensland were, in 1948–52, better than those of non-tropical parts of the continent. Although Western whites—not least the women—obviously dislike tropical heat (why go to the tropics?), the population of Queensland tropics increased from 247,236 to 270,536 between 1933–7 and 1948–52, that is at about half the rate for Australia outside the tropics.[2] It is most important to note, however, that a substantial proportion of this population is Mediterranean (south European) in origin. In 1931 a committee of inquiry found that in the northern sugar lands, which produced 60 per cent. of a crop that more than supplied the needs of Australia, 43·6 per cent. of the employees were foreign or natura-lized. Borrie concluded in 1954 that the picture was one of a minority who, emerging from the vicissitudes of economic depres-sion and war, were still far from completely integrated with the

[1] W.S.T., ch. vi.
[2] Grenfell Price, 'The Social Challenge', in Northern Australia—Task for a Nation, Australian Institute of Political Science, Sydney, 1954; R. K. Macpherson, 'Environmental Problems in Tropical Australia', Report on living conditions in the Northern Territory and New Guinea, Commonwealth Govt., Canberra, 1956; C. S. Christian, 'Developments in Northern Australian Agriculture', R.G.S. of Australasia, S.A. Branch, Proceedings, Dec. 1957.

social and cultural life of the majority; but the turning-point had been reached, and the forces operating in favour of assimilation, whether economic, cultural and social, or demographic, were much stronger than any which were operating against their ultimate fusion with Australians.[1] On the whole the development of a great and prosperous sugar industry in the north-eastern marginal tropics of Queensland is one of the most remarkable and praiseworthy of Western achievements in such regions.

In spite of repeated efforts Australia found that over the monsoonal tropics—the 470,000 square miles of country bordering her northern shores—close settlement by either white or Chinese people was impossible owing to isolation, unreliable rainfall, poor leached soils, and pests. The nation made some progress with the pearl shell and mining industries, including the recent development of uranium, but failure in many agricultural experiments showed that, excepting for some comparatively small areas of good soil, the country was cattle country, capable of considerable development if capital was expended upon the improvement of water and transport, particularly roads, railways, and the lifting of beef by air.[2]

Information from other tropical regions indicates that a coloured population of low living standards might in some favoured spots support life by obtaining a gross return of £2 to £3 per acre.[3] Australians believe, however, that the expanding peoples of Asia would be best served by the extension of birth control and industrialization, and by utilizing for migration some of the sparsely settled regions which, like Borneo or Sumatra, are their own possessions and are nearer to hand than Australia. This viewpoint seems to have the support of fair-minded demographers, who like Irene Taeuber stress the need of birth control, or Maurice Zinkin the need of capital.[4]

[1] Borrie, op. cit., chs. vi, vii, p. 127.
[2] N.A. See also p. 224, note E, for works on this subject.
[3] Grenfell Price, W.S.T., p. 114.
[4] I. B. Taeuber, 'Recent Population Developments in Japan', *Pacific Affairs*, Mar. 1956; M. Zinkin, *Asia and the West*, Inst. of Pacific Relations, 1953, pp. 291 seq.

V

THE HUMAN INVASIONS—SOJOURNER COLONIZATION

(A) EAST AND SOUTH-EAST ASIA

Character of the invasions

FROM the viewpoint of human numbers the most important of the six divisions of the Pacific world is East and South-east Asia, for these regions, together with the sub-continent of India and the island of Ceylon, contain the vast majority of the Asian population which is more than half the total for mankind. In 1955 the United Nations placed the world population at 2,487 million including estimates for the U.S.S.R. and China, and that of Asia, excluding the U.S.S.R., at 1,317 million.[1] (See Pl. IV.) In this connexion it cannot be stressed too strongly that the immense size of the populations of China, India, Japan, Indonesia, and many minor Asian countries is recent, and is due largely to the comparative peace, law, order, health services, and technologically improved production brought about by the white invasions. Certain other factors must also be repeated. First, the Western invasions were but an interlude in the historic outpouring of Asian peoples into other countries and upon other peoples. Second, this Western interlude was extremely brief; the maximum time of contact in lands such as India, the East Indies, and the Philippines dates back only to 1498, and in these lands and in others such as China and Japan, the period of pressure, including conquest or attempted conquest, has been in general very short, although its effects have been immense. Panikkar terms the years from Vasco da Gama's arrival in India in 1498 to the withdrawal of the Western fleets from Asian bases in 1949 'the period of maritime authority', and

---

[1] *U.N. Statistical Papers*, series A, vol. vii, no. 1, New York, 1955.

states that contacts extended over 450 years but that Western dominion lasted for only a century although it transformed practically every aspect of life in most Asian lands.[1] I have stressed, and must stress further in later chapters, the many-sided character of the invasions in which the white peoples were extremely few, and were, from the viewpoint of racial mixture, of very slight importance. Future historians, geographers, and demographers may well give priority of place to factors such as the Western introduction of exotic plants and animals, and to the many aspects of Western culture such as the pioneering of health and educational services, of law, of technological science, of Christianity, of democracy, and of communism, the latest importation from the West.[2] These aspects of the invasions have created, and will continue to create, some of the greatest and most important transformations mankind has seen.

Naturally the character and extent of these transformations varied regionally under the influence of varying factors such as the different environments. As previously indicated, the invaders effected in Asia few changes through racial mixture, nor were their diseases of importance, unless it can be proved that they introduced syphilis and helped to extend malaria, as, for example, when the latter appeared in Batavia in 1731–2 (Chapter VI). The moving frontiers of exotic animals and plants also varied greatly. There was possibly little change in historic agricultural civilizations such as China, whereas the introduction of exotics such as rubber in the plantation regions of South-east Asia and the Indies greatly altered many landscapes, while the development of cities in many regions had considerable effects. Nevertheless, it is probably correct to say that the greatest transformations were those which came from the moving frontiers of culture—e.g. in the spread of Christianity and technological science.

It was unfortunate that these transformations were assisted by and, indeed, to some degree depended upon a colonialism which the West only too often exerted against reluctant indigenous people. Nevertheless, if one takes into account, as is essential, the many-sided nature of the invasions and the immense and rapid

[1] K. M. Panikkar, *Asia and Western Dominance*, London, 1954, p. 479.
[2] Ibid., pp. 494 seq.

results which they achieved in a multitude of fields, the Asian peoples should mingle praise for the good with their magnification and condemnation of the evil. The fundamental difference between the human invasions of East and South-east Asia as compared with the conquests of the Americas, Siberia, and Australasia was that the Asian invasions were of the 'sojourner' variety, whereas the invasions of the temperate and sparsely settled territories were, in the most important cases, of the 'settlement' type. As noted in Chapter III, climatic conditions in lands such as Burma, the immense weight of vast indigenous populations as in Japan, or a combination of both factors as in India and Indonesia, kept the white exotic, and still more his wife and children, as visitors rather than as the settlers which they became in temperate and sparsely populated lands. Any Westerner who paid a lengthy visit to the East could not fail to observe the resentment which Europeans, such as certain British 'Sahibs', created by their attitude to the persons and to the cultural possessions such as the religions of the Asians. To quote the usually moderate Panikkar: 'The racial arrogance of the Europeans, their assumed attitude of mental and moral superiority, and even the religious propaganda to which all the Asian countries were subjected, gave rise to a common political outlook in the Asia of the twentieth century.'[1] Visiting Burma and the Shan States in 1929–30 I saw quite enough Western arrogance to understand the resentment of the Asians. After participating with reasonable moderation in hectic Christmas and New Year festivities, I asked what the charming and courteous Burmese must think of the Europeans. The answer was, 'What does it matter?— they think we are mad anyway'. Nevertheless, observers could not fail to realize that the European and his wife were only too often facing distressing climatic conditions and distressing Asian attitudes and inefficiency which, e.g. in matters of health, required an 'on-guardedness' that was both unceasing and wearying in the extreme.[2] Nor could impartial observers fail to recognize that in the later stages of the invasions, and in the British territories at any rate, a capable and devoted civil service was setting high standards of administrative capacity and, above all, honesty. Guy Wint,

[1] Ibid., p. 494.   [2] *W.S.T.*, pp. 210–13.

using authorities such as Panikkar, draws attention to many of the evils of the British rule in India, but claims that in the early period the British, who were replacing 'collapsed' Indian governments, were not entirely unpopular, and that in spite of many weaknesses their legal system initiated the movement for political and other freedoms, such as the emancipation of women, while their civil service was 'superior to any which had been known before in Asia, the Chinese mandarinate not excepted'.[1]

Authorities and research

Before I give a very brief outline of the major events in the Western advance and retreat in Asia, I should say a word on some of the authorities which are available to the student and upon the necessity of further research upon many aspects of the subject. In the first place it can be claimed that a number of human and historical geographers have published important and unbiased work, and one awaits with interest the results of further research on comparatively recent events, such as the geographical aspects of the famous 'long march' of the Chinese Communists, or the geographical bases of their recent success.[2] The student now has access to many official and institutional studies such as the reports of various officers of the United Nations or the Rockefeller report of 1950, *Public Health and Demography in the Far East*. Institutes of International Affairs and Pacific Relations have made their contributions, and private scholars, many of whom have been participants in, or observers of, great events, have added to the spate of publications. Particularly interesting is the comparatively new school of Asian writers such as K. M. Panikkar, who presents the Asian viewpoint with comparatively little bias, Rajah B. Manikam,

---

[1] Guy Wint, *Spotlight on Asia*, London, 1955, pp. 22–23; *The British in Asia*, London, 1954, ch. iv; Panikkar, op. cit., Part III, ch. 1, for India in the age of empire 1858–1914. Panikkar and Wint both examine the course of events in the more important Asian countries. For the emancipation of women: Panikkar, op. cit., pp. 497–8, and H. Subandrio, 'The Changing Social Position of Women in the East', in *Eastern and Western World*, The Hague, 1953, p. 115: 'Asian women have been granted prerogatives which have only been acquired by their sisters in the West after a prolonged and bitter struggle.'

[2] C. P. Fitzgerald, *Revolution in China*, London, 1952, chs. iii, iv.

who forecasts the development of an Asian type of Christianity, and S. Chandrasekhar, whose pro-Asian attitude is as biased as that of any of the old die-hard Western imperialists.[1] Some of these authorities are noted below, but it must be remembered that both the East and the West are still rather too close to recent events for clear judgement on matters which are not plain records of scientific or other indisputable facts.

Even in the impartial fields of science, many major problems demand research. If, for example, a student considers one of the greatest of modern world problems—the growth of Asian population—he will face the question of how far that growth has been created by indigenous factors such as an increase in agricultural food supplies by historic Asian methods, or how far by Western influences such as the introduction of Western-type medical and health services. The falling death-rate and increasing length of life in many Eastern countries has obviously been due to the latter factor, but I have encountered no general study of the subject, although it is clearly a matter of major world importance (Chapter VI).

The course and character of the invasions

The Portuguese reached India in 1498, captured Malacca in 1511, and penetrated to the Spice Islands in 1512, to Canton in 1514, and to Japan about 1542.[2] Although they were not always successful, their courage, ships, and cannon gained them victories such as the crushing defeat of the Arabian and Egyptian fleets in the battle of Diu in 1509. Some Asian rulers showed interest in

[1] Panikkar, op. cit.; Rajah B. Manikam, *Christianity and the Asian Revolution*, Joint East Asia Secretariat of the International Missionary Council and the World Council of Churches, Diocesan Press, Madras, 1954; S. Chandrasekhar, *Hungry People and Empty Lands*, London, 1954.

[2] Many useful publications provide the facts of the invasions. W. G. East and O. H. K. Spate, *The Changing Map of Asia*, London, 1950; F. B. Eldridge, *The Background of Eastern Seapower*; Panikkar, op. cit.; J. H. Parry, *Europe and a Wider World 1415–1715*; A. G. Keller, *Colonization*, a magnificent study; B. Penrose, *Travel and Discovery in the Renaissance*; H. Heaton, *Economic History of Europe*; O. Hardy and G. S. Dumke, *A History of the Pacific in Modern Times*, Boston, 1949; P. H. Clyde, *The Far East*, New York, 1949; P. E. Eckel, *The Far East since 1500*, London, 1948. Many of these works contain bibliographies which can be consulted for regional and other aspects of the subject.

Christianity, commerce, and particularly cannon, so that the Europeans were able to establish small trading posts and forts which they frequently placed on islands. The Portuguese were followed by four more sea powers, the Spaniards, who established themselves in Manila in 1571, the English and Dutch, who founded East Indian trading companies in 1600 and 1602 respectively, and the French, who made little progress in the Orient until after 1713. All these small Western nations were sea powers who could use the sea to establish little colonies of sojourners, but disunity was the keynote of the period, for the Western invaders were usually bitter antagonists and competitors, while the Asian peoples were frequently divided into small feudal states which tried to make use of the whites for individual aggrandizement rather than combining to resist their onslaught.

In Chapter II, I stressed the fact that the Westerners could never have conducted their invasions without sailing ships and sea-power together with the borrowing from Eastern cultures of such essentials as the lateen sail, the compass, and gunpowder. Although this is true, one would not go so far as Panikkar in his assertions that the domination of the East was due to the Western control of the seas and that the final failure of the European effort to conquer and hold Asia is an example of the limitation of sea-power. Maurice Zinkin saw through this over-simplification when he wrote: 'The techniques which gave the West its victory are not very romantic —joint-stock companies, drill, cannon founding, obedient commanders, ships that could sail against the wind. But behind them lay the whole of the West's political and scientific tradition.' Of the transition from sea to land warfare, Zinkin said:

The most obvious European supremacy was in weapons. In the beginning, in the seventeenth century, it was the superior manœuvrability of Portuguese and Dutch ships, increased still more by the invention of the fore and aft rig in the sixteenth century, and the greater accuracy of their cannon which gave them the victory in every sea fight from the first great battle of Diu in 1509 to the taking of Macassar in 1666. Then it was the better discipline of European and European trained troops, drilled to wheel and advance in formation, and to obey orders even in battle, and the greater range and accuracy of their artillery, which made of a few dozens or hundreds of men the arbiters of Empire. . . . In the great battles of the eighteenth century in India, when half the country was the cockpit of French and English ambition, there were never more than a few hundred Englishmen or Frenchmen involved.[1]

In face of a divided Asia the Western successes were spectacular, particularly with the coming of the industrial and scientific revolutions, the growth of European populations, of technological skill, and of means and routes of transport. Thus during the four and a half centuries from 1500 to 1950 the Westerners conquered and held in sojourner dominion the whole of East and South-east Asia with the exception of Thailand and most of China.

In this struggle Portugal, and later Holland, secured the East Indies; Spain, the Philippines; the British, Burma, Malaya, Singapore, and various islands; the Russians, the Amur region and Manchuria, while the United States later held the Philippines, and for a moment, Japan. For a time it seemed that even China itself would be carved like a melon between Britain, Russia, and France. Nevertheless, it must again be emphasized that the period of serious Western pressure did not open until the nineteenth century, excepting in the East Indies and the Philippines, and then was very short. Thus it was not until 1842, after the Opium war with China, that Britain gained the Treaty of Nanking, which marks the opening of China to the Western influences in the nineteenth and twentieth centuries. In 1853 the American, Commodore Perry, forcibly induced Japan to abandon her partial seclusion. The British obtained control of Singapore and the Malay States from 1819 to 1914, and of Burma from 1826 to 1885. France secured Indo-China as a result of wars and negotiations between the years 1858 and 1907. As all these Asian countries won, or seemed certain to win, complete independence in the 1940's and 1950's, it is clear that with the exception of the East Indies and the Philippines, which the Western peoples occupied in the sixteenth century, Western colonialism afflicted or benefited many parts of Asia for little more than a hundred years. As we have seen, the primary base of early Western dominance

[1] Panikkar, op. cit., p. 17; Zinkin, op. cit., pp. 45–49.

was sea-power, but sea-power alone could never have prevailed against the leading powers of Asia had they shown any real unity. The truth was that, as noted above, much of the area—South-east Asia, the East Indies, and the Philippines—was torn between small and warring feudal rulers, and it was very largely European managerial grouping that produced the extensive and violently nationalistic states of the twentieth century, although it remains to be seen if these large groupings can be maintained.[1]

The Asians opposed the invasions. Japan excluded foreigners, with some slight exceptions, while China repeatedly fought the invaders. As, however, the Russians wanted a sphere of influence in the north of China, the British in the centre, and the French in the south, the Westerners remained sufficiently united to enforce their demands on China, and even, in 1900, to march inland and capture Peking. Nevertheless, the exotics failed to obtain any deep-rooted control of the great East Asian countries, for in most cases they were struggling against either large and densely settled populations or unsuitable climates, and in some instances were contending with both. It is true that the Dutch created some settlement colonization in the East Indies and built up a small mixed population with unhappy results.[2]

The Western retreat

In general the invaders could establish only sojourner colonies, conducting trade, plantations, and mining in South-east Asia, and in China and Japan only sojourner posts engaged in little save missionary enterprise and commerce. This sojourner nature of the European domination of Asia was one of the many causes of a retreat which strangely enough occurred at a time when the Western powers had never been so strongly equipped with weapons of offence. In spite of Chinese suggestions that atomic bombs would have proved useless against a largely agrarian community, the American decision to refrain from using the utmost

[1] Panikkar, op. cit., pp. 501 seq.
[2] P. W. van der Veur, 'The Eurasians of Indonesia—Castaways of Colonialism', *Pacific Affairs*, June 1954. Visiting Java in 1929 I formed the opinion that the Eurasians felt themselves the outcasts of both parent stocks.

strength against a China whose 'volunteer' forces had intervened in the Korean War may rank as one of the turning-points of history, for it reversed the firm attitude taken in regard to Hiroshima and Nagasaki and the firm attitudes of the Western nations in the days of their aggressive greatness. Future historians may decide that a soft answer was a step in turning away the wrath of Asia, yet, on the contrary, they may consider that an exhibition of the full power of the West would have done more to restore European face than half a dozen Colombo plans, which some Asians regard as a white admission of guilt, while others think, quite rightly, that Western philanthropy is being exercised partly because, in the words of the Australian Minister of External Affairs, R. G. Casey, 'we feel the hot breath of international communism on our necks in Australia', for, as he added, 'no nation can escape its geography'.[1] What really happened was that the Western powers had split into two immense camps, idealistically poles apart and mutually antagonistic and apprehensive. Each side was backing different Asian horses and each side was too fearful of Western retaliation to conduct an all-out offensive. Added to this dread was a genuine growth of democratic and philanthropic feeling, which in the British Commonwealth had long expressed itself in doctrines such as Colonial Trusteeship and the Dual Mandate, while as early as 1934 the Americans passed the Tydings–McDuffie Act to give the Philippines their independence in 1946, although America still exercised some economic tutelage and retained some naval, air, and military bases.[2] As Zinkin wrote, the withdrawal of western European power was sudden, but the system was archaic for some years before war broke out. India was the head of the system, and here the British were preparing their departure not without pride in having prepared India for self-

[1] G. Greenwood and N. Harper, *Australia in World Affairs 1950–1955*, Melbourne, 1957, pp. 271–2. K. S. Latourette, *The American Record in the Far East*, New York, 1952, gives the story of MacArthur's desire to bomb the 'privileged sanctuary' of Manchuria and President Truman's recall of the General in 1951. H. V. Evatt, *Foreign Policy of Australia*, Sydney, 1945; W. Levi, *American–Australian Relations*, University of Minnesota, 1947.

[2] C. Robequain, *Malaya, Indonesia, Borneo and the Philippines*, London, 1954, pp. 420, 421.

government.[1] The same process was evident in Ceylon, Burma, Malaya, Singapore, and in Dutch Indonesia, even before the trends of the age were accelerated by the two suicidal European wars. The much-criticized Dutch realized that they would have to leave the East Indies. Thus H. J. van Mook, Lieutenant-Governor of Indonesia, noted that as early as 1819 G. K. van Hagendorp, who had headed the liberation movement in the Netherlands against Napoleon, foresaw a distant day when the Dutch would lose all their colonies but should try and retain the ties of friendship and commerce. Van Mook realized that after the Second World War the Dutch must go, but hoped that they would go at a time most advantageous to the true interests of the Indonesians, a hope which was dispelled partly through the attitudes of the British, Americans, and Australians. 'So', wrote van Mook, 'the plan to achieve a sufficient measure of internal security and administrative and economic reconstruction before the United States of Indonesia was to be declared independent, had failed. The course of events forced the Netherlands government to relinquish its responsibility prematurely.' Later developments were to arouse thoughts that van Mook's ideas were not altogether unsound, together with the realization that the agglomeration of states which the Dutch had created might dissolve. K. S. Latourette is of a similar opinion in regard to the peoples of South-east Asia in general. He writes that a slower transition might have been better for the nations of these areas and might have been followed by more stable and democratic régimes than those which emerged from the Second World War.[2]

The Japanese had long copied certain features of European technological science, particularly military, naval, and air developments. They had finally and decisively broken the prestige of the European in Asia when they defeated Russia in 1904–5, and they turned the last screws in the coffin of European supremacy when they expelled the United States, Britain, France, and Holland from the west central Pacific and, single-handed, kept them at bay for

---

[1] Zinkin, op. cit., p. 3.

[2] H. J. van Mook, *The Stakes of Democracy in Southeast Asia*, London, 1950, p. 262; K. S. Latourette, op. cit., pp. 198–9; W. H. van Helsdingen, ed., *Mission Interrupted*, Amsterdam, 1945.

several years. As Guy Wint writes, 'in the mind of the rest of Asia these shortcomings of Japan were modified by the recollection that in 1941 it was the Japanese armies which gave some of the countries of Southeast Asia their first taste of liberation from Western rule'.[1] The Western powers had, in fact, become too fearful and too philanthropic to risk a ghastly conflict for rewards which had become increasingly unattractive. The important matter was the Western influences that remained behind.

Some results of the invasions

These influences, both psychological and material, were of fundamental importance. First, although comparatively few Westerners stayed on permanently in Asia, there remained vast numbers of Chinese, Indians, and other peoples who had moved to or within the Pacific under the lure of plantation, mining, or other employment.[2] Second, there survived the exotic plants and animals which the whites had introduced and which had become so important in the economy of South-east Asia as to make that area almost worthy of treatment as a separate and seventh division of the Pacific. Perhaps most important of all, however, were the cultural survivals, using the word 'culture' in its widest possible sense. These included weapons other than atomic weapons, technological machinery (a form of capital which was desperately needed to improve living standards), and Western knowledge and ideas adopted both from the Christian-democratic and communist camps. In spite of the retreat of the invaders the desire for Western living standards continued to increase. In Zinkin's words:

So long as the villager lived in a world where few were richer than himself, no one asked for more. Now, however, the spreading knowledge of greater wealth and higher standards which capitalism has made

[1] Wint, *Spotlight on Asia*, p. 53.

[2] I have not attempted to deal with the problem of plural societies in South-east Asia as it has been well covered by authorities such as V. Purcell, *The Chinese in Malaya*, O.U.P., 1948; *The Colonial Period in Southeast Asia*, Inst. of Pacific Relations, New York, 1953; V. Thompson and A. Adloff, *Minority Problems in South-east Asia*, Stanford University Press, 1955; P. Talbot, ed., *South Asia in the World Today*, University of Chicago Press, 1951; R. Emerson, *Representative Government in South East Asia*, Harvard University Press, Inst. of Pacific Relations, 1955; J. C. van Leur, ed., *Indonesian Trade and Society*, The Hague, 1955.

possible in the West, are shaking the old contentment to its foundations, for there is no quick method of attaining the higher standards which the peasant is now learning to want, and his frustration turns easily into an envy corrosive of all settled government.[1]

Population problems

The most immediately dangerous of all the consequences of the invasions is, in all probability, the continuance of the immense growth of population owing to comparative peace in certain vital areas, improved production and transport, and the beneficial effects of Western medical science on the death-rate. Chandra-sekhar says, in an analysis of the dilemma of colonialism, that an advanced imperialistic country sets up a strong and stable govern-ment in a colony, creates peace at home and abroad, introduces medical services, hygiene, and sanitation, and improves the death-without altering the birth- rate. Hence population increases while living standards fall as economic development is directed towards the production of primary goods for the benefit of the metro-politan power rather than towards industrialization and urbaniza-tion which might improve the colonial living standards. This statement is correct in its population aspect. It seems doubtful, however, whether Asian governments, frequently inexperienced and inefficient, and sometimes corrupt, will be able to create urbanism and higher living standards with sufficient speed to avoid the disappointment that Chandrasekhar fears so much.[2]

Returning to the population pattern one finds that from 1750 to 1953 the total Asian population, excluding the U.S.S.R., grew from 500 to 1,317 million. In 1955 the United Nations put the population of East and South-east Asia at some 738 million, and

[1] Zinkin, op. cit., pp. 32–33. Panikkar, op. cit., pp. 497–507, gives an important analysis of the Western influences which at that time seemed likely to be permanent. These were 'an imposing and truly magnificent legal structure', certain political, social, and administrative systems, great cities, vast integrated territories, Western ideas, Western literature, and a realization of the importance of the outside world.

[2] Chandrasekhar, op. cit., ch. v; J. de Castro in his Geography of Hunger, London, 1952, pp. 61–69, puts forward the important theory that hungry com-munities with protein deficiencies are particularly prolific, as shown by 'the sensational experiments' of J. R. Slonaker, who subjected groups of rats to various diets, those rich in proteins reducing the fertility rate and the number of offspring.

that of India and Ceylon at 456 million, while the latest Chinese census gives a population of about 600 million as against former official estimates of some 450 million, which some authorities consider were exaggerated. The Chinese figures, which are for the 1953 census, total 601,938,035. These include 582,603,417 for the mainland, 7,591,298 for Formosa, and 11,743,320 for the Chinese overseas. If correct, these huge totals are of immense importance not least to the advocates of the White Siberian Policy who are China's neighbours to the north, and to the advocates of the White Australia Policy who are Asia's neighbours to the south. Glen Trewartha, G. B. Cressey, and other leading authorities are naturally doubtful about Chinese population figures that are 121 million in excess of the Nationalist Government totals, which themselves exceeded considerably the estimate of non-government demographic experts, and it is not improbable that the communists have 'padded the population figures for propaganda'. Yet even if we accept these statistics as correct, Trewartha's important maps offer some temporary hope as they indicate that the Chinese are neglecting their upland areas and that, as 86·7 per cent. of the population is classified as rural (undefined), the development of these lands, together with increasing industrialism, may help to deal with the population growth.[1] Table IV, from U.N. and other official statistics, indicates the immense increase of Asian population which is taking place.

This table shows clearly why Eastern writers such as Chandrasekhar are suggesting that the Asians should resume their historic policy of pouring out into the territories of their neighbours. Thus while Chandrasekhar advocates planned international migration combined with industrialization, agricultural development, and birth control to right the population disequilibrium, he lays the chief emphasis on migration and writes:

Taking the facts of population and land resources as they are, we can do little to prevent the existence of people already born; we find

[1] G. T. Trewartha, 'New Maps of China's Population', *Geog. Review*, Apr. 1957, pp. 234 seq. As noted in the Conclusion, the American Geographical Society's *Focus* of Apr. 1960 stated that the Chinese population numbered 650 million and was increasing by 20 million a year. Against this the advance of production in certain crops was 'spectacular'.

terribly overcrowded regions and empty spaces scattered almost side by side all over the world. These empty spaces are under the control of peoples who do not desperately need them. In some cases the people who control them are unable to fill these lands, while the people who need them and can fill them are denied access to them. The paradox of millions of square miles of unused and potential farm land scattered about the earth in the face of terrible regional over-population in the world can only be explained in the terms of historical and political *accidents* involving no small amount of aggression, that gave the possession of certain lands to certain peoples . . . our society must make an attempt to effect a peaceful change of the *status quo*, if it is to survive in the long run.[1]

TABLE IV

Asian population increase (to the nearest thousand)

China	1948	468,000,000
	1953	582,603,000
Japan	1950	83,200,000
	1954	88,200,000
Korea	1944	25,120,000
	1949	29,291,000
Thailand	1947	17,443,000
	1954	19,925,000
Burma	1941	16,824,000
	1954	19,242,000
Malaya and Singapore	1947	5,849,000
	1954	7,057,000
Indonesia	1930	60,414,000
	1952	78,163,000
Philippines	1948	19,234,000
	1954	21,040,000

This is a pathetic plea, based on some undeniable facts, but recent history has shown that industrialization with a consequent fall in the birth-rate is a more effective method of dealing with population increase than migration, which is costly and often raises grave problems of racial pluralism, land utilization, the

[1] Chandrasekhar, op. cit., ch. ii, pp. 48–49.

undercutting of labour, living standards, and so forth. The experience of Fiji and other places shows clearly that if a nation introduces Asian migrants, such as Indians, they breed so prolifically that they simply transfer to the new arena the problems which they created in the old. It would, of course, be foolish to say that migration is of no assistance in helping to meet the problem of modern population increase. The highly efficient Dutch did splendid work before their expulsion in moving up to 100,000 Indonesians per annum from crowded Java, with its population of perhaps 930 persons per square mile, to lightly settled Sumatra, that in 1930 had a population of only 46 per square mile, while Borneo offered attractions with a density of only 10, which is less than the present density in non-arid Australia. The Dutch hoped to achieve the migration of 120,000 young couples per annum, which would have met the Javanese increase, but as Robequain says, this was an enormous figure, and was far from being attained even before the advent of war ruined this aspect of Dutch assistance to the Indonesians.[1]

It must not be thought that because certain Western peoples fear that the Asian population frontiers may move in their direction they are opposed to helping the Asians in a situation which has resulted from the best features of Western colonialism, e.g. from medical science. The Colombo Plan is but one instance of the genuine and practical help which the West is giving to meet these difficulties, and the gifts are being made from sincere goodwill and not merely through fear of the material successes of communism. As Guy Wint asked: 'Which of these systems—the Colombo Plan with its liberal system, or the Communist Plan based ultimately on force and the concentration camp—will prove the more effective?'[2] In 1950 the issue was still in doubt and there

[1] Robequain, op. cit., pp. 204 seq.; K. J. Pelzer, *Pioneer Settlement in the Asiatic Tropics*, Amer. Geog. Society, New York, 1945, chs. vi, vii; G. H. C. Hart, 'Recent Developments in the N.E.I.', *Geog. Journal*, London, Feb. 1942; W. Peekema, 'Colonization of the Javanese in the Outer Provinces of the Netherlands East Indies', ibid., Apr. 1943; J. O. M. Brook, 'Diversity and Unity in South East Asia', *Geog. Review*, New York, Apr. 1944.
[2] For the Colombo Plan see Wint, *The British in Asia*, pp. 201–10, and R. G. Neale in Greenwood and Harper, op. cit., pp. 269–77.

was yet no answer to this question. In 1954–5 came the first real gleam of hope. The authorities who in 1950 wrote the very fine Rockefeller report, *Public Health and Demography in the Far East*, had ended their submission pessimistically. There was, they said, ample evidence that the Asians, largely a rural population, showed little interest in restricting child-bearing, and there was then no method of control which could meet their needs.[1] In 1956, however, Irene B. Taeuber published the news that with the official support of the government the Japanese had been able to reduce their natural increase from 2 per cent. in 1947 to 1·2 per cent. in 1954, a most encouraging fall, due to contraception and to the revolting but apparently unavoidable methods of abortion and sterilization. Fifty-two per cent. of Japanese married couples had admitted that they were practising contraception. Reported abortions had increased from 246,000 in 1949 to 1,143,000 in 1954, and in the hands of skilled doctors there had been little loss of life, although the cost per abortion had been lowered to about one dollar. Unfortunately, A. Okazaki (1954) presented a less hopeful picture, as he believed that neither contraception nor migration could deal with an increase which would bring the total to 107,214,000 in 1990 before the numbers begin slowly to diminish. It is inevitable therefore that Japan will face tremendous difficulties, and in the event that Japan's economic strength to support her people is not expanded in proportion to population increase, the standard of living of the Japanese is bound to decline continuously.[2]

If this is the case with an industrialized people such as the Japanese, it will be even more difficult to effect demographic revolutions in backward countries like India with largely agricultural populations who place historic emphasis on the family. Nevertheless, even India is awakening, as is essential, for population pressure may easily drive uneducated peasants into the jaws

[1] M. C. Balfour, R. F. Evans, F. W. Notestein, and I. B. Taeuber, *Public Health and Demography in the Far East*, Rockefeller, 1950, p. 118.

[2] I. B. Taeuber, 'Recent Population Developments in Japan', *Pacific Affairs*, New York, Mar. 1956; L. Finke, 'Population Policies in India, Pakistan and Japan—Some Medical Aspects', in *The Australian Outlook*, Melbourne, Sept. 1954, pp. 146–57; A. Okazaki, *The Present and Future of Japan's Population*, Inst. of Pacific Relations, Japan, 1954, pp. 7–8.

of communist wolves, who promise, and who may temporarily
supply, a little more land per family before they introduce complete socialism as they have now begun to do in China.

The moving frontiers of communism

It is essential that the democratic peoples obtain unbiased information on the successes and failures of communism, and they can
be grateful to authorities such as K. S. Latourette, R. L. Walker,
and C. P. Fitzgerald, who have been able to portray both the good
and evil which the latest Western invader has brought to the
Chinese people. C. P. Fitzgerald, writing in 1952–3, stated that the
communists had distributed land as freehold, a surprising con-
cession from any communist régime, but he thought that in time
the new democracy would give way to communism and that the
land would be collectivized, a process which Walker reported had
begun when he wrote in 1955.[1] As early as 1954 Latourette could
give some details of the price which the Chinese were beginning
to pay, and he painted a ghastly picture of the liquidation of
innocent people whose only fault was their advocacy of indivi-
dualism. At a conservative estimate from 3 to 5 million had been
executed in the first two years of communist control.[2] Walker
stated that the Free Trade Union Committee of the American
Federation of Labour estimated in 1952 that the Mao régime had
been responsible for the deaths of more than 14 million people
over the previous five years, while other authorities estimated
from communist documents that by 1953 the régime had enslaved
more than 25 million labourers.[3]

The return of colonialism?

It is clear that the Russian advances in Asia ended the epoch
when the barbarian nomads of the steppes were able to pour from
the north through the Jade Gate to bring a moving frontier of
conquest into eastern Asia. That age passed into the brief period of
western European contact and colonization, based at the outset

[1] Fitzgerald, *Revolution in China*, ch. vii, p. 172.
[2] Latourette, op. cit., pp. 213 seq.
[3] R. L. Walker, *China under Communism*, Yale University Press, 1955, ch. ix,
'Terror', pp. 214–32.

upon sailing ships and sea-power, and changing into an era of greater pressure which resulted from the growth of Europe in population, technological science, capitalism, and export pro- duction for oversea markets.[1] Again the scene changed when the pressure from the ocean frontiers ceased but that from the historic north was resumed. Once more the Jade Gate opened to admit, on this occasion from eastern Europe, a new colonialism, a colonial- ism of the mind in the form of another European and alien system, although it is operated by Asians and is to some small extent adapted to Asian conditions. The new era has only just commenced, but already it may be fairly claimed from statistics that in the communist areas the Asian peoples are shackled body and soul in fetters of east European design that are at least as heavy and cruel as those which were borne in the very worst days of west European colonization. China is already enchained, and the future alone can show whether or not a slave system can bring sufficient material progress for the communist frontiers to move into even wider Asian fields.[2]

(B) THE PACIFIC ISLANDS

The islands of the central Pacific present a fascinating kaleido- scope of peoples, governments, and industries in lands which have comparatively small economic value but are of considerable popu- lation interest and strategic importance. Here the Western con- querors created sojourner colonies which resembled those in South-east Asia in their introduction of non-European exotic peoples and of plantation economies based for the most part on exotic plants. Where the colonizing process was entirely different

[1] O. Lattimore, *Inner Asian Frontiers of China*, New York, 1940, ch. 1; W. Kolarz, *Russia and her Colonies*, London, 1952, ch. ix.

[2] Nearly all the leading authorities warn the Western peoples that the material successes of the communists and their honesty as compared with previous Chinese régimes may lead to a dangerous extension of their frontiers amongst poverty- stricken and desperate peoples. See Zinkin, op. cit., postscript; Wint, *Spotlight on Asia*, conclusion; Fitzgerald, op. cit., ch. x; Walker, op. cit., ch. xiii; Manikam, op. cit., pp. 79–82, 275–7. M. Lindsay, *China and the Cold War*, Melbourne Univer- sity Press, 1955, ch. 1, explains the 'progressive deterioration in the standards of the Chinese Communist Party'; Lord Lindsay's wife is a very able Chinese woman.

was in the fields of health, for the Western invaders brought European and Asian diseases to non-immune Pacific island peoples, causing the same cycle of decimation and recovery as was experienced by the indigenous inhabitants of Australia, New Zealand, Latin America, Canada, and the United States.

Although the discovery of some of the Pacific islands dated, as we have seen, from almost the beginning of the invasions, the white occupation and development of most of the groups did not come until the closing peak of Western supremacy when, for example, Britannia ruled the waves and Britons claimed that Queen Victoria, the good and great, held dominion over palm and pine in a British Empire on which the sun never set. In the central Pacific the sixteenth century was that of the Spanish explorers who followed the path-finding Magellan across the island-studded ocean. The seventeenth century was that of the Dutch, with the name of Abel Tasman, the discoverer of Tasmania, New Zealand, and Fiji, in the lead. The eighteenth century was the age of Britain and France, when the main features of the whole vast ocean were mapped by James Cook, who discovered many unknown islands such as New Caledonia and the Hawaiian groups, and rediscovered others which, like the New Hebrides, the Spaniards had found and lost under leaders such as de Quiros and Torres. Yet, although Cook perished in Hawaii in 1779, nearly a hundred years were to pass before the great boom in interest in the Pacific sent out traders and missionaries to bring diseases and Christianity to many a lovely isle, whose inhabitants would have been wiser had they continued to eat all new arrivals. Perhaps the worst feature of this unregulated period was the practice of blackbirding—the seizure by several colonizing peoples, from the Australians to the Chileans, of unfortunate natives to serve on plantations in the Pacific borderlands or islands.[1]

Britain, with settler colonies in Australia (1788), was early in the field and occupied New Zealand in 1840 in order to secure strategic areas and economic advantages, to anticipate foreign competition and, above all, to protect and Christianize the island inhabitants. In 1874 she annexed Fiji, took south-east Papua at the

[1] For select bibliography on the Pacific Islands, see p. 224, note F.

insistence of the Australian colonies in 1884, jointly occupied the New Hebrides with France in 1887, and established protectorates over the British Solomons (1893), Tonga (1900), and many other islands. France occupied the rich mineral island of New Caledonia in 1853, the Society Islands, including the lovely Tahiti and other groups, while Germany supported the infiltration of its traders by temporarily gaining north-east New Guinea together with island groups in Micronesia, all of which were taken from her in the First World War by Australia and Japan.

Very interesting was the invasion of certain regions by the young Western settler peoples of the United States, Australia, and New Zealand. From 1893 to 1898 the Americans deposed the last reigning monarch of Hawaii and absorbed the islands; in 1898 they took Guam in the Spanish American War, and from 1899 onwards secured western Samoa, thus building a bridge across the Pacific to the Philippines, which they also acquired from Spain.

This movement of the American frontier, first across the United States, then across the Pacific to the Philippines, and later to Japan, is one of the most important features in the Western invasions and, indeed, in world history. The advance across the Pacific was in a way an accident, due in part to the Spanish-American War, and it was entirely out of step with the American attitudes to imperialism and colonialism. As Allan Nevins says: 'The United States found that it had suddenly been thrust into a career of overseas expansion or imperialism to which it had given no thought, and for which it was quite unprepared.'[1] This unpreparedness was demonstrated by certain aspects of American Pacific policy. At times the Republic could be ruthlessly imperialistic, as was seen when President Theodore Roosevelt realized that the new American obligations in the Pacific demanded the construction of a canal at Panama under American control, and to gain his ends treated the Republic of Colombia in 1903–4 with raw imperialistic methods that 'beat almost anything Europe had been guilty of'.[2] On the other hand, Walter Lippmann bitterly condemned his country for failing to realize the immensity of the obligations to which she

[1] A. Nevins, *A Brief History of the United States*, O.U.P., 1942, pp. 119–20.
[2] J. T. Adams, *Epic of America*, Boston, 1932, p. 357.

had chained herself, with the result that she not only sat on the fence in the period between the World Wars, but deliberately tied the hands of her sister democracies while she herself pursued a policy which incited the Japanese attack.[1] This criticism may be too extreme, but there is no doubt that by her frontier extensions America took over an immense task and became, as her population and resources warranted, the leading democracy, a fact which made her the heartland of democratic strength—a heartland situated in the New World and interested in the Pacific. As Lippmann points out, the Monroe Doctrine pronounced by America in 1823 with British approval, and later supported by British sea-power, was supplemented at the end of the century by the American Pacific advances, with the result that the United States committed themselves 'to defend at the risk of war the lands and the waters around them extending from Alaska to the Philippines and Australia, and from Greenland to Brazil and Patagonia'.[2] As this area of American commitment covered 40 per cent. of the land surface of the earth, but only 25 per cent. of its population, Lippmann was probably right in concluding that the Americans needed friends in the Old World.[3]

Important as were these changes to the nations as a whole, they were vital to the peoples of the Pacific. The American frontier moved forward to occupy a vast if scattered island screen; the Hawaiian Islands, Midway, Wake, Guam, and the Philippines, supported to the south by American Samoa and, even after the disaster of Pearl Harbour and the loss of the Philippines and Guam, American Pacific strength was sufficient to play the leading part in protecting the English-speaking democracies to the south. Yet even here the necessity of New and Old World alliances was demonstrated, for the Americans conducted much of the campaign in the South Pacific from British and French bases.[4]

Meanwhile other Pacific peoples had preceded even the Americans in pushing forward their Pacific frontiers, largely through well justified fears of the advance of European and extra-Pacific powers, such as Germany. The Australians, early alarmed

[1] W. Lippmann, *U.S. Foreign Policy*, London, 1944, pp. 24–26.
[2] Ibid., p. 66.   [3] Ibid., pp. 66–67.   [4] Ibid., p. 77.

by German aggression in New Guinea, obtained through Britain, the League of Nations, and the United Nations the control of south-east New Guinea, Papua—at the northern doors of Australia —of German New Guinea and New Britain, and a share in the island of Nauru with its valuable phosphates.[1] Similarly, New Zealand gained western Samoa, the Cook and other islands, and a share in Nauru.[2] Even Chile joined in the scramble for territory when she annexed Easter Island in 1888.

After the Second World War the Western nations withdrew from Asia excepting where they continued to assist in the defence of key points against the communist advance. The Americans, for example, elevated Japan from an enemy to an ally and a bastion of democracy with such rapidity that the Australians became seriously anxious lest the Japanese regained their desire and ability to assist in another Asian attack.[3] As the geographic and strategic importance of the Pacific islands remained very great, the democracies of the Pacific rimlands retained such possessions or mandates as American Hawaii, Australian New Guinea, and New Zealand Samoa, while even the European powers—Britain, France, and Holland—showed no desire to relinquish their guardianship of island peoples, who, in many cases, were insufficiently advanced to be granted freedom.[4] Nevertheless, there are clear indications that some of the island folk are already looking towards self-government or even independence. The Hawaiian Islands are, of course, an outstanding example of this, but it is perhaps unfair to class them as an example of sojourner colonization, for Western settlers can live permanently in the marginal and mild tropical climate of Hawaii, as they do in Florida and Queensland. Indeed,

[1] *A.C.A.*, ch. v, for references.

[2] For Western (N.Z.) Samoa: McArthur, op. cit., Part III; W. E. H. Stanner, op. cit., Part III.

[3] C. P. Fitzgerald in Greenwood and Harper, op. cit., pp. 213 seq.: 'Japan remained in the view of most Australians the real potential danger . . . the memory of Japan's naval power, and the possibility that it could be reconstructed, presented far more sinister possibilities. Now that Japan must renounce all hope of empire on the mainland of Asia, might she not be led one day all the more surely to seek dominion among the islands of the south-west Pacific, a region which, moreover, was obviously undeveloped and thinly populated?'

[4] Oliver, *The Pacific Islands*, pp. 1–2 and ch. 21.

between 1940 and 1950 the Caucasian population of the islands increased from 104,000 to 115,000.[1] Also Hawaii, like Fiji, is unusual in the fact that exotic peoples, brought in for labour purposes, rapidly outnumbered the indigenous folk, and Chinese, Japanese, and other exotics have accepted American culture and contribute to the movement towards 'statehood'. Far more significant has been the growing demand by the indigenous peoples of New Zealand Samoa for self-government and equality with Europeans in a predominantly Samoan life-context in which some good European things have a place.[2] In American Samoa the United States have established a legislature consisting of a Senate, or Upper House, of highly titled Samoans and a House of Representatives in which fifty members are elected by village units and two by the people who live outside the village system. It is felt that in time the newly organized legislature will develop the trained and capable leaders required in order that the Samoan people may further participate in and control the activities of their government.[3]

Even in tropical, rugged, and primitive lands such as Australian and Netherlands New Guinea, the Western trustee peoples are pursuing the same objectives, although the period of tutelage may be longer. As we shall see later, the administrators of Netherlands New Guinea are working to raise the indigenous peoples to a point where they can make their own decisions.

In considering Samoa one is, of course, dealing with a high-type Polynesian people now recovering from the shock of the Western invasions, a shock which deeply affected the Polynesian, Melanesian, and Micronesian islanders who, as we have seen in Chapter I, probably numbered some 3 to 4 million at the outset of the exotic advance. In this case, although the tropical climate of nearly all the islands enforced white sojourner colonization, the effects on the natives resembled those in the settler colonies, for the Polynesians and Micronesians, and to a lesser extent the Melanesians, went through much that the Red Indians, the Australian aboriginals, and the Maoris had already suffered. Indeed, we see in many

---

[1] Hawaii statistics, Census 1950.   [2] Stanner, op. cit., p. 364.
[3] 1953 *Annual Report of the Governor of American Samoa*, U.S. Dept. of the Interior, Washington, D.C., pp. 6–7.

islands very similar cycles. In the period of moving frontiers the whites destroyed the aboriginals by their diseases, fire-arms, land robberies, and the uprooting of native cultures. In a second period missions took control and slowed down, but did not check, the destructive processes. In a recent period of governmental and scientific management the natives have been recovering, although in many cases, such as Hawaii and Tahiti, they are now far advanced in acculturation to Western ways of life and in assimilation with a number of different types of exotics.[1] As in the American and Australasian regions, the main cause of native decline was the introduction of Western and Asiatic diseases against which the Pacific aboriginals had little immunity. We shall see in Chapter VI that the most dangerous importations were smallpox, measles, pulmonary diseases, social diseases, malaria, filariasis, hookworm, and leprosy. These diseases destroyed the islanders as rapidly and effectively as they, or some of them, had liquidated the Australian aboriginals, the Maoris, and the American Indians. When, however, the Westerners repeated in the islands the medical successes which they had gained in countries such as the United States and New Zealand, the tide turned. Oliver estimated that the islanders decreased from about 3·5 million in 1522 to 2 million in 1939 through diseases, wars, feuds, sterility, and infecundity induced by disease, enforced labour away from home, a later age of marriage, and possibly family instability.[2] The American doctor, S. M. Lambert, who played a leading part in the scientific improvement, divided the Pacific as early as 1934 into three regions from the population viewpoint. The first was eastern Polynesian islands,

---

[1] The cycle of decline and recovery is now quite clear in many island groups. In stage one the moving frontier of disease was the chief destructive factor, although W. H. R. Rivers considered that depopulation was largely due to loss of interest in life (Rivers, *Essay on Depopulation in Melanesia*, C.U.P., 1922, ch. viii). Of the second stage authoritative opinion now seems to take the view that the missions did more good than harm, as they provided the natives some protection, education, and health services, in spite of foolishly wrecking the indigenous social life. For post-mortems see Keesing, *The South Seas in the Modern World*, ch. xi; Furnas, op. cit., pp. 296–302; and Porteus, op. cit., p. 76. The third stage— Recovery—was undoubtedly due largely to government action on scientific lines, particularly in medicine and health. See Keesing, op. cit., ch. x, and bibliography, pp. 367–8.   [2] Oliver, *The Pacific Islands*, ch. 19.

such as the Hawaiian group where the populations had declined to a point which seemed to preclude racial regeneration. Second were the mid-Pacific islands—Polynesian, Micronesian, and Melanesian—which had passed through the period of decline and were safely on the upgrade, and third, the purely Melanesian Islands in the west which were still in the throes of decline. His conclusion was 'that the cause of native decay is largely disease'.[1] Everywhere that one travelled in the Pacific, whether it was in the British, French, or American zones, one found in the 1930's, 1940's, and 1950's that intense and successful efforts were being made to defeat disease, often with considerable success.[2]

Another aspect of the population problem of these Pacific sojourner colonies is that the whites brought to the islands other peoples with the result that the ethnic character of the region— already considerably mixed—became a kaleidoscope of racial types. The Hawaiian Islands are probably the most interesting racial melting-pot in the world, for the Americans introduced for industrial purposes Portuguese, Chinese, Spaniards, Filipinos, Japanese, and Puerto Ricans, who intermixed and bred with the Hawaiians to create a fascinating field for ethnic research. Far more serious, however, is the difficulty in islands such as Fiji, where the British introduced Asian Indians for the sugar plantations and gold mines, with the result that by 1953 these exotics exceeded the native Fijians in numbers and were increasing more rapidly, which had already created a problem of the gravest type. Oliver stated that in 1939 there were some 140,000 whites and 540,000 Asians living in the Pacific islands, but he considered that the greater profits of oceanic enterprise went to companies with shareholders outside the island area, and that most of the whites were sojourners who held to their objective of eventually returning home with their earnings.[3]

Up to the close of our period the French possessions followed the same course as the British and American islands. Chinese

[1] S. M. Lambert, *The Depopulation of Pacific Races*, Bishop Museum, Honolulu, 1934, p. 41; McArthur, op. cit.

[2] I am grateful to the French Government and local authorities for letting me see in 1955 their valuable medical and research services in the Caribbean and Pacific islands.   [3] Oliver, op. cit., pp. 254-7.

exotics numbered 6,000 of the small population of Tahiti and were rapidly increasing, while the French had created similar problems by introducing Tonkinese to New Caledonia and the New Hebrides.[1]

To conclude this chapter I will examine in some slight detail the population problem in three very different island groups: Hawaii, Fiji, and New Guinea.

Hawaii

Authorities consider that in spite of the great variety of exotic peoples now in the islands, the racial conclusion will be almost complete assimilation with a Japanese element predominating. Partly owing to the fact that the population includes many thousands of haolas or white residents, the cultural trends are likely to be white and American.

The following table gives the numbers of the various races at the 1940 and 1950 censuses:

TABLE V

	1940	1950
Hawaiian . .	64,310	86,090
Caucasian . .	103,791	114,793
Chinese . .	28,774	32,376
Filipino . .	52,569	61,062
Japanese . .	157,905	184,598
Korean . .	6,851	7,030
Negro . .	255	2,651
Puerto Rican .	8,296	9,551
All other races .	579	1,618
	423,330	499,769

Figures from 1950 U.S. Census of Population Bureau, *Hawaii, Detailed Characteristics*, 1952, p. viii.

[1] McArthur, op. cit., Part I, for important discussions of the population of the French islands. The 1951 census estimated the Chinese at 6,833. Oliver, op. cit., pp. 226–31, explains the problem of Asian colour in New Caledonia. See also J. Parsons, 'Coffee and Settlement in New Caledonia', *Geog. Review*, no. 1, 1945, pp. 12–21. I found in 1955 that the French had difficulty in repatriating the Tonkinese, as the communists had overrun the homelands.

This table does not give or explain the percentages of race mixture, which do not seem to be presented very satisfactorily as every person of mixed Caucasian blood is classified according to the race of the non-white parent. The following table does, however, cast some light on the subject:

TABLE VI

Census 1950

Race	Total population	Number of mixed races	Per cent. of mixed peoples
Hawaiian .	86,091	73,885	85·81
Caucasian .	114,793	—	—
Chinese	32,376	2,875	8·9
Filipino	61,071	7,680	12·6
Japanese	184,611	4,090	2·2
Other races	20,852	5,692	27·3

Figures from 1950 U.S. Census of Population, *Hawaii—General Characteristics*, 1952, Table 9.

This table, from the method of its preparation, omits the number of mixed-blood Caucasians which is probably high, but it clearly indicates the well-known fact that the Japanese, and to a lesser extent the Chinese, are assimilating very slowly, although this may not apply to acculturation or even to patriotism, for the Hawaiian Japanese behaved splendidly in the Second World War when two combat units were sent to Italy 'where they dived into German fighting in one of the most gruelling theatres of war, with a pluck and skill that made them immortal'.[1] No one can foretell what the future Hawaiian race will be like, but perhaps I received an accurate forecast from an Hawaiian-American official who said that it would be 'one hundred per cent American'.

Fiji

While Hawaii still encounters some slight racial difficulties, the islands face no problem as serious as that created by the introduction of Asian Indians to Fiji. Tasman discovered the archipelago in 1643, and Bligh, during his famous boat voyage, saw some of

---

[1] Furnas, op. cit., p. 190.

the hundreds of islands, including Vitu Levi which has an area of 4,000 square miles. The usual 'rape of the islands' followed when at the beginning of the nineteenth century the Europeans began to exploit sandalwood and bêche-de-mer with the customary results —the introduction of diseases, drink, and fire-arms with consequent undermining of native leadership and the disruption of native social life. European land robbery and settlement increased the difficulties which were not lessened by the arrival of Christianity in 1835. In 1871–2 Commander Markham of the *Rosario* reported that the nefarious system of kidnapping was practised to a most inconceivable extent and that it actually amounted to downright slavery.[1] In 1858, 1859, and 1874 the Fijian chiefs sought to cede Fiji to a reluctant Britain which desired no further obligations nor territories, but in 1874–5 the government gave way and a British governor took office.[1] Meanwhile, from the time of the earliest contacts the moving frontier of Western diseases had swept the islands and depopulation soon followed. 'Lila', a wasting sickness, appeared in 1791–2, and a violent form of dysentery in 1802–3. Smallpox seems to have been held off probably by vaccination, but the year 1875 saw Fijians returning from Britain initiate the famous outbreak of measles, popularly supposed to have caused some 40,000 deaths, a figure which Norma McArthur has reduced to one of from 20,000 to 30,000. Further visitations of measles, together with outbreaks of whooping-cough and influenza, took their toll, and the population began to decrease steadily each year from 1891 to 1900, seeing that the number of deaths exceeded the births. Then followed a period of fluctuations, but from 1912 onwards the superiority of births over deaths was established.[2]

Meanwhile the whites had begun to introduce Indian indentured labour for the plantations,[3] and these exotics increased rapidly in spite of an excess of males, particularly as they showed a better resistance to diseases such as influenza than did the Fijians.[4] By

---

[1] E. A. Benians in *Cambridge History of the British Empire*, vol. vii, Part I, 'Australia', pp. 345 seq.; L. A. Mander, *Some Dependent Peoples of the South Pacific*, ch. vii; Ward, *British Policy in the South Pacific 1786–1893*, chs. xviii, xix.

[2] McArthur, op. cit., Part VI, *Fiji*, pp. 237–40, 260–75.

[3] Ibid., p. 269.   [4] Ibid., pp. 269–75.

1946 the total population amounted to roughly 260,000 of whom 118,000 were Fijians and 120,000 Indians. In 1955 it was estimated that a population of 345,164 included 166,262 Indians and only 146,842 Fijians. Nor was the superiority of the Indian numbers likely to decrease as the Indian women married very young. The Indian birth-rate in 1955 was 42·26 in comparison with a Fijian birth-rate of 34·17, while the Indian death-rate was 7·18 compared with 9·61 for the Fijians.[1] W. E. H. Stanner, E. M. J. Campbell, L. A. Mander, and other authorities emphasize the gravity of a position which cannot be remedied by geographical factors owing to the small size of the islands and the primary character of their industries. Stanner points out that the Indians as in Kenya and Natal are seeking political power, and are conducting 'a peaceful sweepage into every opening left unclosed'.[2] Although depressed by private debt, they are no longer indentured coolies but are an island-born people who cultivate 97 per cent. of the lands devoted to sugar-cane.[2] A Native Land Trust Board protects the Fijians, and better land utilization and the development of other industries may do something to meet the growth of population.[3] Nevertheless, a geographical fact must control the future in that the islands comprise an area of only about 11,000 square miles. E. M. J. Campbell said truly that 'in the long run the Indians in Fiji can maintain and improve their present standard of living only by a voluntary reduction of their high birth rate'.[4] It may be added that if, as in Japan, abortion is to become a fearful but necessary remedy for over-fecundity, the need for doctors will increase; both the Indians and the Fijians have shown an aptitude for medicine, as in the famous school at Suva. Most important of all, perhaps, is the fact that Fiji presents a sombre warning to those people, both white and coloured, who with an ignorance or disregard of history, advocate the removal of migration restrictions by those

---

[1] Ibid., and *Fijian Information*, July 1956, Suva, pp. 4–6; Stanner, *The South Seas in Transition*, Part II, ch. iv; E. M. J. Campbell, 'Land and Population Problems in Fiji', *Geog. Journal*, Dec. 1952; Mander, op. cit., ch. vii.

[2] Stanner, op. cit., p. 179.

[3] Ibid., Part II, ch. vi, outlines the 'Ten Year Plan' and other plans to meet the various problems of a three-sided conflict of race and culture and a rapidly increasing population. [4] Campbell, op. cit., p. 482.

countries whose people have won high living standards. If they were granted free entry to regions such as English-speaking and Latin America, Australasia, and even perhaps southern Siberia, the Indians and probably other Eastern peoples would almost undoubtedly increase with such rapidity that they would produce the same perilous situation that they have created in their own Asian homelands and in Fiji. Indian leaders such as S. Chandrasekhar deliberately close their eyes to two fundamental aspects of the problem—the rapidity of Indian increase and the notorious failure of the Indians to mix with or adopt the social customs of other peoples.[1]

In the case of Fiji, the two main groups—the Indians and Fijians—are living side by side, as yet without any great friction, but also without any physical or cultural assimilation. The political ambitions of the Indians have, however, created difficulties with the whites. These numbered only 9,391 in 1955, while the part-Europeans (mainly Anglo-Fijians) numbered only 7,956.[2] Mander considers that the three-sided conflict of race and culture 'may prove to be the most difficult problem which Fiji will have to face in the coming years',[3] while Stanner believes that the greatest perils will lie in an Indian attempt to impose on a 'Fijians' Fiji' their own 'harsh imperialism' in substitution for what they consider is a British imperialism.[4] Neither conclusion emphasizes the gravest danger of all—the rapid growth of the Indian, and to a lesser extent of the Fijian population. We cannot estimate today the relative weights of the various factors which kept the island populations in check in the pre-invasion days, but diseases, cannibalism, food deficiencies, wars, the killing of widows, the lengthy suckling of children, and abortion probably helped to prevent an excess of people. Most of these checks, like war, have disappeared, or, like disease, are now probably less powerful. Unless Western culture can provide substitutes for the historic checks on population increase the outlook is gloomy in the extreme.[5] (Pl. V.)

[1] Chandrasekhar, *Hungry People and Empty Lands*, pp. 45, 227.
[2] Stanner, op. cit., pp. 192 seq., and *Fiji Information*, July 1956, p. 4.
[3] Mander, op. cit., p. 447.
[4] Stanner, op. cit., p. 258.
[5] In 1953 in Guam, which one imagines enjoys the advantages of American

PLATE V

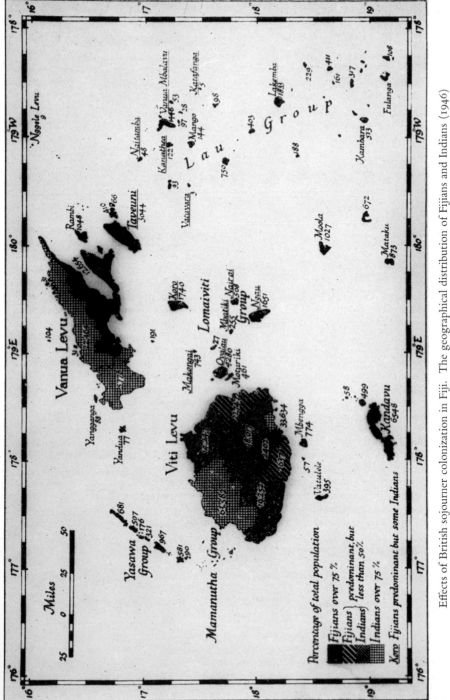

Effects of British sojourner colonization in Fiji. The geographical distribution of Fijians and Indians (1946)

From E. M. J. Campbell, 'Land and Population Problems in Fiji', *Geographical Journal*, December 1952

New Guinea

The vast, rugged, and tropical island of New Guinea offers a totally different picture to Hawaii or Fiji. It is still in most regions a land of backward peoples and of moving pioneer frontiers, yet it presents one of the leading and most explosive problems of current geopolitics. The island, together with the New Hebrides and other groups inhabited for the most part by dark Melanesian peoples, are by law or by fact regions of Western Trusteeship, surviving and worthy examples of the finest type of colonialism when the Westerner so often carried 'the white man's burden' at the cost of his own exile and financial loss.

New Guinea, the second largest island in the world, contains an area of 312,000 square miles and possibly 2·7 million people. The Netherlands control the west of the island—132,000 square miles —with perhaps 1 million natives, and Australia controls the eastern part—180,000 square miles—with perhaps 1·7 million natives. The island is Australian rather than Indonesian in many respects. It is situated on the Sahul or Australian continental shelf, and is separated by the Wallace and Weber lines from Asian flora and fauna.[1] The rugged island contains many and mixed peoples who constitute a great variety of problems for anthropologists as they include people of Papuan and Melanesian types, while there are pygmy and pygmoid peoples in the interior. These groups are certainly not Indonesian in type; some indeed greatly resemble the Veddas of Ceylon, and may also have links with the Australian aboriginals.[2] New Guinea was discovered by the Portuguese and

medical science, the birth-rate was 60·8 and the death-rate 11·9 (U.N. Statistics, Jan. 1955). Recent important research on the problems of Fiji includes: N. McArthur, 'Fijians and Indians in Fiji', *Population Studies*, Mar. 1959; O. H. K. Spate, *The Fijian People—Economic Problems and Prospects*, Suva, 1959; R. G. Ward, 'The Population of Fiji', *Geog. Review*, July 1959.

[1] E. D. Merrill, 'The Correlation of Biological Distribution with the Geological History of Malaysia', *Pan Pacific Science Congress*, Australia, 1923, vol. ii, pp. 1148–55. For east New Guinea (Australian), see Taylor, *A Pacific Bibliography*, section III E, New Guinea (eastern or Melanesian portions); *A.C.A.*, chs. iii and v, for select bibliography; Stanner, op. cit., Part I, *Papua, New Guinea*; McArthur, op. cit., Part VII, *Papua and New Guinea*; Mander, op. cit., ch. iv, 'Papua, New Guinea'.

[2] For recent scientific summary of anthropological theories on the New

partly examined by de Saavedra of Spain in 1528. Holland gained some shadowy rights of sovereignty with the Spice Islands, but an uninviting land peopled by fierce black cannibals offered little attraction, and it was not until 1826 that the Dutch rights were recognized, although even then settlements were not established until 1898 and 1902.[1]

The people of the Australian colonies, however, became justly anxious about the advances of several nations in the Pacific, particularly the French, who sent 121,372 convicts to New Caledonia between 1864 and 1880, and the Germans who began to establish commercial interests in north-east New Guinea. Britain refused a number of Australian pleas that she should annex the island, and in 1883 the Queenslanders sent a party to Port Moresby and annexed eastern New Guinea. The British Government, completely hoodwinked by Bismarck, and with an Egyptian problem on their hands, refused to recognize the Australian annexation until Germany had seized the north-east. These events were a main cause of the federation of the Australian colonies and of Australia's action in astonishing President Wilson and the world when she demanded and gained a mandate over the former German north-eastern New Guinea at the close of the First World War.[2] The nations were reluctant to grant Australia the trusteeship of backward peoples, as the handling of her Stone-Age aboriginals (admittedly a difficult problem) had been on the whole as bad as some of the worst mismanagement by the Westerners of various tribes of American Indians.[3] Nevertheless, Australia did rather better than was expected. In 1943 Dr. Henze summed up the pre-war story fairly and accurately when he wrote: 'The Commonwealth administration in New Guinea has been good

Guinea peoples, see J. P. Kleiweg de Zwaan, *The Papuans of New Guinea—A Physico-anthropological Survey in Antiquity and Survival*, New Guinea, no. 5, 1956, The Hague.

[1] Netherlands Ministry of Overseas Territories, *Report on Netherlands New Guinea to the United Nations*, 1954, p. 5.

[2] *A.C.A.*, pp. 44–51, 92–96.

[3] The outstanding work on Australian Aboriginal Policy is Foxcroft, op. cit. For the comparative management of the American Indians, the Australian aboriginals, and the Maoris, see Grenfell Price, *W.S.N.P.*

. . . and there are few tropical colonies with so clear a record of humane endeavour. On the other hand perhaps Australia has been too recently herself a colony to understand easily that she had now in turn acquired colonial responsibility and the status of "motherland" relative to the Australian dependencies in New Guinea.[1]

Up to the Second World War Australia spent considerable sums in bringing increasingly large areas of wild and almost impenetrable tropical mountains and swamps under the control or influence of the administration, in establishing health services for the natives, in introducing or assisting the missions to promote education, in protecting the natives' lands and labour conditions, and in fostering new and suitable industries. Most important of all, however, was the fact that the White Australia Policy protected the backward Papuan from any large-scale Asian intrusion and permitted his development free from difficulties such as those which followed the Indian penetration of Fiji.

The Second World War and the Japanese invasion of New Guinea proved to the hilt the Australian contention that the island was the northern bastion of the continent and essential to its defence. The Federal Labour Minister to handle the post-war problems was the Hon. E. J. Ward who showed strong sympathy with the natives. A later Liberal Minister, the Hon. Paul Hasluck, the author of *Black Australians*, showed both sympathy and understanding, and proved an excellent choice.[2] The work of Hasluck and the Australian administration in New Guinea is summarized in three useful publications of which details are given in the notes.[3] The statement, which Paul Hasluck gave to the Australian Institute of Political Science in Canberra in January 1958, is a factual record of quite remarkable achievement, particularly in view of the problem of training an adequate civil service to undertake administration and patrols amongst some of the most difficult country and primitive people on earth. It is impossible in this book to outline

[1] *A.C.A.*, p. 96.   [2] Paul Hasluck, *Black Australians*.
[3] Hasluck, *The Progress of Australian Territories 1950–1956* (1957), *Present Tasks and Policies* (1958), and *Australia's Task in Papua and New Guinea*, Roy Milne Memorial Lecture, Perth, 1956. See also Chapter IV, p. 101, n. 2.

and explain this progress, but Table VII presents a brief summary of the main facts.

TABLE VII

	1948–9	1957–8
Finance	£A	£A
Commonwealth grant .	3,197,000	10,802,000
Local revenue . . .	1,233,000	4,938,000
Capital works . . .	629,000	4,464,000
Aviation, &c. . . .	337,000	2,287,000
Transport		
Road mileages . . .	2,763	5,548
Airfields and alighting areas	118	153
Exports		
Coco-nut products . .	2,717,000	7,090,000
Timber	23,000	1,179,000
Rubber	146,000	1,149,000
Coffee and cocoa . .	40,000	645,000
Gold	983,000	1,231,000
Total value of the above and other exports .	4,800,000	13,079,000
NUMBERS		
Stock		
Cattle	1,500	11,708
Patrol posts . . .	24	46
Medical		
Hospitals (all types) . .	106	166
Doctors	64	178
Trained nurses . . .	262	476
Medical assistants . .	200	306
Education (native)		
Schools	2,463	4,205
Pupils	106,038	171,453
Non-native teachers . .	237	685
Native teachers . .	3,316	5,782

From The Hon. Paul Hasluck, Minister of Territories, *Present Tasks and Policies*, Canberra, 1958, Part III.

Since the war the government has further protected the native and his land and has followed on Mr. Ward's policy of preventing the men from remaining away from their villages for long periods of contract labour, and so disrupting the normal social and sex life. As the native groups have acquired some knowledge of civilized life, for example the use of money, the government has set up bodies elected by the natives to manage their local affairs as far as possible by a pyramid of councils.[1]

Relations with the Trusteeship Council and with visiting missions from that body have been reasonably satisfactory, although the invariable criticisms of members from the violently anti-colonial nations are sometimes hard to ignore. This type of ignorant criticism has justified some plain speaking by Paul Hasluck, who has full knowledge of the essential but unbelievably difficult task —the evolution of a new society. As the Minister wrote in 1958:

We cannot predict with certainty the shape of the institutions or the successive stages in the growth of that society. This is the final answer to the stupidity of those positive fools in the United Nations who are always talking of target dates for political advancement. They forget that the Charter itself (articles 73B and 76B) recognises that such advancement is limited by the rate of the more fundamental changes among the peoples.[2]

In July 1958 the United Nations Trusteeship Council commended Australia for the financial assistance given to New Guinea and on the improvements made in administrative machinery and in health. At the same time the Council considered that more rapid progress should be made in training the natives in administration and in commercial pursuits, and expressed regret that the government could not bring the whole country under full administrative control by 1959—this last despite Hasluck's statement that Australia had already gained control of five-sixths of the area.[3] Indian leaders, who since independence have assumed the role of champions of the interests, or alleged interests, of the dependent peoples, have exaggerated beyond all reason the importance of the few but costly remnants of the Western colonial empires and the speed with which their Western benefactors are advancing their indigenous inhabitants. The Australians could well have replied that they were spending about £18 million a year on

[1] Hasluck, *Present Tasks and Policies.*
[2] Ibid., Part I, p. 5.
[3] Ibid. and Nancy Buttfield, 'New Prospect for Natives in New Guinea', *Adelaide Advertiser*, 2/8/58, p. 2.

the natives of New Guinea and they could have spent a great deal more were they not spending £190 million a year on measures to defend, if necessary, the southern approaches to Asia against the communists, and had they not given capital help or technical assistance or both to all the sixteen countries which had accepted Western aid under the Colombo Plan.[1]

In the development of this new society fresh problems are constantly emerging. The replacement of the stone by the steel axe has already created deforestation and erosion. Health services have contributed to the appearance of over-population in certain regions, and large-scale food experiments are being made with rice.[2] Yet in spite of all the progress, or because of its rapid changes, some natives have tended to grow sullen while others have sought relief as did certain American Indians and Maoris of past generations in cults of despair, which in New Guinea have taken the form of cargo cults or vailala madness, abnormalities that have been fomented in part by self-seekers and unstable persons.[3] Senator Buttfield, writing in 1958, noted that the New Guinea natives, like many recipients of colonial bounty, showed no appreciation but treated every type of gift as a right.[4] It is already clear, as in New Zealand Samoa, that the young democratic peoples will have the same experience as the older democracies, namely, that they must move out of their colonies as soon as the colonial people can carry their own burdens, or indeed, sooner, which is the danger. W. E. H. Stanner sums up the reasons why Australia must continue her task in New Guinea no matter how thankless. She is, he writes, the only metropolitan power which has on its doorstep a dependency with three characteristics in common. First, New Guinea is amongst the most backward of the surviving colonial

[1] *Current Notes*, Canberra, Oct. 1957, p. 811.

[2] There are several valuable articles, published reports, and unpublished reports on recent developments in Australian New Guinea. Important are O. H. K. Spate, 'Changing Native Agriculture in New Guinea', *Geog. Review*, Apr. 1953; O. H. K. Spate, J. W. Davidson, and R. Firth, *Notes on New Guinea*, issued in roneo by the Australian National University, 1951. Other reports by members of the Australian National University are in the hands of the Commonwealth Government. See also Chapter IV, p. 101, n. 2.

[3] Stanner, op. cit., Part I, ch. v, 'Native Social Changes'.

[4] Nancy Buttfield, 'New Prospect for Natives in New Guinea', p. 2.

territories. Secondly, it is for ethnological reasons one of the most difficult regions in the world to develop; and thirdly, it is the key to the military security of the Commonwealth.[1] To these we can add a fourth reason enunciated by Senator Buttfield—'if we don't bother, someone else will, and the chances are that the someone else may hold an opposing ideology'.[2]

West New Guinea

West New Guinea, the country controlled by the Dutch for 120 years, presents an equally difficult task and one which is complicated by a flood of Indonesian propaganda and threats of violence. Students will find references in the notes to these Indonesian claims. They rest upon the facts, first that the region was part of the former Dutch possessions which otherwise had passed to the Republic, and second, that it represented 22 per cent. of that area. Outweighing everything else, however, is the consideration that Indonesia wants it for reasons of prestige.[3]

Apart from the legal rights of the Dutch (and, as we have often seen, legal rights have little weight in the modern world), the vital question is—What régime will bring most benefit to the primitive inhabitants? These number about a million and are almost certain to increase under the influence of the highly efficient Dutch medical services, which were partly responsible for the immense growth of the Indonesian population in Java. In present circumstances the Netherlands can claim that there is no case whatever for the opening of western New Guinea to an Indonesian population flood, which before the war the Dutch were skilfully directing to Sumatra, an island that, like Borneo and other Indonesian islands, has a low population density.

In these circumstances the Netherlands report to the United Nations in 1954 was important.[4] After setting out the difficulties of dealing with a tropical mountain terrain and primitive peoples

[1] Stanner, op. cit., p. 163.   [2] Buttfield, op. cit.

[3] For bibliographical detail see p. 225, note G.

[4] *Report on Netherlands New Guinea*; see p. 225, note G. Pelzer, *Pioneer Settlement in the Asiatic Tropics*, ch. vii and Appendix B, contains important information on the Dutch efforts to send Indonesian migrants to the outer islands, including New Guinea. Leading difficulties were cost and the resistance of the Javanese peasants to migration.

with a variety of languages, the Dutch claimed that about 314,000 people were in administered territory and that of these some 200,000 were Christians. The government and the missions were waging an able, though costly, campaign to improve health, particularly against the worst scourge, malaria—for the malaria parasites had in New Guinea a reservoir which is probably unique in the world. Also the natives were proving highly susceptible to tuberculosis, which had entered the areas that were in contact with the outer world. Four leper houses had been established to deal with 260 cases, and filariasis was serious on the south coast.[1] Nevertheless, the Dutch claims that they are making progress in the fields of health were more than fully upheld by Dr. Robert H. Black, who visited several parts of New Guinea and reported to the South Pacific Commission in 1954. He wrote (Technical Paper No. 80) that in 1954 the Dutch budget for the control of malaria was £A62,500, that the Dutch were training native New Guinea students as technical assistants, and that the Netherlands New Guinea Oil Company had reduced in the Sorong oil area the malaria rate of attack from 27 per cent. per month in 1947 to 1·2 per cent. Dr. Black concluded his report by saying that the Dutch were approaching the malaria problem in a realistic manner and that their malaria control service provided a pattern by which other territories in the area could be guided in their plans. He added that the experimental work of Professor van Thiel was of great importance, and his results offered promise for the control of malaria in other regions. Another vigorous campaign was being waged to introduce education. In 1954 the cost of this was 5,962,202 florins. The administration had been conducting experiments in production by the natives of cocoa and other crops, and had been examining the prospects of rice-farming, saw-milling, and sea and lake fishing. The Dutch had been working closely with the United Nations, the South Pacific Commission, and with the Australian authorities in training an indigenous medical personnel.[2]

The Dutch have a far smaller stake than the Australians in New Guinea, and it is difficult to consider their attitude and efforts as other than unselfish, unless, of course, they regard the

[1] *Report on Netherlands New Guinea*, op. cit.   [2] R. H. Black, p. 225, note G.

retention and development of the region as a matter of prestige. One must remember, however, that in spite of the way in which the Indonesians and other freed peoples, and indeed some of the Western peoples, have condemned so many Dutch actions, Holland has been a highly efficient colonial power and, on occasions, unselfish. Anyone who knew Java in the colonial days must pay tribute to that efficiency, and anyone who knows the smaller islands of the Dutch West Indies—St. Martin, St. Eustasius, and Saba for example—must admit that the Dutch are not unprepared to carry losses in order to help their island peoples. On the whole there may be truth in the Dutch claim that the nation faces 'a magnificent task . . . to educate the people of Netherlands New Guinea and to bring about their active participation in a Christian civilization'. When these people reach the point where they can make their own political decisions, 'what they may decide will be their own business and theirs alone.[1] It is unfortunate that in this problem the importance of the few backward and costly remnants of the former great and wealthy Western colonial empire should be so greatly exaggerated and used for propaganda to a very wide extent. Thus Mr. Nehru and other Indian leaders, who have taken the side of the dependent peoples, criticized the Dutch on the grounds that they have been maintaining their historic and detested colonialism. The Dutch, like the Australians, could well have replied that their colonialism no longer includes those features which have been so often open to criticism, and that it is ridiculous for countries such as India to be impatient when they know full well that Stone-Age peoples cannot be converted into self-governing democrats overnight. Above all, the Dutch could have said, with every justification, that Indian and other leaders have no compunction whatever in requiring the sacrifice of the natives of New Guinea at the demand of the Indonesians, a people who have not yet demonstrated their capacity to keep order in the territories which they have already taken over, and who have shown that they have gained no real conception of Western law and justice by their final treatment of those Hollanders and Eurasians who tried to stay on in Indonesia.

[1] Verhoeff, *Birdseye View of Netherlands New Guinea*, p. 80.

The year 1958 saw an awkward international predicament. The Australians who had done much to gain Indonesia her independence had learnt a bitter lesson, and were supporting Holland on the west New Guinea issue in which no compromise seemed likely to result. Moderate people had suggested a Dutch-Indonesian condominium or a Dutch-Indonesian-Australian trusteeship, but no peaceful action seemed to offer the means of ending the deadlock.[1] A short time ago the distinguished Swede, Gunnar Myrdal, the author of *An American Dilemma*, the classic work on the American Negro problem, told me that in his opinion Australia and the Netherlands should hand the whole of New Guinea to the United Nations to be managed by that organization. This action would be opposed by all three parties—Australia, Indonesia, and Holland—the first for the geographical reasons that she herself must control her northern gateway and be able to prevent Indonesian or communist intrusion into eastern New Guinea. The future must decide the wisdom of the various attitudes to this problem of political geography, particularly as the Indonesians and other Asian peoples assert that any remnant of Western colonialism promotes the growth of communism. According to a high authority, J. S. Furnival, 'that is what happened in China. That is how France and America are working to build up a Communist state in Indo-China. That is what Mr. Attlee in his wisdom prevented from happening in Burma.'[2] Nevertheless, the Western peoples may well reply that, as in the case of Japan, the resurgence of Asian aggression had to be stopped. What more just occasion could offer than that of New Guinea where a new, unstable, and unproved nation was threatening the welfare and advancement of over 300,000 primitive people? Every Westerner of goodwill must wish the Indonesians success and progress, but many Australians feel that the efforts of the young republic must be confined to its own geographical territories and its own racial groups.

[1] Greenwood and Harper, op. cit., pp. 256–62.

[2] Ibid., p. 231, quoting J. S. Furnival, 'The Future of the Far East', *Australian Outlook*, 1953, vol. vii, p. 84.

VI

THE MOVING FRONTIERS OF DISEASE

MANY leading universities are now employing in the history of medicine lecturers whose duty it is to bring the importance of this branch of culture to medical undergraduates. Worthy as is this proposition, it misses the real necessity, which is to place the importance of the sadly neglected history of disease before all types of historians, for disease has played and is playing a vital, if little realized, part in world events, including the Western expansion to the Pacific and other areas. Thus when Cortez invaded Mexico, Navarez, according to Castillo, 'brought with him in 1519 a negro who was in the small pox', and the disease spread all over the country to such an extent that it interfered with the assembly of the Aztec armies against the Spaniards, and so facilitated the conquest. G. C. Shattuck believed that 3·5 million Indians perished, amongst them Cuitlahua, the successor of the Emperor Montezuma. As in the early stages of the conflict the Aztecs succeeded in driving the Spaniards and their allies from Mexico City, it seems that disease may well have contributed to the later failure of their defence. Similarly, smallpox, introduced by the invaders, may have reached Peru in 1519–20, some five years after the Spaniards began dealing with the coastal natives, but ten or more years before Pizarro's conquest. According to Pedro de Cieza de León this outbreak killed more than 200,000 Peruvians including the Inca, Huayna Capac. Similar stories of the importance of disease, in many cases exotic disease, can be told of most of the countries invaded by the whites.[1] (See Pl. VI.)

A few medical historians have recorded events in parts of the world other than the Americas.[2] A Sydney doctor, Charles

[1] P. M. Ashburn, *The Ranks of Death, A Medical History of the Conquest of America*, New York, 1947, ch. vi, pp. 85–87.

[2] Paul de Kruif, *Hunger Fighters*, New York, 1926; *Microbe Hunters*, New York,

MacLaurin, put forward revolutionary and sometimes horrifying suggestions, for example that the 'visions' of Saint Joan of Arc were caused by a common female disorder, and that the success of the Protestant Reformation in England was due to Henry VIII contracting syphilis and leaving a sterile daughter, Mary, who had no child by Philip of Spain. With more probability MacLaurin claimed that the history of Europe was greatly affected by the insanity of Juana which influenced the character of her Hapsburg successors, particularly that of the Emperor Charles V.[1] Under the present scientific trend of thought some geomedical biblicist will no doubt claim in the future that the serpent, which caused the fall of Adam and Eve, was in reality a vitamin deficiency due to lack of apples.

Leaving the realms of fancy and returning to the fields of serious history, one finds that eminent authorities, such as Sir Ronald Ross, W. H. S. Jones, and G. G. Ellet, have presented evidence that malaria was an important factor in the decline of Greece and Rome, while the evidence collected by Mooney, Shattuck, Ashburn, and others proves conclusively that disease was an important factor in the white conquest of the Americas. In the words of Ashburn:

We have seen America conquered largely by disease, seen the Indian defeated, not merely because he had no firearms, no horses, no iron, but even more because he had no immunity to most of the diseases that the white man brought with him. So much is plain. But is it not true, even if not at once obvious, that the white man was a conqueror partly because he and smallpox, he and measles, he and alcohol, were long time acquaintances, ancient enemies, whose combats had made them strong?[2]

On the present distribution of disease and on the history of specific diseases in various regions, medical scientists have done

1926; Hans Zinsser, *Rats, Lice and History*, London, 1935–42. In addition to these brightly written books for popular consumption, there are now available for the amateur, and possibly even for professional readers, the Penguin Medical Series, which contains valuable studies such as those mentioned below.

[1] C. MacLaurin, *Post Mortem*, 1923–8; *Mere Mortals*, 1925. Both books were incorporated in *De Mortuis*, London, 1930–5.

[2] Ashburn, op. cit., p. 210.

PLATE VI

Disease amongst the American Indians in the sixteenth century

From D. M. Poole, 'Codex Florentino', *Geographical Journal*, March 1951

or are doing splendid work in spite of the difficulty of making diagnoses from pre-scientific accounts.[1] These scientists include, amongst many others, Jacques M. May, who is publishing the American Geographical Society's maps of the present distribution of disease, and Ernst Rodenwaldt, who is issuing a fine atlas of World Distribution of Epidemic Disease. H. R. Carter's *History of Yellow Fever*, which also deals with the origin of malaria and other diseases, is a classic. Until his much-regretted death in 1957, A. S. Walker was outlining the remarkable progress of Australian medicine in the war theatres, while in many regions such as Central America or the Pacific Islands, leading authorities like M. C. Balfour, G. C. Shattuck, and S. M. Lambert were publishing the results of Rockefeller and other achievements, one of the latest contributions being that of R. H. Black, who in 1955 made, as noted above, a most favourable report to the South Pacific Commission on the splendid medical work of the much and unjustly maligned Dutch in west New Guinea.

A very useful book is P. M. Ashburn's poorly named *The Ranks of Death*, 1947. Ashburn, a widely travelled American army doctor and army medical librarian, spent many years in writing from Portuguese, Spanish, Italian, French, and English sources the story of the effects of disease in the Western conquest of the Americas, but, possibly because of its uninformative title, his posthumously published book seems little known, even to experts on the subject.

In spite of some research results that are in existence, leading authorities seem to feel that no comprehensive survey of the historical geography of geomedicine has appeared since Hirsch's great *Handbook of Geographical and Historical Pathology* in 1883–6.[2] This leaves unfilled, almost incredibly, a gap of seventy years, a gap which seems an even greater discredit to the lack of historical research in medicine when one remembers the remarkable advances of medical science over the period. Fortunately, however, the little research available enables one to paint at least the outlines of the picture.

[1] For details of the works quoted see pp. 225–6, note H.
[2] See pp. 225–6, note H.

Some general considerations

In putting forward some general considerations of importance I am not claiming that any proposition is a proved scientific principle or fact. All that a layman dare do is to suggest that the researches of leading medical scientists appear to indicate the presence of certain tendencies or patterns in a number of instances. Thus in *White Settlers in the Tropics* I tried to show that the scientific conquest of disease, and other factors, had enabled the white peoples to establish some successful groups of permanent settlers in some favourable parts of the marginal tropics, such as Florida, Costa Rica, Saba, and Queensland, and even to estabish some permanent settlement in low and difficult tropical areas such as the Northern Territory of Australia and Panama, facts which seemed to disprove some old and foolish beliefs, e.g. that the white man could not breed or raise progeny in the tropics.[1] Similarly, in *White Settlers and Native Peoples* I gave the opinions of a number of leading authorities who considered that in many countries exotic diseases had been the chief factor in the destruction of indigenous peoples, and quoted amongst many examples the views of J. Mooney on the decline of the American Indians north of the Rio Grande. I also suggested, as noted in Chapter IV of the present work, that a considerable number of indigenous groups had passed through stages of numerical decline, followed by recoveries in which the growth of immunity and the advance in the control of exotic disease had been leading factors. There is no space here to list the many cases of this decline and recovery, but population figures for certain groups of American, Canadian, and central Mexican Indians, and for the Maoris and other inhabitants of the Pacific Islands, are examples.[2] These instances of decline and recovery lead on to a discussion of several vital problems, e.g. the much-disputed origin of outstanding diseases such as syphilis or malaria, the problem of immunity, and the immense increase in medical knowledge and efficiency created by the scientific revolution in the eighteenth and nineteenth centuries.

[1] *W.S.T.*, particularly chs. i and xviii.
[2] *W.S.N.P.*, particularly pp. 18–22 and 196 seq.

The origins and movements of some leading diseases are fascinating subjects which will be touched on later. As regards the way in which these diseases accompanied Western expansion, it is sufficient to quote as an example the views of a number of American scholars who consider that the American Indians were extremely healthy people until the whites arrived with their plagues. Thus G. C. Shattuck wrote in 1938:

One can say with certainty, or with a high degree of probability, that nearly all the more deadly epidemic diseases known in the New World since its discovery by Columbus have been imported from the Old World within historic times. This is probably true, also, of the minor epidemic diseases and of many other infections as well. Much doubt remains as to the origin of typhus fever, of the milder forms of malarial fever, and of various forms of dysentery.[1]

After his extensive study of original authorities, Ashburn reached the same conclusion. He wrote that the various peoples of the Americas

were probably as happy as any, and they were far more healthy than any others of whom we know. . . . There was no devastating smallpox, measles, malaria, yellow fever, perhaps no typhus or typhoid, almost no tuberculosis, probably no venereal diseases, no disease due to over-eating. . . . Into this Arcadian continent came the white man, thirsting for the riches of this world or the next. . . . The white man was speedily followed by his black slave, and white and black brought their diseases. . . . Arcady was no more. Death stalked from Canada to Patagonia. . . . This was the greatest mobilization of disease and of its introduction to new and susceptible peoples. . . . It was the most striking example of the influence of disease upon history.[2]

On one really vexed question, the origin of syphilis, Ashburn wrote:

It seems probable that the three common and widespread venereal diseases, syphilis, gonorrhoea, and chancroid, were introduced to America by the white conquerors. . . . Possibly, however, the transfer of syphilis (not of gonorrhoea and chancroid) was in the opposite direction, from America to Europe. If so, the Indian thereby inflicted

[1] Shattuck, op. cit., p. 48.   [2] Ashburn, op. cit., pp. 4-5.

a more potent revenge upon his conquerors than he was ever able to obtain by warfare, cultivated hatred, and studied cruelty, and the end is not yet.[1]

Leaving the American Indians we find that the explorers and early visitors gave glowing accounts of the health of various other primitive peoples before they were riddled by exotic diseases of various types. Cook said of the Maoris: 'These people enjoy perfect uninterrupted health.' His party never saw any diseased person and was surprised to find a number of well-preserved old men.[2] Elsdon Best wrote in 1934 that 'the simple life, hard fare, and industry of the old time Maori kept him usually in good health, and in many cases he was long lived. No doubt the law of the survival of the fittest caused weakly children to perish, and helped to produce an energetic, healthy, and virile population. Few diseases afflicted them, and apart from the dangers of war and black magic, men reckoned to die of old age.'[3]

Much the same story can be told of the Pacific Islands. S. M. Lambert wrote:

Depopulation follows the visitor. The immortal Captain Cook guessed this over a hundred and fifty years ago. A century ago keen observers like George Turner marked the locust swarm of imported diseases eating their way along the islands. But later, investigators broached a comfortable theory that the natives had begun to die off before the white man came. Nonsense. White men, in the malign form of looters and slavers, Spanish, Dutch and Portuguese, were there two hundred and fifty years before Cook came.[4]

It would be very dangerous to generalize, but it is, perhaps, possibly correct to say that the Pacific Islanders were, in general, free from smallpox, measles, typhus, typhoid, hookworm, leprosy, syphilis, and certain other major ills before the white invasions, although they seem to have been afflicted by filariasis, yaws, and

---

[1] Ashburn, op. cit., pp. 189–90.

[2] Quoted by H. B. Turbott in I. L. G. Sutherland, *The Maori People Today*, Auckland, 1940, p. 229.

[3] Elsdon Best, *The Maori as he was*, Wellington, N.Z., 1934, p. 6.

[4] S. M. Lambert, op. cit., p. 382; Sparrman, op. cit. (pp. 168–70), indicates that Cook found elephantiasis and possibly hookworm in New Caledonia.

PLATE VII

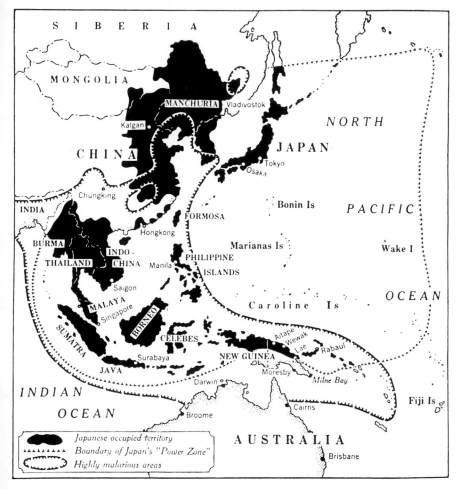

Pacific: Malarious areas

From A. S. Walker, *Clinical Problems of War*, Canberra, Australia, War Memorial, 1952

various skin diseases.[1] In a very interesting map A. S. Walker drew the boundaries of the 'highly malarious areas of the Western Pacific'. These boundaries run from the north-west Australian coast to India, and from Cairns to the Solomons (the zone excluding New Caledonia and Fiji), and then pass north to Korea and South-east Asia including New Guinea, New Britain, the Philippines, and Formosa, but excluding the Carolines, the Marianas, and Japan. This map indicates that northern Australia, New Guinea, the East Indies, South-east Asia, together with most of China and south-eastern India, are malarious areas, but that the remainder of the western and central Pacific lies outside the highly dangerous zone, a fact which is confirmed by Jacques May's map of the distribution of malaria vectors (Pl. VII). H. R. Carter believed that both malaria and yellow fever originated in the Old World—in Africa. This is very probable, as is also the supposition that some of the diseases spread with the advent of sailing vessels which could make long voyages to lands inhabited by non-immune peoples.[2]

As we have seen in Chapters IV and V, one of the outstanding effects of the Western invasions upon primitive indigenous peoples, such as the American Indians or Maoris, was a numerical decline due largely to disease. This was frequently followed by a numerical recovery which was often delayed until the particular group was partly assimilated and absorbed by the whites. A consideration of this cycle of decline and recovery involves a very brief examination of two important matters, the way in which some indigenous folk built up a resistance to exotic diseases, and the immense effects of the improvements in disease control which followed the scientific revolutions. It must be remembered, however, that these improvements affected both the indigenous and the invading peoples, and were the outstanding causes of the population problems which now afflict mankind.

B. G. Maegraith points out that 'certain individuals appear

---

[1] Keesing gives a well-balanced estimate of the relative weight of the indigenous and exotic diseases in his *The South Seas in the Modern World*, ch. x. See also Furnas, *Anatomy of Paradise*, p. 51, and Lambert, op. cit., pp. 382–3.

[2] A. S. Walker, *Clinical Problems of War*, p. 76; J. M. May, Map, 'Distribution of Malaria Vectors', *Atlas of Distribution of Diseases*, Plate III, in *Amer. Geog. Society Review*, 1951, no. 4; H. R. Carter, op. cit., pp. 69, 270–1.

naturally resistant to malarial infections. They may live continuously for years in endemic or hyperendemic areas apparently without acquiring the diseases, and they may fail to become infected after inoculation with parasites.'[1] Also it has long been known that 'continuous exposure to malarial infection over many years leads to the development of some degree of acquired resistance or immunity to the disease'.[1] The ancient Hindus and Chinese knew that it was possible to initiate mild attacks of smallpox with the resultant protection by transmitting matter from the pustule of a smallpox patient to a healthy person, and in the eighteenth century, even before Edward Jenner's experiments with cowpox in 1796, English 'inoculators' had achieved European fame.[2] These facts, which apply to many diseases, probably played an important part in some of the cycles of population decline and recovery before the scientific revolutions. If, as noted in Chapter IV, the population of all central Mexico was approximately 11 million in 1519, 1·5 million in 1650, and 3·7 million in 1793, it is possible that a natural and acquired immunity assisted other factors in producing a striking recovery before the days of modern medicine.[3] The same phenomenon must have occurred in a large number of cases, for example in the disappearance of leprosy in Europe, although this was largely due to stringent laws for the segregation and isolation of lepers. Medical scientists now possess a great deal of scientific information on the facts which underlie the building up of resistance. These phenomena have been clearly explained by a number of writers and need not be examined in this book.[4]

---

[1] B. G. Maegraith, *Pathological Processes in Malaria and Blackwater Fever*, Oxford, 1948, pp. 370–1.

[2] J. Jaramillo-Arango, *The British Contribution to Medicine*, Edinburgh, 1953, pp. 18–20.

[3] S. F. Cook and L. B. Simpson, *The Population of Central Mexico in the Sixteenth Century*, pp. 17–48.

[4] For leprosy see P. H. Manson-Bahr, *Manson's Tropical Diseases*, 7th edn., London, 1921, pp. 501–6. For immunity see F. M. Burnett, *Viruses and Man*, London, 1953, pp. 56 seq.; G. Lapage, *Animals Parasitic in Man*, London, 1957, pp. 173–4, 274–7; J. Drew, *Man, Microbe and Malady*, London, 1940–54. *W.S.T.*, ch. xv, p. 206, notes, with references, that the Negro seems to have a greater immunity to hookworm than the white man and is less heavily infested. Note also the following important statement from the *American Journal of Tropical*

It is also impossible to describe adequately in a work such as this the course of the revolution in medical science and the good deeds which the philanthropic Western peoples wrought throughout their tottering empires and revolting colonies, deeds which affected the course of history and presented mankind with new and almost insoluble problems such as that of Asian population increase. The pioneering explorations of Edward Jenner and of Louis Pasteur, who followed him from 1857 onwards, became in the final quarter of the nineteenth century a torrent of epoch-making discoveries. Medical scientists realized, for example, that there was a geography of disease, that many diseases conformed to a spatial pattern, and that many were entirely seasonal in character. They found that some of our worst afflictions were due to parasites, and that the geography of such diseases was a biological fact, existing in the limitation by temperature and moisture of the range of the parasite. As Jacques May has said of malaria, geographical factors influence the vector, possibly the causative agent, and possibly man in many ways. The two most important of these geographical factors seem to be rainfall and temperature.[1] Finally, it was proved that certain diseases reflected the incidence of social and economic as well as of geographical environments, and that throughout the colonies differences in sanitation, diet, or medical science produced different standards of health.[2] In his *History of Medicine* Arturo Castiglioni has given a brief but useful summary of the partial and sometimes sweeping victories against smallpox, measles, yellow fever, influenza, cholera, hookworm, pellagra, and syphilis, to which one can add plague, typhus, typhoid, malaria, and even leprosy, as knowledge grew of bacteria, viruses, and vitamins and the part which they played in disease.[3] Philanthropic institutions, such as the Rockefeller Foundation, conducted 'pilot projects' to

---

Medicine, Mar. 1947, pp. 111–15: 'The American negro has a marked tolerance, either natural or acquired, to vivax malaria in the U.S., yet when white and negro troops were exposed to vivax malaria in the Pacific, there was no difference in the incidence of primary or recurrent malaria between the two races. Natives of the area, however, exhibit a marked tolerance.'

[1] J. M. May, *Atlas of Distribution of Diseases*, Plate III.
[2] *W.S.T.*, pp. 34–36.
[3] Arturo Castiglioni, *History of Medicine*, New York, 1941.

educate governments and large commercial organizations in the vital need of improving and maintaining health.[1] From Queensland to Costa Rica, from Japan to Fiji, the local authorities saw at least some light and responded with a vigour which in many cases provided joyful retreats in the death-rate and sorrowful advances in population increase. In 1933, on returning to New York from the American tropics, I surprised my Rockefeller supervisor by suggesting that the Foundation might soon be spending millions of dollars in meeting the demographic problems created by its superb work in improving health. When I again visited the United States only six years later, he admitted sadly that it already seemed that my forecast would prove correct.

Deficiency diseases

We will now consider very briefly a few of the diseases which accompanied the invaders or the peoples whom they introduced to the invaded lands. Amongst the first ills to appear were deficiency diseases such as scurvy, the result of a new factor in world history, the long ocean voyages. These ills evolved in days before water and food could be properly preserved, and also stemmed from the famines and hardships suffered by many exotics when first opening up new territories. In many instances these diseases affected the exotic seafarers and pioneer settlers more than the indigenous folk who had evolved satisfactory diet patterns. Nevertheless, the aboriginals frequently changed their diets for less healthy Western foods, and suffered in consequence, as was the case with the Maoris in New Zealand. Writers such as R. S. Allison have termed these diseases 'sea diseases', but this is clearly a misnomer as they have probably affected far more people on land than at sea both in ancient and modern times.[2] They are now known to be due to the lack of various vitamins, a number of which have been isolated and analysed, some synthesized, and their effects in

[1] W.S.T., chs. xv, xvi.
[2] For the so-called 'Sea Diseases', see R. S. Allison, Sea Diseases, London, 1943; L. H. Roddis, James Lind, London, 1951; J. C. Beaglehole, The Voyage of the Endeavour, Hakluyt, C.U.P., 1955, particularly the introduction, and Grenfell Price, C.J.C.P., particularly chs. 1 and 14; May, Atlas of Distribution of Diseases, Plate IX—'Diets and Deficiency Diseases', Amer. Geog. Society, New York, 1953.

the production and cure of disease evaluated. Amongst the best known are vitamin B_1 or F (anti-beriberi), the B_2 complex or G (anti-pellagra), and C (anti-scorbutic).[1]

Scurvy, due largely to the lack of vitamin C, probably existed long before we have any medical recognition or description of it as a peculiar form of disease.[2] Indeed, it may well have appeared amongst the Viking or Polynesian voyagers if these mariners remained a sufficient time at sea. On land, deficiency diseases such as scurvy were known for a long time but without accurate information evolving as to what substances were deficient.[3] In historic times scurvy has appeared on many occasions, particularly during long voyages such as those of Vasco da Gama and Magellan, and in wars like the Crimean, the American Civil, and the Russo-Japanese. Amongst the most famous illustrations are those presented by some of the Manila galleons which sailed the Pacific between Acapulco in Mexico and the Philippines. The outward and westward voyage with the Trades took three months, which was within the bounds of reasonable health, but the eastern voyage, which involved a great sweep with the Westerlies, and a voyage of from four to eight months, was a very different story. Water and food went bad; there was no room for exercise; maggots swam in the broth; and the ships 'swarmed with little vermin and other vermin'. In such circumstances beriberi swelled the body and scurvy putrified the gums and made all the teeth drop out. In 1755 the *Santisima Trinidad* lost 82 out of 435 people in a voyage of seven months, and in 1657 another galleon, probably the *San José*, was found drifting off Acapulco with all on board dead, as the voyage had lasted over a year.[4]

In view of the grave and sometimes crippling losses suffered by European sailors, it seems incredible that, although the scientific causes of scurvy remained unknown, some of the European sea powers had actually hit on the preventive methods necessary, but had declined to use them, probably because they put the cost of preventive measures above the value of human

[1] Castiglioni, op. cit., pp. 772–3.   [2] Hirsch, op. cit., vol. ii, p. 512.
[3] Castiglioni, op. cit., p. 772.
[4] Schurz, *The Manila Galleon*, pp. 264 seq.

life. Thus, as early as 1593, Richard Hawkins cured his crew from scurvy and beriberi with oranges and lemons, writing: 'This is a wonderfull secret of the power and wisdom of God, that hath hidden so great and unknowne vertue in this fruit to be a certain remedie for this infirmite.' Again, when James Lancaster sailed to the East in 1601, the crews of his three small ships suffered severely, which was not the case with the complement of the larger flag-ship, because Lancaster 'brought to sea with him certaine bottles of the juice of limons, which he gave to each one as long as it would last, three spoonfuls every morning fasting, not suffering them to eate anything after it till noone'.[1] The French too seem to have hit on a preventive, as the American Indians taught Cartier in 1536 how to cure his sailors with the juice of the Ameda tree.[2] Yet on his voyage around the world in 1740–4 Anson lost 626 out of 961 men largely from preventable disease, and it was not until the writings of Dr. James Lind, physician of His Majesty's Royal Hospital at Haslar, and the practical work of the great James Cook in his voyages from 1768 to 1779, that the British naval authorities took measures to provide their hapless crews with anti-scorbutics, fresh water, and clean and dry clothing. We have already seen that until Cook's day, any naval seaman who undressed during a voyage was liable to be ducked three times from the yard arm.[3]

The defeat of scurvy on sea and land, and at later dates the defeat of beriberi, pellagra, and scrofula ashore, led to great improve-ments in the health of both the exotic peoples (the chief sufferers at sea) and the invaded folk. R. B. Vance found that much of the inefficiency and comparative lack of energy attributed to the climate of the southern United States could be laid with justice at the door of the so-called concealed diseases. One of these, pellagra, was due to dietary deficiencies, and when this was disclosed in 1907–8, its universal recognition seemed like the outbreak of an epidemic. The Southerners were greatly incensed as they were over the discovery of hookworm, but the resulting health and dietary campaigns had excellent results.[4]

[1] Allison, op. cit., pp. 25–29.   [2] Castiglioni, op. cit., p. 772.
[3] Allison, op. cit., p. 62.
[4] Vance, *Human Geography of the South*, pp. 436–41. *W.S.T.* quotes widely

An examination of the part played by deficiency diseases in the decline of the Maori discloses interesting facts. Several of the reports by pioneer medical officers, preserved in the Wellington Archives, show that scrofula, which seems to have been a tubercular tumour occurring particularly in the neck, was a main cause of Maori death. Hirsch believed that aetiological factors (diet and close confinement) played a prominent part in the disease,[1] while the New Zealand doctors considered that it became 'the curse of the Maori race' as a result of filth, and the fact that many Maori groups had a diet of putrid food including pork and fish, and—a recent acquisition—'stinking maize'.[2]

According to Dr. Thomson, Cook saw no scrofula, but Dr. Martin thought that it 'must have existed all along to a considerable extent, although it may be more frequent and fatal of late'.[3]

Eruptive fevers

These diseases, which include scourges such as smallpox, measles, typhus, and influenza, were outstanding killers in pioneer days in most of the conquered lands. Smallpox, to which the whites were to some extent immune, accompanied many of the invading groups and wrought havoc amongst the non-immune aboriginals. From native foci in central Africa and India this disease spread over much of the Old World, and in 1507, only fifteen years from the arrival of Columbus, began to decimate the aboriginals of the West Indies. We have already seen the destruction which it wrought in Mexico and Peru. These lands saw successions of epidemics as did Guatemala and Brazil, where, as in many other

from Vance's chs. 14, 15, and 16 which deal with climate, energy, diet, and human adequacy in the southern United States, and are extremely valuable.

[1] Hirsch, op. cit., vol. ii, p. 634.

[2] J. Fitzgerald, 'Medical Report on the State of the Native in the District of Port Nicholson, Wellington, N.Z., 1846', MS. N.Z. Archives, Wellington.

[3] A. S. Thomson, *The Story of New Zealand*, London, 1859, vol. i, Part I, ch. xi, pp. 211 seq.; S. M. D. Martin, 'Report on Maori Health', Sept. 1842, MS. N.Z. Archives, Wellington. Later but important works on Maori population and health are: James H. Pope (Inspector of Native Schools), *Health for the Maori*, Govt. Printer, Wellington, N.Z., 1884; A. Joan Metze, *Character of the Maori Population of the Auckland Province*, University of New Zealand, 1951; Noel Ruth, *The Maori Population of New Zealand*, Canberra, 1952.

instances, the outbreaks may have been due to the importation of Negro slaves.[1]

Smallpox was recorded in Canada from 1635 onwards, and aided the Iroquois to defeat the Hurons. Farther south the English described decimating visitations from about 1616, but punctuated their woeful accounts with paeans of gratitude to the Almighty who had so mercifully made room for his elect to settle by the destruction of barbarous savages. As the Puritan Johnson wrote of the plague which ravaged the Indians in 1616–20: 'By this means Christ, whose great and glorious works throughout the earth are all for the benefit of his churches and chosen, not only made room for his people to plant, but also tamed the hearts of those barbarous Indians.'[2] Smallpox also afflicted many indigenous groups in lands other than North America. Hirsch records that it reached Brazil in 1560 and that in later times epidemics followed the arrival of slave ships. The scourge entered Siberia in 1630 from the nearest Russian province, and produced frightful havoc amongst the Ostiaks, Tunguses, Samojeds, and Yakuts. James Cook recorded that it arrived in Kamschatka for the first time in 1767. Hirsch also notes that it was brought to Cape Colony by a ship from India in 1713. Tahiti suffered severe epidemics and the scourge killed 8 per cent. of the population of Hawaii when it appeared in 1853.[3] Hirsch may be wrong in stating that Australia enjoyed an absolute immunity until 1838, as Cleland and other Australian authorities believe that the Malays introduced smallpox in the north just before the first fleet arrived with convicts in 1788, and that it spread southwards amongst the aboriginals, causing grave loss of life. The disease seems to have reached the natives of the Sydney region in 1789. A second outbreak occurred on the north coast about 1828 and extended southwards to New South Wales and South Australia. In 1836 it reduced the aboriginals of Dungog (N.S.W.) from 200 to 60, and was partly responsible for the diminution in the number of natives along the Murray–

---

[1] Ashburn, op. cit., pp. 82–90; Shattuck, op. cit., pp. 40–42; Hirsch, op. cit., vol. i, pp. 128–39.

[2] W. C. MacLeod, *The American-Indian Frontier*, London, 1928, pp. 49–50.

[3] Hirsch, op. cit., vol. i, pp. 128–39.

Darling rivers, facts reported by the famous explorer Charles Sturt after his second journey down the Murray in 1838.[1]

A checking of early medical records in Wellington indicates, however, that Hirsch was almost certainly correct in his statement that the disease failed to enter New Zealand. This was partly due to the fact that the islands were not officially colonized until 1840, whereas vaccination was introduced to the civilized states of Europe as early as 1799–1804. Thus the practice spread to New Zealand in early times, and A. S. Thomson wrote in his *Story of New Zealand* in 1859 that two-thirds of the Maoris had been vaccinated.[2]

One can easily understand the destruction wrought by small-pox in a non-immune community, but it is difficult to realize the damage that was effected by measles which most Western peoples regard as a childish and even harmless disease. Hirsch considers that it is impossible to differentiate between measles and other diseases in Arabic and other early writings, but believes that by the Middle Ages the disease was widely dispersed through the Old World. Ashburn notes the same difficulty of diagnosis in the Americas but says that some definitions are clear, for example the visitation of 1532 in Mexico, and also that in Honduras, where, according to Oviedo, half the population died. Sigaud stated that measles claimed as many victims amongst the Indians of northern and central Brazil as did smallpox, and that in 1749–50 an epidemic killed up to 30,000 on the Amazon.[3]

On occasions the disease was equally destructive in other regions influenced by the invasions. Hirsch notes the mortality which it caused in Astoria in 1829, where half the Indians succumbed, amongst the Indians of Hudson's Bay in 1846, amongst the Hottentots at the Cape in 1852, and in Mauritius and Fiji in 1874.[4] N. McArthur has examined the records of this Fijian disaster when a measles epidemic, which was introduced by infected Fijians from

[1] Hirsch states, vol. i, pp. 133–4, that 'the continent of Australia up to 1838 had enjoyed an absolute immunity from smallpox'. This statement seems inaccurate in the light of later research; see p. 226, note I.
[2] Thomson, op. cit., vol. i, Part I, ch. xi, p. 212.
[3] Hirsch, op. cit., vol. i, pp. 154–70; Ashburn, op. cit., pp. 90–92.
[4] Hirsch, op. cit., vol. i, p. 167.

H.M.S. *Dido*, 'raged throughout the whole group in 1875'. A commission of 1893 noted that the outbreak killed 40,000 out of 150,000 Fijians, but McArthur considers that both these figures are too high and that the deaths probably numbered from 20,000 to 30,000.[1] Measles also had disastrous effects on the Australian aboriginals and the Maoris. Paul Hasluck gives striking pictures of the losses in Western Australia where the scourge may have killed half the natives of the Roebourne district about 1865.[2] Hirsch rightly comments that the degree of severity in an outbreak has often been controlled by the amount of attention paid to the sick. This view is supported by Hasluck who paints sad pictures of the measles epidemic in Western Australia in the 1880's when the white employers, who had to be the mainstay in the case of sick aboriginals, found that the weak and thirsty fell into the rivers while trying to drink, and the dead lay along the roads or in the bush.[3] Measles also produced serious results in New Zealand where the disease entered the South Island in 1838 and killed many natives in the Otago district. In 1854 an American vessel brought measles to the North Island where it spread rapidly and widely, carrying off some 4,000 Maoris. Serious as this was it is doubtful whether measles was as grave a scourge as scrofula (tuberculosis) or the social diseases.[4]

Typhus

A third example of these devastating fevers is typhus which is due to a rickettsial virus of which tick, lice, and fleas are vectors. It is now found over large areas in Europe, Asia, Africa, and North and South America, and Australia, where it appears in epidemic form in times of war or famine when living conditions are low and large bodies of people are in close contact. Only the tick type

---

[1] N. McArthur, *The Populations of the Pacific Islands*, Part VI, *Fiji*, Aust. Nat. University, about 1955, pp. 261–75. All of Dr. McArthur's volumes in this series are of importance to demography and geo-medicine; they are: Part I: *Territories of French Oceania*; Part II: *Cook Islands and Niue*; Part III: *American Samoa*; Part IV: *Western Samoa and the Tokelau Islands*; Part V: *Tonga*; Part VI: *Fiji*; Part VII: *Papua and New Guinea*; Part VIII: *Netherlands New Guinea*.

[2] Hasluck, *Black Australians*, pp. 103 seq.

[3] Ibid., p. 106.   [4] Thomson, op. cit., vol. i, pp. 212–13.

is found in New Guinea, the Solomons, and the New Hebrides, while New Zealand, Micronesia, Polynesia, and parts of Melanesia, such as Fiji and New Caledonia, seem to be free.[1] Ashburn has no doubt that the Western invaders brought typhus to the Americas at very early dates, particularly as it was epidemic in Spain and in the Spanish armies in 1489–90. He considers that the disease was particularly murderous in Mexico and quotes León that in an epidemic of 1576–7 the deaths exceeded 2 million.[2] Hans Zinsser, on the contrary, takes the view that the guilt of the Westerners remains unproved as there is much in historical evidence which suggests the existence of typhus fever among the South American nations in pre-Columbian days, even if there were no rats in South America before 1544–6.[3] Shattuck adopts this view and writes, 'Much doubt remains as to the origin of typhus fever'.[4]

The social diseases

In very many of the invasions the conquering males, often of the roughest type and far removed from their own women, engaged in an orgy of sexual licence with the willing or unwilling women of the conquered, with the result that venereal disease took a terrible toll, which was not only widespread in the colonies, but may have been responsible for very grave repercussions in the metropolitan countries. The story is one of singular interest, first because of its historic importance, second because of the unsolved problem of the origin of syphilis, and third because of the triumph of modern scientific medicine over these diseases.

Authorities such as John Drew consider that gonorrhoea is one of the oldest of the bacterial diseases of man, almost as old probably as the human race itself.[5] Gonorrhoea was, however, a less outstanding curse than syphilis, for, although it could cause death from septicaemia, it yielded to treatment with mercury and

---

[1] May, *Atlas of the Distribution of Diseases*, Plates X, XI, XII, for distribution of rickettsial diseases, 1953–4; see also K. M. Smith, *Beyond the Microscope*, 1952, pp. 32 seq., and G. Lapage, *Animals Parasitic in Man*, pp. 220–3, for the louse.

[2] Ashburn, op. cit., pp. 92–97, 224–8.

[3] Zinsser, op. cit., ch. xiv, p. 258.

[4] Shattuck, *Guatemala*, p. 48, also pp. 43–44.

[5] Drew, op. cit., pp. 118–23.

salvasan, and in recent times to the sulphonamides and penicillin, which gave excellent results. Syphilis, which may end in the terrible lesions of the tertiary stage, in insanity, or in the living death of locomotor ataxy, is a more dangerous and loathsome disease than gonorrhoea and has been called 'the worst scourge of mankind'. John Drew stated in 1940 that according to leading authorities some 10 per cent. of the population of the British Isles were syphilitic; 100,000 fresh cases occurred annually, and from 50 per cent. to 100 per cent. of prostitutes were infected.

Gonorrhoea, in particular, has been called the sailors' disease, but both it and syphilis were undoubtedly carried by the white invaders or their coloured labourers to many lands in which, at the time, they did not exist. Lambert, writing in 1941, gave as an example the rapid and disastrous spread of venereal diseases amongst the amoral and unsophisticated Pacific Islanders. He wrote that he had done his best to inquire into the prevalence of gonorrhoea, the old enemy of racial fertility, particularly in regard to the little-visited island of Rennell in Melanesia. He concluded his investigations with the following sad comment: 'What I found that our sailors had picked up from Rennell alarmed me as to the island's future. The barriers were down, the White Sands were offering the most generous hospitality to visiting sailors. I had seen other island populations sink for similar reasons.'[1] The same story can be told of many of the invaded territories, with New Zealand as an outstandingly sad example of the state of affairs which was not new in Pacific history, and which existed in Tahiti for years afterwards. In the 1830's some 150 vessels with total crews of about 4,500 sailors entered the Bay of Islands annually, and were entertained by the Maori chiefs who greeted them with canoe-loads of Maori women and pigs, which were offered in exchange for rum, tea, sugar, or cash. These rapacious, greedy, and thieving chiefs had no compunction in sacrificing even their sisters and daughters in a traffic which brought in about £11,000 a year by prostitution and theft. As a result, wrote Ramsden, 'venereal disease, a Pakeha gift to the Maori, was rampant. Only one woman in fifty was regarded as free from the scourge; further,

[1] Lambert, op. cit., p. 343.

the disease was of the most virulent kind.'[1] The Bay of Islands was, of course, a particularly bad example, but Dr. S. M. D. Martin wrote in a report on Maori health in 1842 that the first cause of decline was disease which resulted from European intercourse. Half the deaths in New Zealand were, he felt, directly or indirectly due to social diseases. Second to these he placed respiratory diseases, scrofula, and rheumatism, the scourges incidental to the transition from a savage to a civilized state, while he gave third place to the sale of young Maori women for prostitution which created much disease, together with the infanticide of female babies whom the mothers refused to expose to a similar type of life, the tragic degeneration resulting in a great numerical disparity between the sexes.[2]

Fortunately, as we have seen, the Maoris, like many other of the invaded peoples, survived these periods of governmental neglect and missionary ignorance, to reach a stage when official health control and the discovery of remedies such as penicillin repaid with good some at least of the earlier evil.[3]

Many volumes have been written on the origin of syphilis and whether Columbus's crew and other early invaders introduced the scourge to or brought it back from the Americas. Ashburn, who carefully examined both the original authorities and the opinions of recent scholars, gives five alternative theories, which we will summarize briefly. First, there is the possibility of American origin which rests on the question of whether or not certain Indian syphilitic bones were pre-Columbian, and on the general European belief in the sixteenth century that the disease was American. Secondly, there is the opinion that the disease long existed in a mild form in Europe and that it flared up owing to the wars and poverty which were prevalent in Columbian times. Thirdly, a few authorities think that the disease existed in both hemispheres, having been taken to America by Asian migrants. Keizo Dohi, however, believes that the Portuguese first took it to the Orient. In the fourth place there is a theory that syphilis evolved from the

---

[1] E. Ramsden, *Marsden and the Missions*, Sydney, 1936, pp. 66–73.
[2] S. M. D. Martin, 'Report on Maori Health'.
[3] *W.S.N.P.*, chs. viii, ix.

tropical disease yaws which may have preceded the whites to the Pacific and is now widely distributed. The organism *treponema pertenne* closely resembles the organism *treponema pallidum*, which is responsible for syphilis. The two diseases have many points of clinical resemblance and they give cross-reactions of immunity but, unlike syphilis, yaws is not handed on by sexual contact.

A final and most interesting view is that syphilis is a new disease which resulted from the union of the Europeans and Indians and their spirochetal parasites. 'In the bridal night of the two races was syphilis conceived.' Considering the evidence as a whole, Ashburn concludes that all the venereal diseases were probably carried to the Americas by the Europeans, but that the transfer of syphilis was possibly in the opposite direction. In any case, syphilis had such immense historical effects that the problem, although now largely academic, may be worth further research in original documents and accounts.[1]

Tuberculosis

Various medical scientists name this or that disease as the most devastating to mankind and E. R. Baldwin states that tuberculosis 'transcends all maladies in the total number of its victims and the cost to society'. The disease was familiar to the most ancient civilizations, judging from the inscriptions on Babylonian tablets which represent the earliest human records.[2] Ashburn began by believing that the Westerners introduced this curse to America particularly as Aleš Hrdlička adopted this view when he failed to find evidence of tuberculosis in many thousands of pre-Columbian skeletons. Later, however, Ashburn himself visited Mexico and found pre-Columbian figures which in his opinion clearly showed the characteristic spinal deformities of the disease. The same doubt appears as regards the age of scrofula in New Zealand. As noted above, Dr. A. S. Thomson characterized the disease as 'the curse of the New Zealand race' and pointed out that Cook had failed to report any cases of this disease which seemed to have appeared

---

[1] Ashburn, op. cit., pp. 176–90, 238–40.
[2] Ibid., p. 144.

after the white invasions through the Maoris sinking to filthy living conditions and adopting potatoes and stinking fish, pork, and maize as their main diets.[1] Martin, on the other hand, considered that scrofula must have existed all along to a considerable extent, although it might have become more frequent and fatal of late. As noted above, Martin regarded all these complaints of the chest and lungs as incidental to the transition from a savage to a civilized state.[2] Other writers thought that these sicknesses were the result of the Maoris overcrowding and spitting in inadequate dwellings, and the replacement of the healthy and open-work flax cloaks by heavy trade blankets, which were worn over the chest whether dry or wet.[3]

An examination of the records of other invasions of regions inhabited by populations which were not adapted to *Bacillus tuberculosis* and other respiratory diseases gives the same sad result. In the words of John Drew:

man does not possess any natural immunity to *B. tuberculosis* and it is a deadly germ among populations that have not adapted themselves to it. Among the South Pacific Islanders, the negro tribes in Africa, and the Eskimos, tuberculosis has spread with devastating effects since its introduction by white explorers and colonists. We do not yet possess any certainly effective means of artificial immunization against the germ, although work that is now in progress is promising.[4]

Mosquito-borne diseases

Malaria, yellow fever, and filariasis are shocking diseases. The World Health Organization reported in 1955 that malaria killed 2·5 million and affected 250 million persons per annum, or one-tenth of the population of the world. H. B. Carter believed that it was the only disease which could make a region uninhabitable. The cost in medical attention, lassitude, and inefficiency is fabulous.[5] Yellow fever, which made Panama 'the pest-hole of the world'

[1] Ibid., pp. 144–7 and 236–7; Thomson, op. cit., ch. xi.

[2] Martin, op. cit.

[3] Bishop Williams's remarks, 3 Apr. 1860, on F. D. Fenton's 'Observations on the State of the Aboriginal Inhabitants of New Zealand', Auckland, 1859, MS. N.Z. Archives, Wellington.   [4] Drew, op. cit., pp. 97–98.

[5] For the cost of malaria in lives and money see *W.S.T.*, pp. 208–9, quoting Andrew Balfour and H. R. Carter; also Lapage, op. cit., p. 183.

and West Africa 'the white man's grave', and which is still highly dangerous in jungle environments, is due to a virus carried by the mosquito *Aedes aegypti*, once called *Culex fascinatus* or *Stegomyia fascinata*.[1] Filariasis, which can become elephantiasis, with revolting enlargement of parts of the body, is due to a round worm that is carried by some forty-one species of *Aedes*, *Culex*, or *Anopheles* mosquitoes.[2]

Malaria is due to four species of a single-cell parasite, the plasmodium.[3] The scourge has been known in the Old World for centuries. Jaramillo-Arango states that 'malaria is one of the oldest diseases known to man' and 'the suspicion that it and other diseases were transmitted by insects goes back several centuries before Christ'.[4] From the late 1870's onwards, famous scientists of several nations discovered the causes of these and of other diseases, and the world realized that they were environmental scourges dependent upon the climate and other conditions which the parasites and their many varieties of host could tolerate. Thus malaria, whatever form it takes, is a cosmopolitan disease, for one or more species of *Anopheles* can breed in most parts of the world. Fortunately, the mosquitoes cannot in general breed at great heights, say above 9,000 feet, or in dry deserts, so that these regions are often free from the disease. It is also absent from some island groups such as New Zealand, Hawaii, Fiji, Samoa, the Gilbert and Ellice Islands, and the Marquesas, and it is not found north of latitude 60 N. or south of latitude 30 S. It is hyperendemic in some areas, which means that its incidence is much higher than in endemic areas in which it is always present. These hyperendemic regions are Southeast Asia and the East Indies, India, Central and South America with the West Indies, and the south-west Pacific including the northern coast of Australia. Thus it may be said that malaria covers much of the earth including a large part of the territory which the whites invaded.[5]

Yellow fever is far less widely distributed than malaria although its range includes tropical Africa, where it is often mild, and parts

[1] Burnet, op. cit., ch. 13.   [2] Lapage, op. cit., pp. 95 seq.
[3] Ibid., p. 175.   [4] Jaramillo-Arango, op. cit., pp. 96–97.
[5] Lapage, op. cit., p. 175.

of tropical South America. In former times it spread as far north as New York and even England, sometimes with disastrous results.[1] Fortunately, when the causes became known it was found that the *Aedes aegypti* was a house mosquito with a restricted flight, which made its local extermination possible.[2] Later it was discovered that as well as the cycle man–*Aedes aegypti*–man, a monkey–mosquito–monkey cycle also existed which created areas of jungle yellow fever, although the mosquitoes concerned were quite different to the *Aedes*. In this type of country it was impossible to use the techniques of mosquito destruction which rid Cuba of yellow fever and made it possible to build the Panama Canal. In general reliance had to be placed on immunization.[3] It is interesting to note the suggestion of F. M. Burnet that as the virus exists in both the Old and New Worlds, it may have been with the monkey tribe ever since the common ancestor flourished somewhere in Asia or Africa. Jacques May comments, 'still undetermined are the reasons for the mildness of yellow fever in the eastern part of Africa and for its complete absence in Asia and the Pacific area', although, as Burnet notes, the *Aedes* mosquito is prevalent everywhere in the tropics and there are monkeys in much of the region.[4]

Like malaria and yellow fever, filariasis is probably an ancient disease which is now widely spread. Bancroft's filarial roundworms, of which the adult form was discovered by Bancroft in Brisbane, Queensland, in 1876, lives in and inflames the lymphatic system of man causing one variety of the disease filariasis created by worms of this type. Lapage quotes Stoll who estimated in 1947 that *Wuchereria bancrofti* and *W. malayi* infected 189 million people over a vast area which included large parts of the tropics and sub-tropics, particularly the coastal regions.[5]

[1] For the distribution of malaria, see J. M. May, *Atlas of the Distribution of Diseases*, Plate III, *Geographical Review*, Oct. 1951. For yellow fever and dengue, Plate V, ibid., Apr. 1952.   [2] Burnet, op. cit., ch. 13, is very up to date and interesting.
[3] Ibid., pp. 172–3.
[4] J. M. May, *Atlas* above, Plate V in *Geographical Review*, Apr. 1952; Burnet, op. cit., pp. 167 seq.
[5] Lapage, op. cit., pp. 96–100; Manson-Bahr, op. cit., p. 581; J. B. Cleland in *Medical Journal of Australia*, Apr. 1950, pp. 549 seq.

How far are the Western peoples responsible for the advance and, in some cases, the retreat of these and similar diseases ? Although there has been an immense amount of scientific dispute on the subject, it seems probable that the developments of Western scientific transport, the sailing ship, the steamer, and the aeroplane, carried the parasites, and even the mosquitoes, far and wide. Jacques May writes: 'As *Aedes aegypti* has a restricted flight range, dengue fever owes its ubiquity to man-made means of transportation. Epidemics follow lines of communication by road, rail, water and air'.[1] There is no space to examine the various views on the spread of these diseases, and in particular the controversy as to whether or not the whites and their slaves brought such scourges from the Old World to the New. One can, however, quote the views of the leading medical scientists such as H. R. Carter and G. C. Shattuck, views which are supported by P. M. Ashburn and other authorities. On the subject of yellow fever Shattuck writes that 'Carter's epidemiological study of yellow fever all but proves that this disease was imported from Africa'. Although Shattuck thinks that a mild form of indigenous or imported malaria may have affected Cortez's forces, he notes that Stitt, in *Our Disease Inheritance from Slavery*, referring to the United States of America, lists tropical malaria (aestivo-autumnal) and blackwater fever among the diseases probably introduced from Africa, and adds that Carter is inclined to think that malaria did not exist in America prior to its discovery. It would of necessity have been introduced early by the Europeans and Negroes, and *Anopheles* being generally present, it would have spread.[2] Ashburn states that there is no real evidence that malaria existed in any part of America before the conquest. Of filariasis he notes that the Spanish chroniclers of the invasion can hardly have failed to notice and mention the monstrous

[1] May, *Atlas of Distribution of Diseases*, Plate V, 'Dengue and Yellow Fever', in *Geographical Review*, Apr. 1952; Burnet, op. cit., pp. 167 seq., for the far-reaching and disastrous spread of yellow fever with the introduction of the ocean-going sailing ship.

[2] Shattuck, *Guatemala*, p. 39, for opinion on Carter's work on yellow fever; p. 49 for reference to E. R. Stitt, *U.S. Naval Med. Bull.*, no. 26, 1928, pp. 801–33, U.S. Public Health, *Science Reports*, 7 Mar. 1919. For Ashburn's conclusions on malaria see *The Ranks of Death*, pp. 125–6.

PLATE VIII

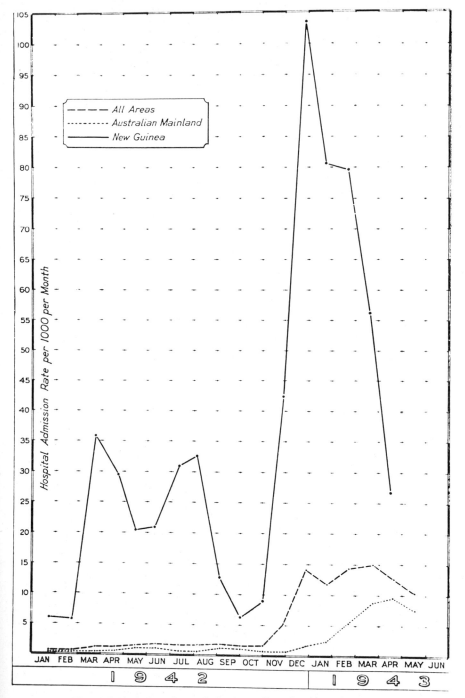

Hospital admissions for malaria, Australia and New Guinea, 1942–3
From A. S. Walker, *Clinical Problems of War*, Canberra, Australia, War Memorial, 1952

deformities of elephantiasis, and as they failed to do so 'it was probably introduced to America with slaves, as the Europeans were not apt to have had the parasite in their home countries'.[1]

Turning to the western shores of the Pacific and to the islands in the ocean, one finds that Hirsch has published an immense amount of information from authorities who have reported on these diseases. Again it is impossible to trace their spread in any detail, but again, as in the Americas, there is evidence of the advance of exotic diseases under the influence of the invasions. B. H. M. Vlekke states that malaria suddenly appeared in Batavia in 1732 with the result that the city declined, for instead of being the pearl among European settlements in the Orient it got the reputation of being one of the most unhealthful places on earth.[2] R. H. Black gives an interesting account of malaria in the south-west Pacific, where very early explorers encountered it in infected areas such as New Guinea, the New Hebrides, and the Solomons. He considers that it is not clear whether malaria was endemic or not in pre-European times, but it seems probable that in northern Australia there had always been repeated introductions of the disease by Malays and by the native traffic across Torres Strait. He also gives instances of the spread of the disease and the danger of aircraft transporting *Anopheles*.[3] Lambert notes the advance of filariasis in the Pacific Islands, when civilization broke down the barriers of primitive savagery which had maintained an inter-island quarantine.[4]

Efforts to control mosquito-borne diseases

Many writers have traced the long battle which medical scientists have waged against mosquito-borne diseases, e.g. the discovery of the causes of yellow fever and malaria and the victories over yellow fever won by the medical scientists Reed, Carter, and Gorgas in Havana and later by Gorgas in Panama. Unfortunately, some

---

[1] Ibid., pp. 173–4.

[2] B. H. M. Vlekke, *Nusantara*, Harvard, 1945, pp. 175–6.

[3] Black, *Malaria in the South West Pacific*, Technical Paper no. 81, South Pacific Commission, Noumea, 1955, pp. 1–8. See also p. 224, note E.

[4] Lambert, op. cit., pp. 169–70.

of these authorities, such as Gorgas, developed exaggerated hopes as a result of these successes, for even today malaria confines the Americans at Panama to what is really a series of fortified stations along the Canal. Thus it can be said that the battle has not been a complete victory but a series of advances on a very long front over a period of at least eighty years.[1]

As an example of recent methods of control one can take the case of malaria. Here scientists are attacking mosquitoes by spraying houses and aeroplanes to prevent the latter transporting insects. They are also draining infected areas, and are killing the larvae by Paris green or with spreading oil on water surfaces. Not least important is the use of drugs to kill parasites within human bodies. Of these drugs quinine has been known since 1638 when it cured the Countess d'El Cinchón, wife of the Viceroy of Peru, from which it gained its name Cinchóna. Later, laboratory workers discovered other anti-malarial drugs such as atabrine and paludrine in efforts which quickened when, during the Second World War, the Japanese overran Java and Malaya and secured the chief supplies of quinine.[2] During the war the American and Australian forces showed what could be achieved by the use of DDT and drugs such as atabrine and paludrine. At Milne Bay, New Guinea, in a rainfall of 104 inches per annum, the Australians in four months reduced the malaria rate from 4,264 attacks per 1,000 men to 420 per 1,000 men. (See Pl. VIII.) The American scientists set out to guard their forces, to prevent troops returning to the United States bringing back exotic diseases, to train medical personnel, to develop research, and to apply the results of that research in the war areas. To this end the authorities gave short courses on tropical medicine at Tulane and conducted intense research on repellants, insecticides, protective clothing, penicillin, and vaccines, with the result that many diseases, such as yellow fever and sleeping sickness, failed to appear. DDT protected millions of troops from diseases such as louse-typhus in Africa and rodent-borne bubonic plague. The *American Journal of Tropical Medicine* gave in January 1945 the following rate of hospital admissions:

[1] *W.S.T.*, pp. 148–51.
[2] Lapage, op. cit., pp. 180–3.

Disease	Cases	Rate per 1,000 for troops in the area
Malaria . .	460,872	18·9
Dengue . .	84,090	3·4
Sand-fly fever .	12,434	0·5
Scrub typhus .	6,861	0·28

At the outset the Americans had some trouble in the uncon trolled areas, but the rate of malaria fell from a peak of 160 per 1,000 in 1943 to 25 per 1,000 in 1945.[1] The problems of applying the lessons of these military successes in the civilian fields lie in the spheres of care and cost. Forces under military control can be compelled to take care, and under pressure of war the governments protect their personnel regardless of cost. Even in recent years the tide of combat has ebbed and flowed. In 1929–30 the mosquito *Anopheles gambiae* was transported by fast French destroyer or by aeroplane from Africa to Brazil, where it produced an epidemic of malaria so severe that by 1938 practically the whole population became infected, economic life was disrupted, and between April and October 1938 20,000 people died. Yet by 1941 the Brazilians had conquered the *Anopheles gambiae* and in that year no mosquito of that species, bred in Brazil, could be found.[2]

Leprosy

In conclusion a word may be said about leprosy, which was for ages a terrifying disease, although it possibly slew fewer individuals than did diseases such as smallpox, malaria, or influenza. At the time of the invasions it was probably widespread in Europe, Africa, and Asia, although certain populations seem to have been developing some immunity. Hirsch and other authorities believe that the Americas had no leprosy until the Westerners brought in Negro slaves, and it is possible that the Westerners also spread it

[1] The *American Journal of Tropical Medicine*, Baltimore, published a number of very important articles after the Second World War, e.g. J. S. Simmons on 'Tropical Medicine and the Challenge of Global War and Global Peace', Jan. 1947.

[2] Lapage, op. cit., p. 166.

through the Pacific Islands by introducing Asian migrants. It is now located in parts of Europe, Asia, Africa, Latin America, and the Pacific Islands, particularly in hot countries where living standards are low and populations crowded.[1] It has not been prevalent in British America or New Zealand, but it has gained a serious hold on the unfortunate aboriginals of north Australia. Dr. C. E. A. Cook, now in the Commonwealth Department of Health and at one time Protector of the Aboriginals in the Northern Territory, summed up the matter as follows:

Leprosy, introduced by Chinese railway construction workers in the last century, has long been endemic amongst the remnants of the de-tribalized native population in the vicinity of the Darwin–Katherine railway. Up to the outbreak of war in 1939, it seemed probable that the medical service would be successful in controlling and ultimately eliminating this disease. Involvement of the white population, common some years ago, has, for the time at least, been successfully arrested. The intervention of the war, however, led to the dispersion of infectious cases to Missions, and the concentration of formerly nomadic tribes in contact with them there has precipitated a wide extension and increasingly heavy incidence.[2]

Fortunately, if the disease is detected and treated in time, it is curable with the new drugs available. In the leprosarium near Papete in 1955 we found the French doctors very optimistic, while of western Samoa and the Cook Islands, N. R. Sloan wrote in 1954: 'It seems probable that the adequate programme of diagnosis and treatment now under way will bring the disease under control within a reasonable time.'[3]

Conclusion

Taken as a whole a great mass of evidence indicates that the diseases of the Western invaders and of their labour forces were a powerful factor, perhaps in some cases the most powerful factor,

[1] May, *Atlas of the Distribution of Diseases*, Plate VII, *Geographical Review*, 1953; Hirsch, op. cit., vol. ii, ch. 1; Ashburn, op. cit., pp. 191–4, 240–2.

[2] C. E. Cook in *N.A.*, p. 200. See also p. 224, note E.

[3] N. R. Sloan, 'Leprosy in Western Samoa and the Cook Islands', *South Pacific Commission*, Technical Paper no. 69, Noumea, 1954, p. 22.

in the defeat of the indigenous peoples, and not infrequently in their destruction.

This chapter and *White Settlers and Native Peoples* present evidence which shows that in many instances the eruptive fevers such as smallpox and measles, together with social diseases, led the attack, but that other ills, particularly the respiratory diseases such as tuberculosis, did the mopping up. In English-speaking America the well-known authority J. H. Mooney gave in order the agents of destruction as: 'smallpox and other epidemics, tuberculosis, social diseases, whisky and attendant dissipation, removals, starvation and subjection to unaccustomed conditions, low vitality due to depression, and wars.'[1] Ivan Petroff, in his report on Alaska, places the destructive agents in order as pulmonary tuberculosis, scrofulous diseases, paralysis, inflammation of the bowels, and rheumatic troubles. Syphilis 'was probably first introduced in Alaska by the Russians, . . . at any rate Captain Cook records that several of his crew contracted the disease during their brief stay on Unalaska Island in the year 1778'. Measles, which had fatal power over the natives, ravaged Kadiak Island and the mainland on several occasions. Typhoid and pneumonia from time to time wasted whole settlements. The most devastating disease of all, however, was smallpox, which entered Alaska as an epidemic from 1836 to 1840, doing little damage to the Russians and Creoles, but killing hundreds of natives before the authorities could organize widespread vaccination.[2]

On the other side of the Pacific in the case of the Maoris of New Zealand, an entirely different race in an entirely different environment, Dr. S. M. D. Martin attributed, as noted above, a similar decline in numbers to causes which strikingly resemble those on the east of the Pacific. Martin considered that half the Maori deaths were due to social diseases, the result of European intercourse. Then came complaints of the chest and lungs, tuberculosis, rheumatism, scrofula, the killing of female infants, bad diet, and lack of salt, which may have caused the scrofula, filthy houses and

---

[1] Quoted in *White Settlers and Native Peoples*, p. 19.

[2] Petroff, *Report on the Population, Industries and Resources of Alaska*, pp. 229–32 and 344–5.

habits. Then at the end of the Maori Wars came land robbery and mental depression which caused the Maoris to believe that they would disappear before the Westerners 'as the native rat disappeared before the European'.[1]

We have seen that the development of resistance and immunity, the growth of medical science, and the spiral of trusteeship in the metropolitan or colonial governments resulted in the recovery of many indigenous groups, some of whom joined their conquerors and the great Asian peoples in those vast population advances by which modern medicine has created many of the chief problems of our age.

We must leave others to discover and relate whether or not the Western impacts had evil as well as good effects on Asian health. Authorities often find difficulty in making completely reliable diagnoses from the descriptions of Oriental or Arabian doctors in ancient times, but it is clear that Asia contained many of the worst diseases such as smallpox, plague, and leprosy, and that the frequent Asian invasions of Europe carried these scourges into Western territory.[2] Nevertheless, the Western invasions of East Asia probably reversed the current in a number of instances; for example, Castiglioni notes the opinion of Chinese writers that syphilis was brought into China at the beginning of the sixteenth century by a vessel from Europe touching at the port of Canton.[3] Again, as noted above, malaria suddenly struck Batavia in 1732 with devastating results. 'Death means nothing here', wrote James Cook in 1770, when the crew he had saved from scurvy died around him, and his scientists Banks and Solander fled to a country house with a Malay woman apiece, 'hoping that the tenderness of the sex would prevail even here, which indeed we found it to do'.[4]

Much as one would like several more lives in which to learn the Asian languages and attempt the research necessary to pursue this subject, all one can do is to follow Asian experts such as Panikkar

---

[1] Martin, op. cit.   [2] Hirsch, op. cit., vol. i, ch. 10; vol. ii, ch. 1.
[3] Castiglioni, op. cit., p. 103.
[4] See p. 167, n. 2. For Banks and Solander see Beaglehole, *The Voyage of the Endeavour*, p. 441. Beaglehole states that the fullest account of the murderous sickness is in Banks but that Parkinson deserves to be quoted. See also Grenfell Price, *C.J.C.P.*, p. 87.

and Chandrasekhar and record the vital importance of the Asian population growth, adding, however, one outstanding historical truth which Asian writers tend to omit, namely, that the world is now blessed by the presence of hundreds of millions of additional Asians largely through the virtues of Western medical science. What science achieved through a vast number of discoveries such as vaccination, inoculation, insecticides, and drugs, has been frequently referred to in the above chapter, while a few of the population advances have been mentioned in Chapters IV and V, but one does not know of any general work in geomedicine that correlates the growth of medical and hygiene services with population increases, although this question has been and is of the utmost consequence. Fortunately, the Rockefeller Report of 1950 on health and demography in a number of Asian countries in the western Pacific—Japan, China, Formosa, Indonesia, and the Philippines—does something to remedy the deficiency as far as this important region is concerned.

The Rockefeller surveyors showed that in Indonesia and the Philippines, lands under the direct management of European powers, which introduced health and hygiene services, the populations registered substantial growth. They wrote that in Java, civil disorder, ignorance of the basic principles of sanitation and nutrition, a fluctuating food supply, and epidemic and endemic diseases retarded population growth severely until the early nineteenth century. Then the colonial administration of the Dutch began to penetrate every phase of the life of the people. It maintained peace and order, introduced public health measures, spread elementary notions of hygiene, and improved agricultural techniques. As previously noted, the admittedly inadequate estimates indicate that the native people of Java and Madura increased from about 5 million in 1826 to 13 million in 1861, 30 million in 1905, and 41 million in 1930. Activities were sufficient to limit mortality, particularly from epidemic diseases, but in contrast with the activities in the West they were limited. Gradually preventive measures were extended to the general population. Except for malaria, the major epidemic diseases were controlled. Excellent laboratories and institutes of research and biological production were functioning and were effective on a quantitative basis. The committee felt, however, that the rate of preparing medical and auxiliary personnel was much too slow if the people were really being prepared for independence.[1] The surveyors paid an even more favourable tribute to the American health work in the Philippines and to its effect on population increase. In the forty-eight years of United States government and guidance, the general education and health of the island's population received special attention. 'Public health and medical care have played', wrote the committee, 'an important part in the demographic transformation of the Philippines. Population growth was rapid and continuous. Numbers increased from 7·6 million in 1903 to 10·3 million in 1918, 16·0 million in 1939, and 19·2 million in 1948.'[2]

The surveyors showed that Western medical practice had similar results on the population growth in the hands of the capable and energetic Japanese. After describing the improvements in public health and medical care the surveyors wrote:

These comprehensive health and medical services, combined with generally increasing food supplies and advancing educational levels, produced the declining rates of mortality that were primarily responsible for Japan's increasing population throughout most of the 75-year period between the Meiji Restoration and the Surrender. The statistical picture is blurred during the period between 1868 and 1920, but for the twenties and thirties the presence of mortality declines, comparable in speed and incidence to those that occurred earlier in the West, is indisputable. Crude death rates declined from 21·9 in 1921–5 to 17·9 in 1931–5. Infant death rates, 174 per 1000 live born children in 1916–1920, declined to 121 in 1931–5, and to 83 in 1942. The life expectancy of males at birth increased from 42·1 years in 1921–5 to 44·8 in 1926–30 and 46·9 in 1935–6.[3]

Figures of a similar if of a less striking type could be produced for many other lands to which Western settlers and sojourners

[1] M. C. Balfour and others, *Public Health and Demography in the Far East*, Rockefeller Report, pp. 90–93; Van Helsdingen and others, *Mission Interrupted, The Dutch in the East Indies and their Work in the Twentieth Century*, ch. 13, 'Welfare Policy—The Dutch Work in Health'; ch. 11, 'The Conquest of Natural Resources'; and ch. 12, 'From Four to Forty-four Million Souls in Java'.
[2] Rockefeller Report, 1950, pp. 90, 93, 103.   [3] Ibid., p. 22.

brought their scientific medicine, or in which the indigenous inhabitants introduced Western medical practice. Even Australia, a region of white settler colonization for which Warren Thompson and other writers incorrectly predicted a population decline, showed remarkable increases in the expectation of life. In 1881–90 the male expectation was 47·20 years; in 1901–10 55·2 years; in 1920–2 59·15 years, and in 1946–8 66·07 years, while the female expectancy throughout was about 4 years longer.[1]

I do not claim that the population increases which resulted from the advance and spread of Western medical science were advantageous to the world as a whole or even to the particular countries concerned, which only too often faced population pressures, decreased living standards, and wars. For these reasons we find certain governments attempting to direct medical scientists to the task of remedying those demographic difficulties in which they have been, even if indirectly, the chief causative agents. Above all, however, stands the need of research into little understood problems of demography, health, social science, and technology. As the Rockefeller Committee stated: 'Systematic work in demography is essential. At present scant attention is given to the subject either by governments or by universities.' Again they wrote: 'We believe there is need for more knowledge of the interplay or changes in health with those in the economy and society, particularly as they affect population growth. Specifically we would welcome work seeking to use health, which is one of the few universally accepted values, as a strategic carrier for other essential but less immediately acceptable elements of social change.'[2]

[1] *Year Book of the Commonwealth of Australia*, 1956, p. 647.
[2] Rockefeller Report, 1950, pp. 114–15.

VII

THE MOVING FRONTIERS OF
ANIMALS AND PLANTS

The effects of the invasions on flora and fauna

THE changes in flora and fauna which resulted from the Western invasions were so important that in many regions human replacement of the indigenous plants and animals by exotics resulted in greatly transformed landscapes. Nevertheless, it is probably fair to say that since von Humboldt founded plant, and Wallace animal, geography, the research on the subject has been less than its importance warranted. As early as 1864, however, G. P. Marsh published his famous *Man and Nature*, later entitled *The Earth as Modified by Human Action*. Interest in the subject was kept alive by the Russian, A. I. Woeikof, and other scientists until in recent times the studies of many authorities such as those quoted below have really begun to turn attention to the immensity of the changes wrought by Western intervention in many areas, including the Pacific.[1] In general these invasions by plants and animals resembled in their sweeping and ruthless nature the influx of Western peoples with their diseases and culture. If the incomers thought a region suitable for white settlement or for sojourner colonization with a plantation economy, and if the indigenous people, plants, and insects were incapable of effective resistance, the exotics used fire, axe, plough, gun, and later the more advanced instruments of scientific technology to establish their settlements, fisheries, farms, pastures, towns, and secondary industries.

For the development of their civilization and culture in the new environments, the Westerners introduced a multitude of exotic plants, mammals, birds, and insects, but they soon discovered that both they themselves and their introductions were accompanied

[1] For bibliography see pp. 226–7, note J.

by an unwelcome multitude of associated weeds and pests. This question will be discussed in detail a little later, for, as Marsh realized nearly a century ago, the ravages committed by man subvert the relations and destroy the balance which nature has established between her organized and her inorganic creations, and she avenges herself upon the intruder. Marsh saw with extraordinary clarity and perception the effects of the emigrant swarms on newly occupied Pacific lands such as the Americas and Australia, and it is a tragedy that the warnings which he uttered as early as 1864 passed unheeded.[1]

The destruction of natural resources—man the despoiler

As the conquests began in some areas owing to the demand for whale oil for lighting and for furs for warm and lovely clothing, an early and rapid aspect of movement was the slaughter of sea life. The Portuguese and French were fishing on the Newfoundland Banks soon after the voyages of Columbus and Cabot, and although in these seas the cod appeared virtually inexhaustible, the fishing folk came ashore for various purposes, and destruction followed—e.g. the extinction of the Newfoundland Indians, the Boethucs.[2] When the Europeans occupied the Atlantic coasts of the Americas, they began the decimation of whales in the North Atlantic, and as the supply decreased moved on to attack the whales and seals of the South Atlantic and Pacific. The Russians reached the latter ocean as early as 1639, but the great period of slaughter followed the return of the crews of the explorers Bering

[1] G. P. Marsh, op. cit., 1882 edn., p. 43.
[2] D. Jenness, *The Indians of Canada*, National Museum of Canada Bulletin, no. 65, Ottawa, 1934, pp. 266–7. The European fishermen 'resented their petty pilfering and shot them down at every opportunity, the French even placing a bounty on their heads'. The Micmac also hunted them into the interior; the last of the tribe, a woman, died in 1829. The whole story is very similar to the destruction of the Tasmanoids, whose last full-blood survivor in Tasmania (a woman), Truganini, died in 1876. As noted in Chapter V, the Western settler invasions resulted in the extinction of many aboriginal tribes in many countries, and these extinctions have figured in romantic and imaginative literature, which includes: Fenimore Cooper, *The Last of the Mohicans* (North America), and *The Last of the Udege*, a novel by A. A. Fadeev, whom Kolarz (*The Peoples of the Soviet Far East*, p. 83) considers 'the only prominent living Communist who can be considered a Far Easterner'.

in 1742 and Cook in 1780 with furs that obtained high prices in the Chinese markets.[1] The history of the destruction of North Pacific sea life by hardy whalers and sealers of Russian, American, and other nationalities is a tragic romance which included the extinction of the beautiful sea otter and of the huge edible sea cow, together with the near extinction of the fur-seal and the steady movement of the great salmon canneries northwards up the Pacific coast as the salmon population was decreased by fishing, or by the use of the hatching rivers for power or irrigation, under what Russell Smith termed, as we have seen, 'another of those perfect and sickening examples of what we have done with our natural resources'.[2] A classic example of the follies of the invaders was, as previously noted, the near extinction of the fur-seal in the great seal breeding grounds of the Pribilof Islands, a tragedy that was checked by American efforts to halt the butchery by securing international co-operation, and to re-establish the famous herds which the Westerners reduced from 2 million in 1873 to 127,000 in 1911. The decline was largely due to the slaughter of the females, so the numbers recovered when the Americans limited the killings to the superabundant young bachelors.[3]

As the various Western invaders spread out over the waters of the Pacific similar destruction followed. Bay and ocean whalers slaughtered the cow whales indiscriminately with the consequent decline of many of the whale populations. In later years two attempts were made to prevent, by international agreements, the industry drawing to a tragic close. One of these was the establishment of an international whale commission by means of which, after conferences in 1937 and 1946, fourteen countries attempted to preserve the number of the whale population, particularly in the Antarctic. The other was the Santiago Agreement between Chile, Peru, and Ecuador, under which these nations endeavoured to conserve the whales off the western South American coast.[4]

[1] C.J.C.P., p. 282.

[2] J. R. Smith and M. O. Phillips, *North America*, p. 742.

[3] Ibid., pp. 744–5, and *Seal and Salmon Fisheries and General Resources of Alaska*, vol. iv; special references to the Pribilof Islands, pp. 477–88, 549–61, 708 seq.

[4] M. Graham, 'Harvest of the Seas', in W. L. Thomas, op. cit., pp. 487–503, with references.

Nevertheless, before the decimation of the mammals was complete, whaling played an important part in opening up the Pacific. In Australian waters the returning ships of the first convict fleet sighted whales in 1790, and the destruction of the Australian whales and fur-seals soon began with such vigour that sea industries provided a considerable part of the Australian and Tasmanian exports. Governor King of New South Wales stated, for example, that the seal fishing was 'the only staple yet discovered', and as late as 1833 whale products amounted to more than half the total exports of New South Wales, 'exceeding the value of wool and of all other products put together'.[1] The disgraceful behaviour of the whalers was largely responsible for the British occupation of New Zealand, as even a government bent on non-intervention could hardly stand by and tolerate British seafarers leasing a British ship to enable North Island Maoris to destroy a South Island Maori village and to use the ship's coppers to cook a cannibal feast.[2] Whaling also assisted in the Western occupation of Tahiti and other islands of eastern Polynesia. In the 1850's Papete saw each year the arrival of dozens of whaling vessels for rest and refreshment.[3]

Land resources

The advances of the Western frontiers on land—particularly in North America, Siberia, Australia, and New Zealand—saw similar events. In the north of North America the unfortunate musk ox formed defensive circles and waited for the annihilating bullets. White and Indian used horse and gun to slaughter the buffalo until in the 1880's the herds failed to appear, and the Plains Indians faced starvation. Similarly, Indian tribes who had carefully conserved the beaver, found themselves bereft of a main support of life. Even in Australia the Westerners drove the unfortunate aboriginals from their water-holes, slaughtered the marsupials upon which they lived, and then sent out punitive expeditions to shoot them down for spearing cattle and sheep.[4]

[1] *A.C.A.*, pp. 10–12.   [2] *W.S.N.P.*, p. 154.
[3] Oliver, *The Pacific Islands*, ch. 8, pp. 76–78, for Pacific whaling.
[4] *W.S.N.P.*, pp. 22, 72, 79, 106.

As settlement increased the incomers used the steel axe, and in later times technological machines to destroy the forests to give space for agricultural and pastoral settlement, creating over vast areas grave problems of erosion. In this connexion Carl Sauer has given important descriptions of the way in which the United States has led the modern world in the destruction of land.[1] Russell Smith has been equally emphatic and has quoted Dean Davenport of the University of Illinois as follows:

> 'Here's a fine animal,' said the frontiersman, 'let's kill it.
> Here's a big tree, let's cut it down.
> Here's a thick sod, let's plough it up; I'll skin this farm
> and go get another.'

Russell Smith continues:

> This has been the practical motto of entire generations. We have slashed and let it burn, deforested and let the soil wash away, degrassed and let it blow away. We have trampled the resources as dumb cattle trample their hay in mud as they eat. The speed of the sacking of the continent is dumbfounding.[2]

The same plaint echoes from Latin America, Australia, New Zealand, and other regions of Western settlement. In many parts of Latin America the erosion problem had by 1950 become extremely serious. The Food and Agriculture Organization of the United Nations reported in 1954–5 that erosion surveys in Chile and other countries showed a discouraging picture. In Chile, of the country surveyed, only 12·6 per cent. was not affected, and 40·1 per cent. was heavily damaged. Few countries were by then conducting active programmes of conservation. The Conservation Foundation of New York, headed by Fairfield Osborn, reported in 1954–5 that it was conducting a soil erosion survey of Latin America which emphasized 'the seriousness of resource depletion in parts of Latin America having a high potential productivity'.[3]

---

[1] Carl O. Sauer, *Agricultural Origins and Dispersals*, Bowman Memorial Lecture, Amer. Geog. Society, 1952, pp. 100–3; 'The Agency of Man on the Earth' in W. L. Thomas, op. cit., pp. 49 seq.

[2] J. R. Smith and M. O. Phillips, op. cit., pp. 20–21.

[3] *Prospects for Agricultural Development in Latin America*, Food and Agriculture

In Australia authorities such as S. M. Wadham, F. N. Radcliffe and G. W. Leeper have drawn attention to the serious effects of wind erosion on the dry pastoral inland and the dry margins of the wheat belt, together with the widespread destruction wrought by water in the form of sheet erosion and of gullying in the higher rainfall areas of New South Wales and Victoria. When these authorities wrote in the late 1940's, little had been done to survey or map this grave problem.[1]

In New Zealand the destruction of forests, including the damage wrought by pests such as deer, the overburning of tussock country, and the overgrazing of sheep and rabbits have had such grave effects that A. H. Clark has described the hill-slopes of the Central Otago plateau as 'a man-made desert'. Here one motors for many miles amongst the scars and gullies which may well indicate the beginnings of economic disaster.[2]

Very interesting is the way in which even primitive peoples can and do destroy natural resources as soon as they are provided with Western scientific appliances. As noted above, the North American Indian wrought havoc on the buffalo when he secured fire-arms and horses, and fire-arms also enabled him to decimate other native animals such as the beaver, musk ox, and caribou.

As recently as 1956 O. H. K. Spate gave an important and vivid picture of the results of the moving frontier of Western technology in the highlands of New Guinea where the primitive peoples had established a non-nomadic culture based upon ash fertilization and the stone axe. Here the introduction of the steel axe wrought

Organization of the U.N., Rome, 1954–5, pp. 84–85; The Conservation Foundation, New York, Report, 1954, p. 9.

[1] G. W. Leeper in G. L. Wood, ed., *Australia—Its Resources and Development*, New York, 1947, ch. iv; *Soil Conservation*, Dept. of Commerce, Melbourne, Vic., 1953. This work considers the problem in the United States, Latin America, China, and other countries, in addition to Australia; F. N. Ratcliffe, *Soil Drift in the Arid Pastoral Areas of South Australia*, C.S.I.R.O., Melbourne, 1936, and *Further Observation on Soil Erosion and Sand Drift with special reference to South-western Queensland*, C.S.I.R.O., Melbourne, 1937; R. M. Moore, *The Effects of Wool Growing on the Australian Vegetation*, Aust. Nat. University, 1957, with important bibliography of work on Australian flora; N. C. W. Beadle, *The Vegetation and Pastures of N.S.W.*, Dept. of Conservation, N.S.W., 1948.

[2] A. H. Clark in H. Belshaw, ed., *New Zealand*, University of California Press, 1947, ch. 2, p. 46.

a revolutionary change. Forests were rapidly destroyed and population numbers advanced. Serious erosion followed, however, and, with the development of swamps, malaria increased.[1]

Conservation

On the subject of the necessity of conserving natural resources as a result of the invasions there were in 1955 two schools of Western thought. W. B. Fairchild, Vogt, Fairfield Osborn, and others depicted in works such as *Our Plundered Planet* the disasters which man faced through his reckless destruction of non-renewable resources such as oil, or of renewable resources such as forests, which might provide permanent wealth if conservation was adopted soon enough and conducted upon a world-wide scale. Other authorities, such as C. E. Kellogg, de Castro, and A. D. Stamp, on the contrary stressed the inventive genius of man which had hitherto produced ever-increasing resources. Moderate opinion like that of Sir J. B. Orr or Dr. James Prescott emphasized the necessity of co-operative action such as world-wide afforestation, and the concentration of scientific effort on the phosphorus question, the most vital of food problems then unsolved.

In this connexion, Sauer, Scarlott, and other scientists warned the world that the loss of phosphorus from the soil by modern destructive methods was enormous, and that the reserves left were comparatively slight. In power resources the position seemed more satisfactory; Ayres and Scarlott noted that in addition to atomic developments scientists were considering the possibility of increasing plant resources by growing algae in shallow sea water, as experimental yields had been as high as 15 dry tons per acre per annum or considerably higher than the customary land growth.[2]

A detailed examination of efforts to conserve in the Pacific the flora and fauna which the invasions endangered would be an immense task, far beyond the scope of this book, even if confined to the Pacific. Reference is made, however, to a number of

[1] O. H. K. Spate, 'Changing Native Agriculture in New Guinea', *Geographical Review*, Apr. 1953; Jenness, op. cit., pp. 255-7.
[2] Ayres and Scarlott, op. cit., pp. 239-43.

examples of conservation or restoration, as, for example, the American success in preserving the Pribilof Island seals, but unfortunately there is no room to discuss such matters as the Canadian attempts to protect wild life, or the American efforts to check erosion problems such as that created by the overgrazing of Navajo stock in the American south-west. One may, perhaps, mention, however, the recent and important example of Japan which has been accepting American technological aid to meet those economic problems that have become so grave in view of the population growth. The restoration of the depleted fishing grounds, seed improvement, fertilization, mechanization, and lumbering have all made headway. As American writers have indicated, the outcome of the Pacific war enabled the allies to direct all their wisdom and goodwill towards mitigating the results of the tragedy in Japan, and the work of the occupational forces became of the first magnitude in its historical significance. The psychological results of this goodwill may be speculative, but it is already evident that the American efforts in the cause of restoration and conservation have had important effects.[1]

Movements of flora and fauna

Leading botanists such as E. D. Merrill and Edgar Anderson have in recent years thrown much light on the exchange of animals and plants between the Old and New Worlds, and the routes along which these exchanges were effected. These movements of plants and animals, which accompanied the Western invasions, were immense, widespread, and swift and have become of outstanding importance in the story of mankind. Thus E. D. Merrill wrote:

It is doubtful if it is generally appreciated, even among many botanists, that since the close of the fifteenth century, man intentionally or inadvertently has been the greatest single factor in extending the

[1] *Agriculture in Asia and the Far East—Development and Outlook*, Food and Agriculture Organization of the U.N., Rome, Oct. 1953, outlines some of the assistance being given to Japan and other Asian countries in very many ways, such as the supply of better plant seed, plant protection, livestock improvement, control of stock diseases, and so forth. Nevertheless, the slow progress in the use of pesticides shows how much has still to be achieved.

range of plants. This applies to plants characteristic of both the tropical and temperate regions of the globe. Up to about 450 years ago there were, with the well known exception—*Lagenaria*—no cultived economic species, and apparently none of the aggressive weeds common to either the temperate or tropical parts of the two hemispheres. To these we must add the sweet potato and the coconut, both with limited distribution in parts of the Eastern and Western tropics.[1]

Yet when Edgar Anderson gave in 1952 a list of 100 of the world's most important crops, he could include some twenty of American origin, some of which are of great economic value and are now widely distributed in the Old World. These include maize, cocoa, tobacco, sweet potatoes, peanuts, tomatoes, avocados, guavas, papayas, strawberries, and pineapples.[2]

Similarly, Franz Verdoorn pointed out that in spite of the tremendous number of native food plants already available and in cultivation in the New World at the time of the Spanish conquests, economic plants from the Old World, such as bananas and sugar, gained great importance in the Americas.[3] Australia, now a leading world exporter of primary products, contained at the time of conquest no indigenous plant or animal of substantial food importance, so that the whole of her vast production and export trade is now based on exotics.

There is neither time nor need for this study to examine in detail the historic controversy on the extent to which Asian plants and animals moved eastwards and American plants moved westwards in the Pacific Ocean area itself. E. D. Merrill as a botanist joins the anthropologists and other scientists who consider that almost all kinds of Pacific Island flora and fauna which were not indigenous were, like the culture of the Pacific Island peoples, Asian in origin and type. Argument may continue even over the sweet potato, which authorities in general believe must have been brought to the Pacific Islands from America by Polynesian canoe or by balsa raft, but vigorous controversy is more likely to rage

[1] E. D. Merrill, *The Botany of Cook's Voyages*, p. 223.
[2] E. Anderson, op. cit., ch. x, pp. 154–85.
[3] F. Verdoorn, *Plants and Plant Science in Latin America*, Chronica Botanica, Waltham, Mass., 1945, p. 23.

over the diffusion of other plants such as cotton, gourds, and coconuts. Nevertheless, although E. D. Merrill has been bitterly and perhaps unduly critical of his fellow botanists and other scientists, his expert examination of the botanical collections made by Banks, Solander, and the Forsters, all of whom accompanied James Cook to the Pacific Islands, led to conclusions which may be hard to contradict.

Turning to the weeds found by Banks and Solander in Tahiti in 1769 Merrill wrote:

we find not a single species that we may positively say came from America, although probably a few may have originated there. On the other hand a surprisingly high percentage of the Tahiti weeds, at the time indicated, are clearly of Indo-Malaysian origin, some of which have not as yet reached America. . . . As the rather numerous introduced food and economic plants, with one exception, clearly came out of Malaysia and some of them, like the seedless breadfruit, had to be transported in earth as established young plants, it is rather clear how these Old World weeds reached Tahiti in early times.[1]

In his *Vikings of the Sunrise*, Peter Buck, a famous anthropologist, himself part Maori and an outstanding authority on Polynesian tradition, traced the routes by which the Pacific islanders carried Asian flora and fauna to their new habitats. In Buck's opinion the only exception was the sweet potato which he believed the Polynesians secured by canoe voyage to America. On the other hand, Heyerdahl may be right in assuming that this plant was carried by balsa raft from Peru, provided that Indians blown off the coast were carrying sweet potatoes on their rafts, and that these potatoes survived the long voyage. To make confusion worse confounded Merrill ended his work by claiming that the sweet potato may have been an Old World plant which originated in Africa and was transported to America across the Atlantic.[2]

[1] Merrill, op. cit., p. 219.
[2] Ibid., ch. 4, pp. 212 seq., chs. 6 and 7, particularly pp. 321 seq. R. A. Silow gives as references: J. B. Hutchinson, R. A. Silow, and S. G. Stephens, *Evolution of Gossypium*, together with S. G. Stephens, 'Cytogenetics of Gossypium', *Advances in Genetics*, vol. i, pp. 431–2, New York, 1947. The controversy over Thor Heyerdahl's theories is outlined in part in articles in the *Geog. Journal* by Heyerdahl,

In this controversy the scientific evidence provided by cotton is important. Dr. R. A. Silow, in addressing the Waite Agricultural Research Institute of Adelaide in 1949, gave the following views. First he considered that although the white man might have been far longer in the Americas than had been realized, biological and ethnological data indicated that the cultivated cottons of the New World arose in comparatively recent prehistoric times, and that man himself was responsible for the transfer of one of their parents across the Pacific Ocean by a warm route, as cottons had a complete intolerance of frost. Silow continued: 'So we are led to the conclusion that man must have taken cotton along with him on early colonising expeditions from southern Asia across the South Pacific to South America.' Silow then gave cytogenetical and biological evidence that the cultivated cottons of the New World originated comparatively recently, together with archaeological evidence that the desert graves of pre-Inca Peru contained spindles of the type used by fine spinners of Dacca muslin in India, while in the cotton areas of the New World was found the complex double-bar loom, which was developed in the cotton and silk areas of the Old World, and which was an intricate piece of apparatus involving at least eleven independent inventions. I do not propose to enter the controversies which surround the drift theory of A. Sharpe or Heyerdahl's views that some groups came westwards from South America. No layman ignorant of the highly specialized technique by which botanists and other scientists reach their conclusions can do more than record these views, and express the hope that at some future date the experts will produce new evidence and become unanimous (Chapter I, text and note B, pp. 222–3).

Apart from the historic land routes across Asia, and the sea and land routes across the Atlantic and the Americas, there were two seaways to the Pacific—the major route around the Cape of Good Hope, and the minor and difficult route via the Straits of Magellan or around Cape Horn. The earliest and most important seaway

R. Heine-Geldern, and Marion Smith, Mar. 1950, Dec. 1950, Mar. 1951, and Dec. 1953. For Sharpe's 'drift theory', see A. Sharpe, *Ancient Voyagers in the Pacific*.

was the Cape of Good Hope route, pioneered by the Portuguese (Chapter III) and later used by the Spanish, Dutch, English, and French. From the time of the great voyage of Vasco da Gama, western European, Mediterranean, and South African plants, weeds, animals, and insects could enter the Indian Ocean, and a few years later, the Pacific. Some authorities have, however, failed to recognize and emphasize the fact that, after the discovery of South America and its occupation by the Portuguese, a frequent route, with favourable winds, was to Brazil and thence to the Cape of Good Hope, the Indian Ocean, and the Pacific. Students of early voyages to Australia will find records of plants and animals, together with their unofficial, and sometimes unnoticed, accompaniment of weeds and pests which the voyagers picked up at Rio de Janeiro and the Cape of Good Hope. Thus the first fleet which sailed to New South Wales left South Africa with 500 animals of different kinds, including a few Indian hair sheep. Again in 1797 Governor Hunter imported from the Cape 49 black cattle, 3 mares, and 107 sheep.[1] Many of the exploring, trading, and migrant-carrying vessels must have resembled extremely uncomfortable travelling zoos. The good-natured farmer king, George III, loaded Cook's ships with living presents to South Sea Island chiefs on the voyage of 1776–9, not altogether with the leader's approval. Similarly, one reads in the diaries of Australian pioneers of the additional discomfort created on vessels such as the *Buffalo* commanded by the first governor of South Australia, Sir John Hindmarsh, who was vigorously criticized for allotting so much space to animals such as 'filthy hogs', including his own stock.[2]

The second sea route, via Cape Horn or the Straits of Magellan, was less important than two land ways from the Atlantic; the one crossing the isthmus of Old Panama, and the other running from the Gulf of Mexico to Acapulco and other Mexican ports on the Pacific. Sailing from Lima in Peru, Mendana, Quiros, and other explorers made brief visits to a few Pacific islands such as the Solomons and New Hebrides, but the important development

[1] M. H. Ellis, *John Macarthur*, Sydney, 1955, ch. 17; Merrill, op. cit., pp. 229–30.
[2] *F.P.S.A.*, Adelaide, 1929, pp. 98–99.

was the evolution of the famous Manila galleon route, by which Spanish galleons, usually built in the Philippines, sailed with the Westerlies to Mexico and back to Manila with the Trades.[1] This route had undoubted effects on flora and fauna. Merrill states that in 1912 the 40 square miles covered by the flora of Manila included 175 plants from Mexico and Brazil out of 1,000 known species. Similarly, the island of Guam, which lay on the galleon route, and which contained only 212 square miles of territory, acquired 113 Mexican and Brazilian plants of 550 known species. We will later see that J. E. Spencer notes the case of the Philippines, which were settled so early and so long by the Spaniards, and now contain a number of American plants. Maize, a major crop, was, he says, 'brought to the islands and popularised by the Spanish', as were various root crops and fruits.[2]

Changed and transported landscapes—man the creator

We will now look at the changed and transported landscapes produced by the invasions in many parts of the six regions under which we are examining the Pacific. At the same time it must be remembered that, as Merrill and Bates have pointed out, these alterations have been due not only to the plants and animals, which the invaders introduced deliberately, but also to their accompanying weeds and pests. Thus Merrill notes that weeds are transplanted in packing material, the clothes of man, the hair of domestic animals, and by wind over limited areas, particularly when a weed is introduced to a new region, while birds and animals help. Thus there were no weeds on Christmas Island until settlers arrived in 1888. In 1890 there were four species; in 1897, twelve; in 1904, thirty—a rapid increase over the very short period of white settlement and deforestation.[3] One of the best summaries of the whole process was contributed to that splended symposium

---

[1] Schurz, *The Manila Galleon*; Merrill, op. cit., pp. 229–39.

[2] J. E. Spencer, *Land and People in the Philippines*, University of California Press for Inst. of Pacific Relations, 1954, ch. 5, pp. 61–67; Merrill, op. cit., ch. v, pp. 235–7; C. Robequain, *Malaya, Indonesia, Borneo and the Philippines*, London, 1954, ch. 18, pp. 351–8.

[3] E. D. Merrill, *Plant Life of the Pacific World*, pp. 123–5.

of 1955, *Man's Role in Changing the Face of the Earth*, by Marston Bates, under the title of 'Man as an Agent in the Spread of Organisms'. In this Bates outlined not only the deliberate or accidental introduction to the Pacific and other countries of domestic mammals and plants together with the reasons for such introductions, but also the transport of insects, weeds, and pests.[1]

Transported landscapes in Pacific regions

Probably because my time for research was brief in Europe, and even more brief in the United States during a third visit in 1955, I could find in the libraries little evidence in English of transported landscapes in Siberia, although it is probable that the establishment of primary industries in the form of exotic crops, together with the development of manufactures in the south-east of this region, have already effected some change. In densely settled countries like China and Japan, with long-established practices of production based on historic crops, such as rice, the introduction of exotics has naturally been on a smaller scale than in regions of Western settlement or in those of sojourner plantation economy. Yet, although the Western peoples wrought in China and Japan changes less sweeping than those produced by the cultivation of rubber in South-east Asia or of wheat in the Americas and Australia, Cressey noted in 1934 that sweet potatoes, maize, peanuts, potatoes, and tobacco—all of American origin—had become fairly important Chinese crops. Similarly, Trewartha stated in 1939 that Japan had 278,000 cho under sweet potatoes; 166,000 under Irish potatoes, and 53,000 under maize. The sweet potatoes represented 3·4 per cent. and the Irish potatoes 2·1 per cent. of the crops, while their respective values were 2·8 per cent. and 1·8 per cent. of the totals.[2]

[1] M. Bates in W. L. Thomas, op. cit., pp. 788–804; E. V. Wulff, *An Introduction to Historical Plant Geography*, ch. vii, 'Artificial Factors in the Geographical Distribution of Plants', for the difficulties experienced by exotic plants in adapting themselves to new environments and in competing with indigenous species. Many plants are dependent upon cultivation by man.

[2] G. B. Cressey, *China's Geographic Foundations*, p. 100; G. T. Trewartha, *Japan*, University of Wisconsin, 1945, p. 214.

Western culture has also affected the historic domestic plants of Asia through Western methods of plant protection and seed breeding and through assistance given by the introduction of fertilizers and mechanical appliances. The influence of exotic flora and fauna was more important in South-east Asia and Indonesia where the Dutch, French, and British conquerors introduced plants such as rubber and cinchona for their plantations, and improved the Asian animal stocks, e.g. by the importation of Dutch and Frisian bulls. Merrill stated that the number of exotic genera and species imported into Malaysia is very great and is increasing rapidly. He added that although there had been little study of the problem in tropical regions, C. A. Backer had done pioneering work on Javanese weeds, while Merrill himself had published research on the exotic flora of Guam and the Philippines. Spencer, Robequain, and other authorities give interesting details of the changes effected by the introduction of exotics to South-east Asia and by plantation economy. Spencer notes that the Philippines possessed only a few indigenous domestic plants out of an extremely numerous wild flora. Rice, coconuts, and mango reached the islands before the Spaniards, who, in the sixteenth and seventeenth centuries, imported American crops such as maize, sweet potatoes, cassava, and tobacco. Pigs, water buffaloes, and chickens were transported in early times from Asia, and the Chinese brought in the duck and possibly the goose. The Spaniards made numerous efforts to introduce domestic animals including horses, cattle and sheep, some from the New World and some from China, but had varied success.

Robequain noted that in Java in the nineteenth century the Dutch added new exotic crops of tea, cinchona, and rubber to the long-established exotic crops of tobacco and coffee. Rubber, an American exotic, covered the largest plantation area of 557,000 acres, after which came tea, 259,000 acres; coffee, 223,000 acres; sugar-cane, 206,000 acres; tobacco, 73,000 acres; kapok, 57,000 acres; and cinchona, 38,000 acres. Yet in 1937 this plantation area, largely under exotics, represented only 7 per cent. of the total land cultivated, which indicates both the continued value of the historical Asian staples and the importance of the production which the natives secured by using exotic floras under their own economy and control.[1]

One observes that in the Pacific Islands the moving frontiers and changing landscapes wrought by exotic plants vary greatly. Already the sugar and pineapple plantation areas of islands such as Fiji or Hawaii may be said to represent changed and transported landscapes, whereas exotic plants have not yet altered greatly the wilder parts of islands such as the New Hebrides. New Caledonia presents an interesting picture, as transported landscapes of exotic crops alternate with exotic Australian eucalypts and an indigenous flora which in part resembles in appearance that of Australia.

Of the works on Pacific fauna, J. L. Gressitt's extensive survey of the *Insects of Micronesia* seems outstanding. Gressitt considers that the early migrants, probably coming from South-east Asia and carrying food and plants in their canoes, brought ants, cockroaches, flies, and certain household pests, such as beetles and moths which attacked dry foods. They also introduced certain insects associated with plants, but on the whole the number of these was small compared with those transported by the early Western voyagers and traders. Rough as they were, and much as they admired the pliant Tahitian women, even Cook's sailors were horrified at seeing these dusky beauties catching and eating the lice from one another's heads.[2] Gressitt considers that the exotic plants which were most effective in creating changes in Micronesia were the coconut palm and the sugar-cane. The former eliminated much native vegetation and facilitated the spread of coconut pests.[3]

Landscape changes in regions of Western settlement—North America

Perhaps the most important and sweeping changes of landscape which have occurred in recent centuries are those which the invasions produced in what were at one time European colonies

[1] Merrill, op. cit., pp. 230–9; Spencer, op. cit., ch. 13, pp. 168–77; Robequain, op. cit., ch. 17, pp. 331–2.

[2] J. C. Beaglehole, *The Voyage of the Endeavour*, p. 124. For various types of lice see Zinsser, op. cit., chs. ix, x.

[3] J. L. Gressitt, *Insects of Micronesia*, Bishop Museum, Honolulu, 1954, p. 11.

in the Americas, Australia, and New Zealand. Under the heading of 'Man and his Transported Landscapes', Edgar Anderson has painted a charming picture of the autumnal changes in the area running westwards from Boston and Philadelphia on the American east coast to Minneapolis and Kansas City in the interior. Here the American flora, bred for the violent American climate, 'goes into winter condition with a bang', leaving an autumnal green of trees and grasses that are European.[1] Similarly, a transported flora covers the rolling hills of California, in this case Mediterranean weeds and grass which probably came out with the Spaniards.[2] Merrill quotes M. L. Fernald to the effect that in 1950 the north-eastern United States contained perhaps some 284 exotic plants as against 849 indigenous species, and W. C. Jepson, taking a conservative view of the limits of the species, recorded that there were in California in 1924, 292 naturalized exotics out of a total of 4,019 species. The naturalized species were mostly from those parts of the world with a Mediterranean type of climate. Merrill considered that the periods of introduction covered some 350 years in the North-Eastern States and 200 years in California. The number of 292 exotics in California gave, according to Jepson, 'no proper concept of these alien populations, since the species are often very aggressive'.[3]

It is a remarkable thought that so many species of flora and fauna in these New World lands are, like the languages and cultures of their inhabitants, to a large extent exotics which have stemmed from the Old World. Nevertheless, the migrant character of the American civilizations can be exaggerated, for in some cases the incoming peoples gained very substantial benefits from the indigenous groups, such as the American Indians, and made extensive use of their cleared fields, crops, and methods of transport. As Sauer points out, the early American settlers supported themselves on Indian fields and, in Latin America, on Indian labour. In an article on 'The Agency of Man on Earth' he writes that 'the colonists of all nations largely used the Indian ways'.[4]

---

[1] E. Anderson, *Plants, Man and Life*, ch. i, pp. 9–10.
[2] Ibid., pp. 12–15, and Merrill, *Botany of Cook's Voyages*, ch. 5, pp. 223 seq.
[3] Ibid.   [4] Carl O. Sauer in W. K. Thomas, op. cit., pp. 62–64.

Australia

The changes in flora and fauna were even more striking in British Australasia. Neither Australia nor New Zealand possessed the indigenous crop plants or animals upon which the invaders could base the industries essential to their advanced cultures and high living standards, so they were forced to transplant exotic economic plants and animals which could be established in the new habitat, and they effected this so efficiently that they became the creators of immense areas of changed landscapes, changed not only through the effects of economic plants and animals, but through the influences of the accompanying weeds and pests. In Australia a C.S.I.R.O. publication of 1950—*The Australian Environment*—is most illuminating on one aspect of the plant invasion, the spread of exotic flora in the interests of the pastoral industries which provide the greatest wool production in the world. It is now quite clear that exotic grasses and clovers are widely developed in southern New South Wales, in Victoria, in the coastal regions of central and eastern South Australia, and in the south-west of Western Australia. It is also evident that the vital production of wool, meat, and dairy products is becoming more and more dependent upon these exotic plants which, under human guidance, continue to form moving frontiers that are followed by transported and altered landscapes.[1]

The botanists J. M. Black and J. G. Wood have examined the growth of naturalized flora in South Australia—a region of Mediterranean climate. Black wrote in 1909 that the alien plants formed the greater part of the herbage near the coastal towns, and that many had found their way into the far interior. His list also included several ornamental plants that had gone astray from gardens or hedges, and all the 'noxious weeds' which had been proclaimed as such by the government. Of the 368 plants described, 128 came from Europe and western Asia, and 92 from the Mediterranean region (Europe and North African coasts). Sixty of these were cosmopolitan; 44, including the soursob (*Oxalis pes-caprae*), came from South Africa, another Mediterranean area;

---

[1] *The Australian Environment*, ch. 7, pp. 97 seq.

15 came from South America, 10 from Asia, 6 from temperate North America, 6 from East Australia, 1 from Western Australia, 3 from Mexico, 2 from the Canary Islands, and 1 from Abyssinia. It was noticeable that the plants which succeeded best came from lands of similar climate to South Australia, such as the Mediterranean region, South Africa, and temperate South America. At the time when he wrote Black knew of no Australian work covering the same field.[1]

Writing nearly thirty years later in 1937, J. G. Wood stated that the naturalized alien plants included the commonest weeds in South Australia, and were found especially in the well-watered southern parts. Like Black he pointed out that the majority came from climates akin to that of the State. There were 381 species of naturalized alien plants belonging to 160 genera. Of these 151 were Mediterranean species, 118 were European and West Asian, 42 were South African, 37 cosmopolitan, 13 South American, 10 western North American, and 3 Indian. Wood also gave an interesting description of the exotics which had invaded the savannah woodlands, the country in which the aliens were most prominent. He stated that following the settlement by Western man with his flocks and herds, the composition of the vegetation had in many areas 'undergone a profound change', whereas in closed communities such as the scrub layer, few alien species could compete with native species, unless there were disturbances. The indigenous grasses of the savannah forests, usually within easy reach of Adelaide, served as valuable pastorage, in which the grazing destroyed the native grasses and herbage, their place being taken by more hardy annual alien plants or by plants with a tufted or rosette habit. On the drier slopes of the foothills bordering the Adelaide plains, the whole *facies* of the community had been changed owing to the colonization of the soil by the Mediterranean olive, the South African cotton bush (*Gomphocarpus*), the European briar, and the South African box thorn (a noxious weed), while the change in the ground flora was no less profound owing to the establishment of plants such as alien grasses. Once again it was clear that the successful alien plant exotics came from

[1] J. M. Black, *The Naturalised Flora of South Australia*, Adelaide, 1909.

PLATE IX

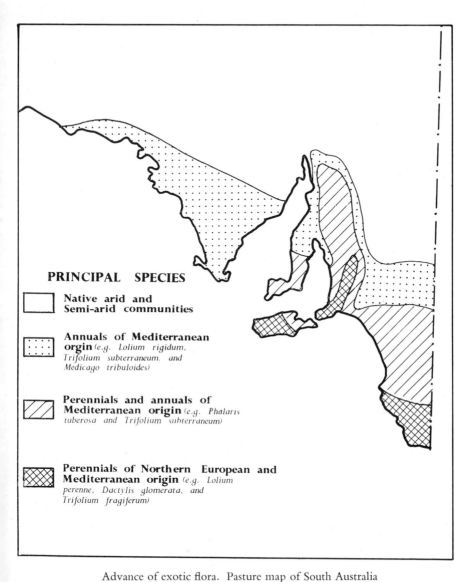

Advance of exotic flora. Pasture map of South Australia

From C. M. Donald, 'The Pastures of South Australia', *Introducing South Australia*, A.N.Z.A.A.S., Adelaide, 1958

the European and South African areas of a Mediterranean climate similar to the Gulf region of South Australia.[1] (Pl. IX.)

In an important paper issued by the Australian National University, Canberra, in 1957, R. M. Moore discusses the effects of wool-growing on Australian vegetation. He concludes that in the savannah woodland regions which cover large parts of New South Wales, Victoria, South Australia, Western Australia, and Tasmania, the once luxuriant kangaroo grass (*Themeda australis*) has disappeared under sheep-grazing, and in the higher rainfall parts of these zones native pastures are being deliberately replaced by introduced pasture species usually based on white clover and perennial grasses such as *Phalaris tuberosa* or perennial ryegrass. For example, the area under sown grass in New South Wales increased from 1·8 million acres in 1951 to 4·8 million acres in 1955, and in Australia from 18 million to 27 million acres in the same period.

In the south-west of Western Australia grazing by sheep and the use of superphosphate and subterranean clover have almost entirely eliminated the native perennial grasses which have been replaced by Mediterranean and South African species.

In the field of fauna, D. C. Swan has published important research. His detailed analysis of insect and acarina pests in Australia indicates that of 214 imported insects, 79 came from northern Europe and 40 from the Mediterranean—a total of 119, or 55 per cent. Swan also believed that the introduced pests now greatly outnumber the native and that many of these exotics, unlike the Australian insect pests, are free from predators and parasites, and hence have become serious problems under Australian conditions, whereas some have been of relative insignificance in their country of origin. Swan's thesis gives support to a point which has been, I hope, strongly emphasized in the previous chapter on disease. Had the Western peoples invaded the Pacific regions after they had acquired their later scientific knowledge, some at least of the conquered lands might have been spared the

[1] J. G. Wood, *The Vegetation of South Australia*, chs. 5 and 10. See also R. H. Pulleine, 'The Botanical Colonization of the Adelaide Plains', *Proceedings, R.G.S. of Australasia, S.A. Branch*, vol. xxxv, 1935.

introduction of Old World diseases, pests, and weeds. In many cases it is now too late to close the door, but, as previously noted, the recent defeat of the mosquito *Anopheles gambiae* after it had actually reached Brazil, indicates that science can still win victories, even when a disease or pest penetrates the first and essential line of defence, which consists of a scientific and unsleeping quarantine.[1]

Amongst the many campaigns against exotic diseases and pests, one of the most interesting is the Australian use of the imported *Cactoblastis cactorum* against the exotic pests—the prickly-pears *Opuntia inermis* and *O. stricta* (Pl. X). Prickly-pears were brought to Australia from various parts of America from very early times. Indeed, the first fleet picked up prickly-pear plants and cochineal insects at Rio de Janeiro in 1787, as Governor Phillip wished to dye his soldiers' coats red. In later years many varieties of prickly-pear were imported for the cochineal industry, for their fruit and flowers, and as botanical curiosities. Of these a number became pests, the chief being *O. inermis* and *O. stricta*, both natives of Florida and Texas. The rapidity with which prickly-pear increased in Australia is regarded as one of the botanical wonders of the world, but equally remarkable is the fact that the plants adapted themselves so successfully to new environments in Queensland and New South Wales, although the Australian regions were drier, higher, and farther from the sea than the American habitats. By 1925 the two main pest pears had overrun some 60 million acres, of which 30 million had become useless from a productive viewpoint.

At this moment the Commonwealth Prickly Pear Board imported eggs of the *Cactoblastis cactorum* from the Argentine, and made in early 1926 the first trial liberations which were followed by a mass distribution from 1928 to 1930, during which 3,000 million eggs were released in the pear territory. The insects carried out a spectacular conquest of the pear. Great tracts of country, utterly useless on account of the dense growth of the weed, have been brought into production. The prickly-pear territory has been

---

[1] D. C. Swan, 'The Composition and Origin of the Australian Insect and Mite Fauna of Economic Importance', MS. Paper, Pan-Indian Ocean Science Conference, Western Australia, 1954.

PLATE X

Defeat of an exotic pest by an exotic control. Destruction of prickly pear by
Cactoblastis, Queensland, 1928–9

From A. P. Dodd, *The Biological Campaign against the Prickly Pear*, Brisbane, 1940

PLATE XI

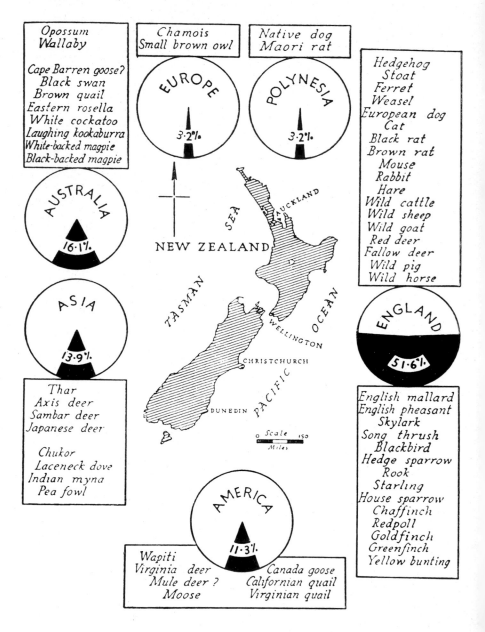

Opossum
Wallaby

Cape Barren goose?
Black swan
Brown quail
Eastern rosella
White cockatoo
Laughing kookaburra
White-backed magpie
Black-backed magpie

EUROPE
3·2%

POLYNESIA
3·2%

Chamois
Small brown owl

Native dog
Maori rat

Hedgehog
Stoat
Ferret
Weasel
European dog
Cat
Black rat
Brown rat
Mouse
Rabbit
Hare
Wild cattle
Wild sheep
Wild goat
Red deer
Fallow deer
Wild pig
Wild horse

AUSTRALIA
16·1%

ASIA
13·9%

Thar
Axis deer
Sambar deer
Japanese deer

Chukor
Laceneck dove
Indian myna
Pea fowl

NEW ZEALAND

TASMAN SEA

AUCKLAND

WELLINGTON

PACIFIC OCEAN

CHRISTCHURCH

DUNEDIN

Scale
0   150
Miles

ENGLAND
51·6%

English mallard
English pheasant
Skylark
Song thrush
Blackbird
Hedge sparrow
Rook
Starling
House sparrow
Chaffinch
Redpoll
Goldfinch
Greenfinch
Yellow bunting

AMERICA
11·3%

Wapiti
Virginia deer
Mule deer?
Moose

Canada goose
Californian quail
Virginian quail

LIST OF ANIMALS AND BIRDS ESTABLISHED IN NEW ZEALAND

-Successful introductions to New Zealand of mammals and birds.

New Zealand: Exotic animals and birds, including pests

From K. A. Wodzicki, *Introduced Mammals of New Zealand*, Department of Scientific and Industrial Research Bulletin 98, New Zealand, 1950

transformed as though by magic from a wilderness to a scene of prosperous endeavour. Moreover, the *Cactoblastis* proved capable of dealing with any recurring pear growth and with resistant types of pear if these types were supplied with nitrogen. The Board took great care to exclude the American parasitic enemies of the insect, and although *Cactoblastis* was attacked by certain Australian birds, ants, and internal parasitic insects, the resulting mortality did not endanger its existence.[1]

Moving frontiers and changing landscapes in New Zealand

The invasion of the islands of New Zealand by exotic flora and fauna is particularly interesting for a variety of reasons. First, the islands with their total area of 104,000 square miles, although comparatively small, show remarkable variations in climate, elevation, soil, and native plant life. Second, the British invaders, for reasons to be discussed later, introduced a quite unusual number of animals and plants with their accompanying diseases, weeds, and pests. Thirdly, while animals and plants varied as to their powers of acclimatization and survival, some became of great economic importance, so much so that authorities consider that the future of the country depends largely upon the advance of exotic plants. Fourthly, the transition from forests to agricultural land was far more rapid and complete than in North America or Australia, and finally, New Zealand has been singularly fortunate in that the history of her invasion, and the problems which it created, were carefully observed and examined in detail by a number of very able contemporary scientists, such as G. M. Thomson, H. H. Allen, K. A. Wodzicki, and A. H. Clark.

At the time of the Western occupation, about 1840, the country consisted of regions of high mountain ranges, of dense forests, of swamp and tussock grasslands, and of fern and scrub. So immense and rapid has been the impact that now, in a little over a century, almost half the country lies under artificially sown pasture or modified tussock grassland, the native forests being reduced from 40 to 3 million acres between 1840 and 1940. The replacement of

[1] A. P. Dodd, *The Biological Campaign against Prickly Pear*, Commonwealth Prickly Pear Board, Brisbane, 1940, pp. 1–13.

indigenous grasses and trees by exotics has given New Zealand two floras and two vegetations. The great bulk of the country is now covered by a vegetation composed of an intermediate grouping of displaced plants with displacing plants. Its study from this angle, whilst most of the steps in the amalgamation processes are still discernible and interpretable, is one of the most fascinating and urgent tasks of the native botanists.[1]

This process has, in the short space of little more than a century, wrought dramatic changes both in the vegetation communities, whether they were plants or weeds, and in the populations of mammals, insects, and birds, whether they were of value to man or undesirable pests. Wodzicki, in his study of the *Introduced Mammals of New Zealand* (1950), divides the mammalian invasions into four periods, the first three of which are certainly applicable to plants. Prior to the arrival of the 'Great Fleet' of Maoris in the thirteenth century, the 'Moa hunters' had possibly exterminated, or almost exterminated, the moa and native swan. Then came the Maoris, who, during Wodzicki's 'First Period', burnt large areas of forest, but, as they had no domestic grazing animals, could create no permanent harm.

In the second period, which dates from Cook's second voyage of 1774, explorers, sealers, whalers, and traders intentionally or accidentally brought in animals, plants, weeds, and pests, but the really important changes came in the third period when, in the 1840's, official settlers poured in and, for a variety of reasons—food, economic needs, shelter, sport, nostalgia, and so forth—brought in a miscellany of mammals, plants, fish, and insects, often with their accompanying weeds and pests. The settlers even formed a large number of 'Acclimatization Societies', which were permitted to introduce virtually any type of animal or bird. Wodzicki estimated that the New Zealanders liberated 53 types of mammals and 125 birds, and that of these, 65 types (34 mammals and 31 birds) became established. Twenty-seven types of mammals were brought in for food or fur, and five for the biological control of other pests. Escapees and stowaways numbered ten.[2] (Pl. XI.)

---

[1] C. M. Smith, 'Changed and Changing Vegetation', in F. R. Callaghan, op. cit., p. 136.   [2] Wodzicki, op. cit., ch. 1, pp. 8–14.

The same story applies to plants, insects, and fish. C. M. Smith stated in 1957 that the then tally of recorded adventive plants came to over 1,400 species, which had changed the landscape in ways dramatically described by A. H. Clark, who made a just and balanced estimate of the good and bad results. On the credit side lay the establishment of superb pastures and the widespread improvement in the fertility of indifferent soil; on the debit, the reduction in the North Island of a nearly continuous cover of magnificent forest to scattered patches of low grade and inaccessible native timber.[1] The introduced flora and fauna naturally included many types which became bancs instead of blessings, while the exotics also included many insects, weeds, and pests. The grey rabbit adapted itself and increased to millions, and through the mountains and forests ranged 100,000 or more red deer and 50,000 wild goats, with grave erosive effects. The Australian wallaby and opossum became pests as did the ferret, stoat, and weasel which were introduced to control the rabbit. Sparrows, once sold to the nostalgic settlers at 20s. a pair, starlings, and other imported aliens developed as destructive birds.[2]

The insect invaders were particularly interesting and important, not least to their unfortunate native counterparts which had to adapt themselves to an increase in pasture and pasture-type country from 13 to 30·5 million acres, together with a vast reduction in forests and a widespread draining of swamps. The number of species of exotic insects is not known with any certainty, but David Miller stated in 1957 that there were over 300 exotic types, mainly European or Australian, the latter largely attacking Australian exotic trees.[3] Unfortunately, there is no room to discuss in this work the many fascinating aspects of the invasions such as the introduction of cattle and sheep, of pasture and plants, and of trees, such as the Northern Hemisphere larch. Similarly, it is impossible to examine the problems created by weeds, pests, and

[1] C. M. Smith in F. R. Callaghan, op. cit., p. 123, and A. H. Clark in H. Belshaw, New Zealand, ch. 2, p. 44.
[2] E. G. Turbott, 'Native and Introduced Birds', in F. R. Callaghan, op. cit., p. 99. Turbott quotes G. M. Thomson, op. cit., 1922.
[3] D. Miller in F. R. Callaghan, op. cit., p. 72.

diseases, e.g. the question of the virus which has threatened to exterminate the *Phormium* (native flax), or the scale insect, which the farmers are now using deliberately to destroy the native tea tree, the manuka.[1]

In the fourth and final period set out by Wodzicki—that is from 1907 on—the New Zealanders could see the practical results of the invasions. First, as J. D. Hooker had foretold in very early times, the advent of the Westerners with their 'usurping tendencies' had destroyed many small local genera. Nevertheless, far more indigenous life had survived than the early settlers anticipated. Secondly, while the New Zealanders realized that their economic prosperity lay with the exotic flora and fauna, and that much of their economic future depended upon the extension of these exotic animals and plants, they realized that far more selectivity and indeed quarantine were essential to avoid mistakes such as those made by their forefathers in the days of the acclimatization societies. This realization resulted in legislation, such as the Acts of 1907 and 1921–2, protecting indigenous species of fauna and controlling more closely the entry of exotics.[2] Nevertheless, even as late as the 1950's the country still faced innumerable problems owing to Western destruction of the balance of life. The islanders, for example, had succeeded in controlling the rabbits by treating them as vermin, but the rabbits had controlled the exotic sweet briar, which promptly took its turn as a widespreading pest.[3]

I have dealt in detail with New Zealand for the reasons previously mentioned, particularly the small size of the country, the dramatic transformation during its brief history, and the splendid basic work of botanists and zoologists such as G. M. Thomson and K. A. Wodzicki. If one had several lives it would be a fascinating task to examine on similar lines the entry of exotic life into regions such as the United States, Canada, and Alaska (where there is a great wealth of wild life material), Latin America, and the Pacific Islands, but such a review would require a team of expert scientists.

[1] C. M. Smith in F. R. Callaghan, op. cit., for the destruction of New Zealand flax (*Phormium tenax*), pp. 126–8; for destruction of manuka or tea tree (*Leptospermum scoparium*), pp. 128–30.

[2] Wodzicki, op. cit., pp. 8–10.

[3] Personal communication by Professor G. Jobberns, Christchurch, N.Z.

Nevertheless, the broad outlines of the invasions and their results are clear. By no means the least important of these is the growing scientific knowledge of the people of the settler regions of the Pacific, their appreciation of the beauty and value of their own indigenous flora and fauna, and their realization that they themselves are now fundamentally Pacific peoples, with decreasing affinities with their relatives in Europe.

After I had written this chapter T. G. B. Osborn kindly gave me his brief but valuable paper on the 'Effect of Introduction of Exotic Plants and Animals into Australia'. He makes the important point that for the great number of plant and animal species along the Pacific coast, the discovery of that region by Captain Cook in 1770 was a tragedy of the first magnitude. Not only did the invading peoples destroy the indigenous flora and fauna for their settlements, and introduce exotics both domestic and pests, but they disturbed the biota in an important manner which has received little emphasis, namely, by permitting native species of subordinate importance to become prominent as did the *Bursaria spinosa* pest shrub, and the Tasmanian underground grass grub.[1]

Even more recently Dr. M. M. Cole, a leading authority on tropical vegetation, drew my attention to further aspects of the invasion of Australia by exotics. She noted the effects of the destruction of brigalow and mallee, and of burning, and the spread of black spear grass. Also of importance were the introduction to Queensland of tropical pasture grasses and the work of the South Johnson Experimental Station, and the Tropical Division of the C.S.I.R.O.

[1] T. G. B. Osborn, 'Effect of Introduction of Exotic Plants and Animals into Australia', *Pan-Pacific Conference*, Canada, 1933, vi, 8, pp. 809-10.

[Since this book has been with the publishers my attention has been drawn to Charles S. Elton, *The Ecology of Invasions by Animals and Plants*, London, 1958, 1960. This is a valuable work, containing references to important biological changes in the Pacific and its continents.]

VIII

GEOPOLITICS AND SECURITY IN THE PACIFIC

A THESIS on the historical geography of the Pacific territories should not close without a brief reference to those grave problems of geopolitics and security which evolved with and from the Western invasions, although it is impossible to probe deeply into any of their many aspects.[1] We have seen that in the lightly populated lands of suitable climate the invasions created great new nations, such as the United States, Brazil, and Australia. In lands of dense population, often with unsuitable tropical climates, such as India and Indonesia, the whites solidified a variety of peoples and comparatively small and unstable political units into large groups. In the majority of cases Western peace and law together with technological science as applied to production, transport, and health, increased population at a fantastic rate, a phenomenon that also occurred in the unconquered lands such as China, which gradually accepted certain aspects of Western culture, particularly medical and technological science. These new or revolutionized political groups for the most part developed Western nationalism so strongly that the Pacific world produced contending nation states, even greater in size than those which had previously evolved in Europe.

These developments did not alter the importance of the Northern Hemisphere which maintained its superiority as the seat of the most important human civilizations, but the chief centres of

[1] It is difficult to make an adequate selection from the masses of official documents, institutional reports, and private research theses which are pouring from the United Nations and other sources on problems of political geography, both current and in the immediate past. The brief sketch in this chapter is based mainly upon United States official documents, on publications sponsored by the American and Australian Institutes of Pacific Relations, and on the report of the Convention on International Relations held in Christchurch, New Zealand, in 1955.

power changed their geographical positions, as they now lay farther north than Greece, Rome, and other historic leaders, and in cases such as Russia and the United States, adjoined or were fairly near a comparatively small Arctic Ocean, which was navigable by aircraft above and by atomic submarines below its ice.[1]

In the Southern Hemisphere the new Western peoples evolved important states in South America, Australasia, and South Africa. Yet, although in cases such as Australia, Argentina, and Brazil these nations surpassed, or seemed likely to surpass, their European progenitors in size and resources, they had not developed into the immense power groups which dominated the Northern Hemisphere under the leadership of two 'Heartlands', the United States in north-eastern America and Soviet Russia in Siberia and eastern Europe.

For several generations far-sighted geographers and historians had been noting the dangerous growth of these vast conglomerations. Halford Mackinder (1861–1947) began to glimpse new global concepts about the beginning of the century. He realized that the world was now a closed system in which power on land and in the air had become mobile to a degree undreamed of in the Victorian age of sea power. By evaluating the conception and possible clash of sea and land power Mackinder concluded that the 'pivot region of the world's politics' would lie in the regions that he named the 'Heartland' and 'World Island' of Eurasia. In 1904 he said: 'The century will not be old before all Asia is covered with railways. The spaces within the Russian Empire and Mongolia are so vast, and their potentialities in population, wheat, cotton, fuel and metals so incalculably great, that it is inevitable that a vast economic world, more or less apart, will there develop inaccessible to oceanic commerce.' From this 'Heartland' in its central position Russia could exert, as Mackinder foresaw, great pressure

---

[1] For geographical changes in the importance of the Arctic, see *Survival in the Air Age*, Report by the President's Air Policy Commission, Washington, 1948, p. 11; Kimble and Good, *Geography of the Northlands*, ch. xiii; E. P. Hanson, *New Worlds Emerging*, chs. i–iv, xiii–xv; Weigert, Stefansson, and Harrison, *New Compass of the World*, chs. i, iv; J. C. Reed, 'The United States turns North', *Amer. Geog. Review*, July 1958, pp. 321–35.

westwards into Europe and southwards into the Near East and India.

By the close of the First World War in 1918, some of Mackinder's prophecies were being fulfilled and he could write: 'Who rules Eastern Europe commands the Heartland; who rules the Heartland commands the World-Island; who rules the World-Island commands the World.' Yet by 1944 and the Second World War Mackinder was revising and expanding his views to include in his fulcrum of world power western Europe and the western shores of the Atlantic. This North American, British, French, and Russian bloc contained 1,000 million people, for the most part Western, and neatly balanced the 1,000 million in the monsoon lands of India and China. Containing as it did the vast majority of the Western peoples and industrial centres, this bloc could probably have dominated the earth had it not split into democratic and communist spheres of influence centred respectively on the two heartlands mentioned above—Mackinder's old heartland of Eurasian Russia and the new American heartland, the eastern United States to which eastern Canada could be added in certain respects.[1]

Strangely enough, while Mackinder was emphasizing the growth of the Russian heartland at the beginning of the twentieth century, a famous British historian, J. R. Seeley of Cambridge, was approaching nearer to the truth, although even he perceived that truth but dimly. Nevertheless, Seeley realized and stated as early as 1902 that Russia and the United States would be predominant forces in the future. 'How is it possible', he asked, 'to question Russia's power or her will to make distant conquests? Has she not conquered in the north the whole breadth of Asia, and in the centre has she not penetrated to Samarcand and Khokand? What Power ever equalled her in successful aggression?' He continued: 'Russia already presses somewhat heavily on Central Europe; what will she do when with her vast territory and population she equals Germany in intelligence and organization, when

[1] For a study of Halford Mackinder see *New Compass of the World*, chs. xi, xii, pp. 80–90; D. W. Meinig, 'Heartland and Rimland in Eurasian History', *Western Political Quarterly*, Sept. 1956, pp. 553–69, references p. 554. Meinig has also published an interesting paper 'Culture Blocs and Political Blocs—Emergent Patterns in World Affairs', *Western Humanities Review*, Summer, 1956, pp. 203–22.

all her railways are made, her people educated, and her government settled on a solid basis?—and let us remember that if we allow her half a century to make so much progress, her population will at the end of that time be not eighty, but nearly one hundred and sixty millions.' Against Russia Seeley set the United States, which by the end of the century would have a population of some 80 million in a territory of 4 million square miles, and which had shown the ability 'to combine free institutions in the fullest degree with boundless expansion'. At a time which many people of his day would live to see, said Seeley, 'Russia and the United States will surpass in power the states now called great, as much as the great country-states of the sixteenth century surpassed Florence'.[1] Thus, while Seeley may have failed to anticipate Mackinder's conception of a heartland, he certainly saw as early as 1902 that Russia and the United States were becoming the two nations of outstanding strength.

There is no need in this treatise to examine in detail the tragic situation which now exists. If the Western nations were working in harmony they could achieve endless good for mankind, but they are as divided as their predecessors of the early invasion days, and they have divided the majority of important races ideologically, and to some extent geographically, into democratic and communist camps under conditions which, in the opinion of Lord (Bertrand) Russell and other leaders of thought, as noted above, may quite possibly put an end to the human race.[2] The evolution of this crisis has been in no small measure due to the application of Western technological science and, in particular, atomic energy to preparations for war.

As we have seen in this book, the early stages of the Western invasions were made possible by the invention of the European sailing ship equipped with the Arab lateen sail and the Chinese compass and gunpowder. Sea power, or sail power, dominated the early stages of colonialism, e.g. the English defeat of the

---

[1] J. R. Seeley, *The Expansion of England*, London, 1902, pp. 290–1, 300–1.

[2] Statement by Lord Russell, Professor Albert Einstein, and others, Appendix II of *International Relations*, the Report of the Christchurch Convention on International Relations, Christchurch, N.Z., 1955, p. 108.

Spanish Armada in 1588 enabled England to begin the founding of British America in 1607 in the teeth of the might of Spain.[1]

For more than three centuries after the Armada, British industry and sea power increased so greatly that the little islands played a predominant part in world affairs throughout the later years of sail and during the whole period of steam. Until the Second World War of 1939–45, particularly in the days of the three- and two-power naval standards, when Britannia really ruled the waves, the British peoples, secure behind their navies, could endure what Sir Keith Hancock has termed 'the long haul'—the period of travail during which an unprepared sea democracy conducted the long haul of economic, military, and political effort, until the initial inferiority of British strength had become a crushing superiority of allied power against which the land enemies at long last met their Waterloo.[2] This phenomenon of 'the long haul' was characteristic of the years of struggle against Napoleon and of the World Wars of 1914–18 and 1939–45. In the First World War— the Kaiser's War—British sea power held Germany and her allies at bay until the United States with her immense resources assured an allied victory on land. In the Second World War—Hitler's War—English-speaking sea power just succeeded in holding back the Germans and Japanese until the democracies had built up sufficient strength to invade Europe and, with the aid of Russia, to crush Hitler.

By this time, however, many new factors were emerging. First, air power was becoming more important than sea power, and battles such as Coral Sea and Midway were decided in the main by aircraft based on ships as mobile airports. Again, although Hitler's armies could at the outset no more invade sea-girt England than could those of the Kaiser or Napoleon, the British naval defence might ultimately have faced almost insoluble problems had it not been for the victory gained by British airmen in the famous Battle of Britain. Finally, while American sea power played a vital part in the reconquest of the north-west Pacific, it was

---

[1] Sir Norman Angel, 'Speaking of Colonialism', *E.S.U.*, May 1957, p. 21.
[2] Sir Keith Hancock, 'War in this Century', Address to A.N.Z.A.A.S., *Adelaide Advertiser*, 23 Aug. 1958.

American aircraft which carried to Hiroshima and Nagasaki the atomic bombs that caused the immediate surrender of Japan.

By 1948 an Air Policy Commission, appointed by the President of the United States, declared that the defence of America must be based on air power.[1]

There was a time [stated the report] when the United States could tolerate with safety a world in which war was the final way of settling disputes among nations. For even if war came the United States could be reasonably sure not only of winning it, but even of keeping enemy forces away from its shores. Our geographical position, our Navy, our industrial capacity, our manpower, and the armies, navies and air forces of the nations allied or associated with us, protected us against direct attack in the two World Wars through which we have just passed. But with the recent revolution in applied science for destruction which is still going on, these safeguards are no longer enough. Our national security must be redefined in relation to the facts of modern war. Our security includes, as always, winning any war we may get into; but now it includes more than that. It includes not losing the first campaign of the war. . . . It includes not having our cities destroyed and our population decimated in the process of our winning the first campaign.[2]

In this statement the American Commission was simply voicing truths which had become increasingly obvious during the preceding years. First, from the viewpoint of communications and transport, the world had decreased in size to an unbelievable extent. Countries, long separated by the Arctic, Atlantic, and Pacific oceans, were now in instantaneous touch by wireless, and were but a few hours apart for the transport of people and goods by aeroplanes. In such circumstances only remote and unimportant peoples could hope to remain in happy seclusion, while even the United States faced the permanent abandonment of the historic Washingtonian policy of isolation. The report of the Air Policy Commission showed that the Americans realized some very hard facts which cut right across their historic policies and beliefs. The United States had become part of Mackinder's 'closed world system'. They were no longer isolated, no longer safe from attack,

---

[1] *Survival in the Air Age*, pp. 8–10.   [2] Ibid., p. 4.

and no longer sure of winning a war if the enemy staged an initial and devastating onslaught.

Evidence before the commission indicated the possibility that within five years from 1947 Russia would be mass-producing guided missiles with a range of 5,000 miles and the capacity to hit 'sizeable targets' such as cities, although the rate of interception might be high. In these circumstances the commission named 1 January 1953 as A-day—the target date when the United States' air arm must be ready to meet an atomic attack.[1] Nor were air power and atomic weapons the only dangers. The President's commission believed that biological weapons were being studied in all parts of the world. Such weapons could be used from the air or distributed by enemy agents. They were a potential threat, not only in times of war, but in times of peace.[2]

During the decade which followed this report, the danger from aircraft and atomic weapons greatly increased. The age-long struggle between the means of attack and defence—the spear and the shield, the arrow and armour, the gun and steel plating—took one of its frequent turns in favour of the offensive weapons, but in a form so vast and terrible that it is difficult for the mind to grasp the consequences of entirely ruthless warfare. Atomic weapons of several kinds could effect the complete annihilation of every form of life over extensive areas. Submarines could lay atomic mines, aircraft drop atomic bombs and guided missiles cross oceans to create devastating explosions, which would, in addition, produce deadly rain or dust. In these circumstances the best experts were unanimous in saying that 'a war with H. bombs might quite possibly put an end to the human race'.[3]

A leading authority, Air Marshal Sir Basil Embry, summed up this new and terrifying position in an article on 'Australia's Role in Global Air Strategy', contributed to the *Adelaide Advertiser* on 17 and 18 September 1957. He wrote that the new offensive weapons not only had an incredible range and strength but were, for the moment, 'well in the lead of defensive measures'. In the field of bombing alone one 5-megaton thermo-nuclear bomb

[1] *Survival in the Air Age*, pp. 18–19.   [2] Ibid., pp. 14–15.
[3] Note 2, p. 205 above, Christchurch Convention, pp. 107–10.

could release twice as much energy as the half-million block-buster bombs dropped in the last war. In other words, one aircraft on a single mission could carry more high explosive than 250,000 bombers in 1945. Furthermore, the advent of long-range rockets had changed the whole philosophy of air defence. It was essential for a modern defensive system to destroy the enemy's offensive weapons before they could do extensive damage, but although progress had been made, this was still impossible.

Lord Russell spoke equally emphatically when he stated that a bomb could now be manufactured 2,500 times more powerful than that which destroyed Hiroshima, and that the radio-active particles released in a war conducted with such bombs could condemn mankind to a death by slow torture and disintegration.[1]

Applying these gloomy facts to the geopolitical situation, particularly in regard to the Pacific, one could in 1958 deduce the following propositions as possibly correct. First, as noted above, the Western peoples of the two heartlands could almost certainly control the world by the ruthless use of atomic weapons, and this despite the claims of the Chinese communists that their agricultural civilization was so widely dispersed that it could not be destroyed by atomic attacks. The truth was that no one knew in 1958 how long any military or civilian population could tolerate a nuclear bombardment, and whether or not the survivors would continue to resist or become distraught, lynch their leaders, and make unconditional surrender. Secondly, it appeared that on the new map of the world, the Russian heartland and its satellites (if China could be termed a satellite) not only controlled Mackinder's 'World Island', but had an inside position and a vast territory connected by land communications, facts which aided the communist policy of a sequence of outbreaks, or threats of outbreaks, in various directions. Thirdly, it was possible, but by no means certain, that the communists' control of an immense and seemingly united land block might have helped them to disperse their industrial cities and areas, and at the same time establish the means of transporting materials more safely by land than was possible by sea. Fourthly, any 'all out' struggle between the democratic and

[1] Ibid.

communist groups was likely to be decided in the Northern Hemisphere. South America was strategically too remote to be of vital importance to the contestants, and although Australia was useful as a base from which the Americans could first halt and then attack the Japanese in the Second World War, and might be a future target of further Asian aggression, British-Australia was probably too remote and too small in population and industry to play a vital part in an atomic conflict, although the Australians and New Zealanders had shown on several occasions their readiness to do their utmost in the cause of freedom. Nevertheless, world wars had in the past continued far longer than was anticipated, and if mankind proved capable of enduring nuclear warfare or was sufficiently fearful to confine a struggle to the older types of weapons, as was the case in Korea and Indo-China, some of the resources of the Southern Hemisphere might well prove of use.

Another important point was the increasing significance of the North Pacific. It is true that the vital industrial areas of the Russian and North American heartlands were situated nearer to the Atlantic than the Pacific, and that the shortest air or rocket routes between the rival heartlands lay across Greenland, which meant that the chief emphasis had to rest on the North Atlantic and the Arctic.[1] Nevertheless, the North Pacific was of great importance for several reasons. First, it provided both outer and inner zones of North American defence. These included the long arc from Alaska and the Aleutian Islands through Japan and Formosa, with their adjoining islands, to the Philippines, while behind this arc lay island groups such as Hawaii, Guam, and American Samoa. Secondly, as America had good grounds for placing no faith whatever in the communists, whose avowed policy was continuous aggression, she was leading the free world in defence of the non-communist rim-lands—Japan, South Korea, Vietnam, and the others, which lay along the borders of communist Asia. The American policy and the practical help afforded to these countries was set out in official publications such as the Reports to Congress

[1] For analyses of air developments and air routes: E. G. R. Taylor, *Geography of an Air Age*, O.U.P., 1945; K. R. Sealy, *The Geography of Air Transport*.

on the Mutual Security programme.[1] Weigert and his co-authors discussed in *New Compass of the World* the advantages and dangers of the United States securing and holding remote strategic bases. Another difficulty lay in the fact that most member states of the United Nations were prepared to assist in the defence of various parts of the free world to the extent, and only to the extent, to which they were vitally interested in the particular region concerned.[2]

It should be noted that during the later years of our period, differences of race and colour seem to have had little effect on the alliances which Western powers, whether democratic or communist, contracted with Asian peoples, or on the aid, either warlike or peaceful, which the West gave to the East. There was no longer indignation, such as that which was aroused in Europe by the alliance of Francis I of France with 'the unspeakable Turk', who later became the welcome ally of several groups of Western powers and who in 1958 was providing an essential base for American defence against any Russian advance upon the Middle East. Thus the Pacific of 1958 saw the Russians in alliance with the Chinese whom they had expelled from Siberia in direct contradiction to communist principles, and the Americans co-operating with the Japanese in spite of the bombing of Nagasaki and Hiroshima. Indeed, the American rehabilitation of Japan, as a bulwark against Russian and Chinese communism in Asia, was extremely disturbing to the Australians, who naturally feared the restoration of the Japanese forces and industries which the former aggressor might put to war purposes.[3]

Nevertheless, mistrust based on race and colour was not infrequently close to the surface. It was evident, for example, in works

[1] Report to Congress on the Mutual Security Programme, Washington, June 1954, and Committee of Congress on Foreign Affairs, *The Strategy and Tactics of World Communism*, Washington, 1948–9.

[2] *New Compass of the World*, Chapter IV above.

[3] N. Harper, 'Australia and the United States', in Greenwood and Harper, *Australia in World Affairs, 1950–1955*, ch. v, pp. 167–8, and *Australian Policies toward Asia*, Institute of Pacific Relations Conference, 1954, Australian Institute of International Affairs, Melbourne. Various authors; note particularly Part IV, W. Macmahon Ball and H. A. Wolfsohn—'Australia's Relations with Japan since 1945'.

such as Chandrasekhar's *Hungry People and Empty Lands* which was mentioned in Chapter VI, and in the Bandung Conference of 1955, which was attended by twenty-nine non-Western nations from Africa and Asia. This interesting conference passed resolutions which vigorously attacked the remnants of Western colonialism, including the Dutch action in continuing their philanthropic work in western New Guinea, sought with more justification the extension of cultural co-operation between Asia and Africa, and urged the adoption of a more liberal attitude by the South African whites towards their native Africans and towards the peoples from India and Pakistan who were resident in the Union.[1] Amongst the participants in this conference were India and other Asian countries, some independent and some part of the British Commonwealth. The position was rather a strange one, for these countries were accepting Western help under arrangements such as the Colombo Plan and yet were strongly criticizing the Western powers which retained colonial possessions to assist the indigenous inhabitants. The Asian neutral bloc was of considerable strength, and in the opinion of various authorities its attitude to the advance of communism might prove of fundamental importance. An outstanding problem was that these peoples needed extensive capital assistance from the Western powers to alleviate their extreme poverty.

Many public bodies and private scholars had tried to analyse the relative strength of the democratic and communist groups, although, as indicated above, the results of an atomic war were likely to depend more upon an initial and annihilating attack than on reserves of strength. Amongst private researchers O. H. K. Spate, a leading authority on the geography of India, published in 1954 'The Pacific: Some Strategic Considerations'. This careful examination of Pacific geography, geographical patterns, arsenals, manpower, and mineral resources, together with its conclusions, was sound at the time, particularly as the author recognized even in 1954 that if an initial blow was 'devastating enough to be decisive, no more need be said; air distances would be almost the only logistic fact to count and the Pacific might indeed be devalued

[1] *International Relations*, Appendix I, pp. 101–6, n. 2; p. 205 above.

in favour of the Arctic. If, however, the opposing powers were able to adopt offensive and defensive counter measures, the Pacific might become important with Australia playing a part.'[1]

In 1955 the United States Government published a very important study prepared for the Joint Committee on the Economic Report by the Legislative Reference Service of the Library of Congress.[2] This paper recorded that the then economic capacity of western Europe, the United States, and Canada was significantly greater in therms of absolute magnitude, diversity, and flexibility than the combined strength of the Soviet bloc. The surveyors stated that in the period 1938–53 the United States increased its production twice as rapidly as did the Soviet Union and that an examination of the various factors of production (growth of labour input, agriculture, housing, &c.) in the United States and in the Soviet Union gave strong grounds for expecting that the absolute gap in the size of the two economies would widen over the next two decades. The national production of the United States had been growing at about three times the rate of that of independent western Europe, which was in danger of falling behind owing to certain 'bottle-necks'. Nevertheless, western Europe was in a better position than eastern captive Europe, which had been drained by the Soviets and had lost much of its trade with its neighbours to the west. The study concluded that the West has tremendous economic strength, whereas the Soviet bloc through propaganda and unfulfillable promises, has been hiding its economic weakness. Three matters were, however, of the utmost importance by 1958. First, it was becoming clear that the democracies would have to consider not only the vast manpower but the growing industrial development of China and other Asian countries in making any estimate of relative strength. Second, it was essential that the democratic countries intensified their efforts to train adequate numbers of scientists, engineers, and technicians, and to keep raising the general level of education if they were to compete with

[1] O. H. K. Spate, 'The Pacific: Some Strategic Considerations', in *Australia*, Commonwealth Relations Conference, 1954, Australian Institute of International Affairs, Melbourne, Part V.

[2] *Trends in Economic Growth*—A comparison of the Western powers and the Soviet bloc, Washington, 1955, particularly summary and conclusions, pp. 1–5.

the communists. Thirdly, the democracies had to recognize that economic strength did not ensure political and military security against a weaker economy, if that economy was prepared and organized for war. Once again we reach Hancock's conclusion that in the days of nuclear weapons the democracies can no longer rely on the policy of 'the long haul', but must be fully prepared to thwart and indeed to anticipate atomic attacks.[1]

[1] M. L. E. Oliphant gives a striking summary of the present situation in 'Science and the Survival of Civilization', Presidential Address, A.N.Z.A.A.S. 1958, *The Australian Journal of Science*, Sydney, Nov. 1958, pp. 8–16.

SUMMARY AND CONCLUSION

THE RESULTS OF THE INVASIONS
THE SETTLER AREAS — SOME RACIAL ASPECTS

I CONCLUDE by summarizing very briefly the results of the Western invasions as set out in this book. In the environments which offered fertile lands, suitable climates, adequate resources, and comparatively sparse indigenous populations, the whites built up new nations, a number of which soon became greater than their metropolitan parents. Some of these peoples came almost wholly from European stocks. Some were a mixture of European exotics with the indigenous inhabitants. Some were composed of Europeans, indigenous peoples, and races such as Negroes, Chinese, Japanese, and Asian Indians whom the whites brought to or moved within the Pacific. We have seen that these new nations, of various types, number at least 300 million persons of exotic blood.[1]

Up to 1958 anthropologists had made little examination of the races which were evolving, for their interests lay more with the indigenous folk. It appears that the young Western peoples were firmly entrenched in the Americas, but less firmly established in Siberia and British Australasia to the north and south of the vast agglomerations of Asian peoples which the whites themselves had done so much to organize and increase. For this reason the survival of the white Siberian and white Australian policies was a matter of considerable interest.

It should be added that the main factor in the decimation, or even occasionally the complete destruction, of the indigenous peoples of the settler regions was their lack of immunity to Western diseases. In many cases the outstanding killers in the pioneer days were the eruptive fevers such as smallpox, and the social diseases, with tuberculosis taking the lead at a later date.[2]

[1] p. 68 above. [2] Chapter VI above.

Culture

If we turn from the racial to the cultural aspects of the invasions in the settler areas, we find that the changes were equally sweeping. We can adopt for our purpose Clark Wissler's broad definition of culture as the way of life of this or that people, namely, all that is inherited or transmitted through society, which, as Ellsworth Huntington explains, would include every object, habit, idea, institution, and mode of thought or action which man produces or creates and then passes on to others, especially in the next generation.[1] Thus, in spite of the fact that their diseases were the main cause of the destruction of the indigenous peoples, the Westerners developed medical and sanitary cultures, which in the settler regions immensely increased the length of life. They introduced and developed a very large number of economic animals and plants which, unfortunately, were only too often accompanied by weeds and pests. On so vast a scale were these introductions made that the exotics not merely created moving frontiers of plant and animal life, but in many regions completely changed the landscapes.[2] While the incomers adopted some cultural practices of the indigenous peoples, they, in general, transported their traditional forms of government, laws, ideology, and scientific and other knowledge. Most of the new peoples, other than those in communist Siberia, adopted some form of Christianity. Most of them established democracies which assured their citizens of freedom and self-government. Most of them used every public and private means to develop those technological practices which were productive of higher living standards and increased wealth. Taking their contributions as a whole, the Western peoples, including the younger nations, fundamentally changed the distribution and status of mankind on earth. Authoritative examinations of this process will be found in works such as *Man's Role in Changing the Face of the Earth*, in which, for example,

[1] Clark Wissler, *Man and Culture*, 1923, p. 1, quoted by H. G. Duncan in *Race and Population Problems*, London, 1929, ch. viii, pp. 139–40; E. Huntington, *Mainsprings of Civilization*, New York, 1945, pp. 7–8.
[2] Chapter VII above and Carl O. Sauer, 'The Agency of Man on the Earth', in W. L. Thomas, op. cit., pp. 62–64.

F. S. C. Northrop discusses human progress from a non-techno-logical to a technological civilization, and the effect of the change on man's aesthetic, ethical, and legal values.[1]

Unfortunately, the Western peoples, who possessed immense potentialities for benefiting all mankind, remained as divided as they were in the days of the invasions, and even more dangerously, for the outstanding rivals—the leading democratic and com-munist powers—had, in the opinion of certain leaders of thought, gained a scientific knowledge 'which might quite possibly put an end to the human race'.[2]

The sojourner areas—race

In the regions of sojourner colonization the Western peoples faced physical difficulties such as unsuitable climates, or large indigenous populations. Nevertheless, under the inspiration of 'Gospel, glory, gold', the whites conquered at one time or another all the peoples of the Pacific regions with the exception of those in parts of China and Thailand. From the racial aspect, however, the effects of these conquests were comparatively slight. In some places the conquering males created only small groups of mixed peoples such as the Eurasians of Indonesia, the 'Outcasts of Colonialism'.[3] Yet these small groups were infinitesimal in com-parison with the immense populations of China, Japan, or South-east Asia.

In the face of grave environmental difficulties the period of Western domination was brief. The Japanese successes in the Second World War, even though of a temporary nature, destroyed the last remaining illusions of white superiority, and, when the defeated Japanese left their ideology and weapons behind them, the Western retreats from the conquered territories were both general and swift. Indeed, for the good of some of the conquered peoples, certain retirements were probably too pre-cipitate.[4]

[1] F. S. C. Northrop in W. L. Thomas, op. cit., pp. 1052–67. See also E. Ayres and C. A. Scarlott, *Energy Sources of the World*.
[2] p. 205 above.   [3] Paul W. van de Veur, op. cit.
[4] p. 112 above.

Culture

Very different to this rapid rise and fall of Western political supremacy was the story of culture, if we accept the wide definition of culture mentioned above. Western government, law, and peace moulded many scattered and frequently warring groups of Asians into comparatively large nation states, in which Western techniques of production, transport, and, above all, medicine and sanitation created an immense population growth. The American Geographical Society in 1960 published a very brief but authoritative survey of Chinese agriculture, which contained the information that the population of China was advancing at the rate of about 20 million people a year, 'the equivalent of a new United States in less than a decade'. The study claimed that this 'staggering increase in numbers' was due to the large population to start with, its youthful composition, peace, and stability, the defeat of famine by roads and railways, improved health and sanitation which had lowered the death-rate, and State responsibility for children which removed the economic checks that frequently curtail the size of families.[1] This statement simply carries farther the thesis propounded in earlier chapters that since the Western invasions the growth of Asian population has been stupendous and unless it is controlled it may prove calamitous both to the Asians and to the rest of mankind.

Although little work has been done on the subject, the Western introduction of plants, animals, insects, and pests to the sojourner areas was important. Particularly in the plantations Western innovations transformed landscapes and changed economic life. Very valuable, too, was the introduction of Western languages, law, and education, to take only a few of many examples. K. M. Panikkar writes that the first, and perhaps the most abiding, Western influence in Asia was in the field of law, for the legal systems of many Asian countries were fundamentally changed according to the post-revolutionary conceptions of nineteenth-century Europe. The imposing and truly magnificent legal struc-

[1] Alice Taylor, ed., Chao Kwo Chün, and others, 'China's Agriculture', *Focus*, American Geographical Society, New York, Apr. 1960, with references.

ture, under which the millions of India, Pakistan, and Burma lived, changed the basis of society in a manner which few people realized. Japan, too, voluntarily brought in a modern system of law which has been in operation for over half a century.[1] India and Indonesia defined the legal position of women, granted them equal citizenship with men, and gave them the vote under general adult franchise. In the words of Hurustiati Subandrio: 'Asian women have been granted prerogatives which have only been acquired by their sisters of the West after a prolonged and bitter struggle.'[2] When one finds Asian scholars expressing such sentiments one feels that the popular opinion may have gone rather too far in its complete condemnation of 'colonialism', particularly before the succeeding systems have shown that they are as unselfish, honest, and efficient as were those of a number of Western peoples at the close of their trusteeship.

This book has not attempted the immense task of examining from the geographical aspect the advance of Western culture in the sojourner lands, particularly as some aspects of the problem were outlined briefly in the second annual address given to the Australian Humanities Research Council in Canberra in 1958 and published by the Council in 1959.[3] In that address I drew especial attention to two features of Western culture in the Asian borderlands of the Pacific—Christianity and technological science. Although Christianity had succeeded in many settler regions and the Christian Church had done some splendid work, for example in its efforts to protect the Indians of Spanish America, this religion had been far less successful in Asia where many people regarded it as the faith of the Western conquerors—repulsively foreign, repulsively occidental, repulsively white.[4] Yet Asian churchmen such as Rajah B. Manikam believed that if Western Christians assisted without trying to dominate, Asian Christianity would make progress, particularly if its adherents adapted it to Asian

[1] K. M. Panikkar, *Asia and Western Dominance*, pp. 497–8.
[2] H. Subandrio, 'The Changing Social Position of Women in the East', in S. Hofstra, ed., *Eastern and Western World*, The Hague, 1953.
[3] Grenfell Price, 'Western Influences in the Pacific and its Continents'.
[4] M. T. Price, *Christian Missions and Oriental Civilizations—A Study in Culture Contact*, Shanghai, 1924, pp. 107–16.

needs as Mao-Tse-tung adapted communism in the early stages of its growth. This may seem optimistic as after centuries of missionary endeavour the Christians of East and South-east Asia numbered only 28 million Roman Catholics and 13 million Protestants— some 3 per cent. of a population of 1,200 million. In contrast the United States contained in 1954 some 90 million Christians in a population of 160 million people—about 56 per cent.[1]

Far more spectacular than the centuries-long battle of the Christian missions to gain Asian converts was the rapid growth of technological science, first in the hands of the Japanese, whom the West completely underestimated, and then, in very recent years, in the hands of the Chinese communists. By 1958 it was abundantly clear that the white peoples would have to rid themselves of the illusion that many Asians despised modern science and would make slow technological progress.[2]

Information from communist China through sources such as the American Consulate in Hong Kong, pictured immense progress in the production of food, fertilizers, iron and cement, textile and other manufactured goods, together with the successful construction of additional railways to link the Chinese with the Russian communists.[3]

Such progress was alarming to the Western democracies because communist successes and the raising of living standards would obviously induce more Asian countries to enter the communist fold. The fundamental point, however, was that despite the political retreat of the Westerners, certain features of their culture seemed likely to spread even more widely and deeply in Asia, and this in the long run might prove to be the most important results of the Western invasions in the sojourner areas.[4]

[1] Rajah B. Manikam, *Christianity and the Asian Revolution*, Madras, 1954, p. 1. For Christianity in Asia see also Panikkar, op. cit., pp. 375–457, and K. S. Latourette, *A History of Christian Missions in China*, London, 1929. For the number of Christians in the United States, see *World Almanac*, New York, 1955, pp. 703–4.
[2] For this view see L. Abegg, *The Mind of East Asia*, London, 1952, pp. 5–6.
[3] *Weekly Survey of the China Mainland Press*, American Consulate, Hong Kong.
[4] For the development of Chinese communism see K. S. Latourette, *A History of Modern China*, London, 1954; C. P. Fitzgerald, *Revolution in China*, and the authorities listed in *Focus*.

Defining culture in a somewhat narrow sense, Macaulay wrote in 1833 that 'the imperishable empire of our arts and our morals, our literature and our laws' was 'exempt from all natural causes of decay'.[1] More than a century later another British authority, C. E. Carrington, could state that the empires of British expansion were the empires of conquest, settlement, trade, finance, language, and ideas, and that of these the empires of settlement and ideas would prove the most enduring.[2] Writing in 1953 Victor Purcell emphasized similar opinions in comments on South-east Asia when he stated: 'In an ideological sense Europe is by no means withdrawing. Its institutions, its legacies of education and above all its technology will continue to exert an influence, and will ever be reinforced from the West.'[3]

These words ring true. Although the Western nations have retreated, or will retreat, from practically all their Asian and Pacific island conquests, where in general they have produced little white and coloured mixture, the frontiers of their exotic animals, plants, ideologies, and institutions are likely to move forward and promote even further those improvements in the cultural landscape, which together with the changes that the Westerners wrought in their settlement areas are the greatest mankind has seen. It is as yet too soon to estimate the permanent effects of these Western advances, but it is not too soon to assert that far too much emphasis is being laid on certain evil aspects of the process and far too little on the splendid results that many of the white invaders achieved.

[1] Quoted by C. E. Carrington in *The British Overseas*, C.U.P., 1950, ch. 21, p. 1032.
[2] Ibid., pp. 1020–36. An excellent historical narrative of British colonialism in advance and retreat.
[3] Victor Purcell, *The Colonial Period in S.E. Asia*, New York, 1953, p. 65.

NOTES

INTRODUCTION

NOTE A. F. J. Turner's famous thesis on the moving frontier in the United States is set out in *The Frontier in American History*, New York, 1921. W. K. Hancock outlines his views in *Australia*, London, 1930; *Survey of British Commonwealth Affairs*, Oxford, 1940, vol. ii, Part I, pp. 4 seq., and *Argument of Empire*, London, 1943. F. Alexander discusses certain aspects of the question in Presidential Address, Section E, History, A.N.Z.A.A.S., vol. xxv, Adelaide Meeting 1946, as does R. O. Buchanan in 'Some Aspects of Settlement in the Overseas Dominions', *Advancement of Science*, Sept. 1952. I outlined the plan of this book in Presidential Address, Section P, Geography, A.N.Z.A.A.S., Dunedin Meeting 1957, published in *Australian Journal of Science*, vol. xix, no. 5a, May 1957, and in 'Western Influences in the Pacific and its Continents' in *Annual Report of the Australian Humanities Research Council*, Adelaide, 1959.

CHAPTER I

NOTE B. Peter Buck, *Vikings of the Sunrise*, New York, 1938. Interesting research has been published on the origin of the peoples of the central Pacific islands, some of whom are believed by Thor Heyerdahl to have come from America, whereas most anthropologists insist that they came from Asia. Heyerdahl's views, which are supported by his *Kon-tiki* voyage and by his archaeological research on Easter Island, were set out in *American Indians in the Pacific, The Theory behind the Kon-tiki Expedition*, London, 1952, and *Aku-Aku, The Secret of Easter Island*, London, 1958. References to the criticisms of Heyerdahl by R. Heine-Geldern and others were set out by M. W. Smith in *Geog. Journal*, London, Dec. 1953, p. 476. In this article M. W. Smith reviewed *American Indians in the Pacific*. She reviewed *Aku-Aku* on the whole favourably in *Geog. Journal*, Sept. 1958. A. Sharp, *Ancient Voyagers in the Pacific*, Polynesian Society, Wellington, N.Z., 1956, and London, 1957, published excellent summaries of the evidence, but his main object was to show that lengthy prehistoric voyages were accidental drifts. Much weight has been placed on the distribution of plants, e.g. E. D. Merrill, *The Botany of Cook's Voyages*, Chronica Botanica, Waltham, Mass., 1954; J. B. Hutchinson, R. A. Silow, and S. G. Stephens, *Evolution of the Gossypium*, O.U.P., 1942, and S. G. Stephens, 'Cytogenetics of Gossypium', *Advances in Genetics*, New York, 1947, vol. i, pp. 431–42. Less emphasis has been placed on the distribution of animals, which seems unfortunate, as the pig, which was probably Asian, reached the Hawaiian, Society, and other islands, and the dog reached New Zealand and other groups. Thus A. Sparrman, a Swedish scientist, who was with Cook on the second voyage, wrote in *A Voyage round the World*, London, 1953 ed., p. 61: 'The Otaheitan hogs are similar to those found in China, having long backs and pendent bellies.' A recent valuable analysis of the problem was made by Gilbert Archey, Director of the Auckland Museum, 'Maori and Polynesian' in F. R. Callaghan, ed., *Science in New Zealand*, Wellington, 1957, pp. 55–69. On the whole it seems likely that man has voyaged on the Pacific from remote times and that he has drifted with winds and currents both east and west.

CHAPTER III
NOTE C. There is a substantial bibliography covering the Spanish voyages in the Pacific, which have been frequently described in texts such as G. A. Wood's charmingly written *Discovery of Australia*, London, 1922, or J. C. Beaglehole's *The Explorations of the Pacific*, London, 1947, and his very fine introduction to *The Voyage of the Endeavour*, Hakluyt and C.U.P., 1955. Special research works on the subject include: W. L. Schurz, *The Manila Galleon*, New York, 1939; W. Borah, *Early Colonial Trade and Navigation between Mexico and Peru*, University of California Press, 1954; R. A. Rydell, *Cape Horn to the Pacific— The Rise and Decline of an Ocean Highway*, University of California Press, 1952; P. W. Powell, *Soldiers, Indians and Silver*, University of California Press, 1952, the story of the Spaniards' difficulties in advancing north from Mexico 1550–1600.

NOTE D. ENGLISH-SPEAKING AMERICA: R. H. Brown, op. cit.; Russell Smith and Phillips, op. cit.; W. D. Wyman and C. B. Kroeber, 'The Frontier in Perspective', Part II, *The American Frontier*, University of Wisconsin Press, 1957; H. N. Smith, *Virgin Land*, Harvard University Press, 1950; R. B. Vance, *Human Geography of the South*, University of N. Carolina Press, 1932, chs. iii, iv; F. R. Dulles, *America in the Pacific*, with bibliographical notes, Riverside Press, Cambridge, 1938; W. F. McCaleb, *The Conquest of the West*, New York, 1947.

LATIN AMERICA: P. E. James, *Latin America*, London, 1942, sections on the currents of penetration and settlement, with maps, pp. 15 and 589; S. de Madariaga, *The Rise of the Spanish-American Empire*, New York, 1947, with bibliographical notes.

AUSTRALIA: S. H. Roberts, *History of Australian Land Settlement*, Macmillan and Melbourne University Press, 1924 (ch. 3 is good on the importance of the crossing of the Blue Mountains); A. L. G. Shaw, *The Story of Australia*, London, 1955; A. Grenfell Price, *Australia Comes of Age*, Melbourne, 1945, pp. 141–54 for references and bibliographies.

NEW ZEALAND: H. Belshaw, *New Zealand*, University of California Press, 1947.

SIBERIA: R. J. Kerner, *The Urge to the Sea*, University of California Press, 1946, pp. 66–88 for the eastward expansion of Russia, with maps. Walter Kolarz notes, however, in his *Peoples of the Soviet Far East*, London, 1954, pp. 12–13, that Russian colonization did not enter a really active stage until the completion in 1900 of the trans-Siberian railway which reduced the crossing to the Siberian far east to thirty days.

CHAPTER IV

NOTE E. For the Australian tropics see *H.P.N.T.*, *W.S.T.*, chs. vi, viii, *W.S.N.P.* chs. vi, vii; P. Hasluck, *The Progress of the Australian Territories*, Dept. of Territories, Canberra, 1957; Macpherson, 'Environmental Problems in Tropical Australia' reviewed in *South Pacific*, Sydney, Jan–Feb. 1957; E. C. Chapman, 'Pioneer Settlement in the Darwin Hinterland', *The Australian Geographer*, Sydney, 1958. The Australian Academy of Science Symposium on *Man and Animals in the Tropics*, University of Queensland, 1956, published 1957, is important for the discussion of many problems both in Australia and New Guinea. The participants in the symposium examined tropical climatology, human and animal adjustments, and lack of town planning and air-conditioning, and, above all, the situation in regard to health. The conference asked for the establishment of tropical research institutes in both northern Australia and New Guinea, for the chief problems differed, not least in the fact that in northern Australia they chiefly concerned a growing population of 300,000 whites, while in Australian and Netherlands New Guinea they were the key to the welfare of 3 million natives. The importance of health was shown by the claim that malaria had made the New Guinea native 'indolent, ill-healthy and ill-nourished'. 'Control malaria . . . and in seventeen years you will double the population.' See review by the author, *Geog. Review*, July 1959, pp. 446–7.

CHAPTER V (B)

NOTE F. FOR THE PACIFIC ISLANDS IN GENERAL: Taylor, *A Pacific Bibliography*; F. M. Keesing, *The South Seas in the Modern World*, London, 1942; D. L. Oliver, *The Pacific Islands*, Harvard, 1951; O. W. Freeman, ed., *Geography of the Pacific*, New York, 1951.

FOR THE PEOPLES AND HISTORY: F. M. Keesing, *Native Peoples of the Pacific World*, New York, 1947; Buck, *Vikings of the Sunrise*; A. Sharp, *Ancient Voyagers in the Pacific*; L. A. Mander, *Some Dependent Peoples of the South Pacific*, New York, 1954; N. McArthur, *Population of the Pacific Islands*, Aust. Nat. Univ., Canberra—see Chapter VI, p. 158, n. 1 of this book.

PACIFIC RELATIONS: G. Greenwood, *Early American-Australian Relations*, Melbourne, 1944; J. M. Ward, *British Policy in the South Pacific, 1786–1893*, Sydney, 1948; Greenwood and Harper, eds., *Australia in World Affairs 1950–55*.

REGIONAL: POLYNESIA (INCLUDING HAWAII): J. C. Furnas, *Anatomy of Paradise*, London, 1950; S. D. Porteus, *Calabashes and Kings*, London, 1954; H. Conroy, *The Japanese Frontier in Hawaii, 1868–1898*, University of California Press, 1953; W. A. Du Puy, *Hawaii and its Race Problem*, Washington, 1932, ch. v. *W.S.T.* sets out in Chapter XII, nn. 44, 45, 46, the publications of S. D. Porteus, M. E. Babcock, L. C. Dunn, K. O. Moe, H. L. Shapiro, A. W. Lind, R. C. Adams, and E. E. Muntz, on the peoples, race mixtures, and anthropological problems of Hawaii, Pitcairn and Norfolk islands. The *1950 U.S. Population Census of Hawaii* has detailed statistics which are useful. The classic work on race mixture in Hawaii is H. L. Shapiro, *Race Mixture in Hawaii*, New

York, 1931. I called on Dr. Shapiro in 1955 and ascertained that he had a great deal more material, but no leisure to publish it.

MELANESIA (INCLUDING FIJI): W. E. H. Stanner, *The South Seas in Transition*, New Guinea, Fiji, Western (N.Z.) Samoa, Sydney, 1953; C. S. Belshaw, *Changing Melanesia*, O.U.P., 1954, with bibliography; R. A. Derrick, *History of Fiji*, Suva, 1946; McArthur, op. cit., Part VI for statistics.

EAST (AUSTRALIAN) NEW GUINEA: Taylor, *A Pacific Bibliography*, pp. 367–70 for culture contacts; A.C.A., pp. 92–96 and 148 for references; McArthur, op. cit., Part VII—*Papua and New Guinea, Pacific Islands Year Book*, Sydney, 1944; D. C. Gordon, *The Australian Frontier in New Guinea 1870–1885*, New York, 1951; L. P. Mair, *Australia in New Guinea*, London, 1948; Greenwood and Harper, *Australia in World Affairs*. The Australian Government holds important reports, and there are a number of authoritative articles in journals, e.g. O. H. K. Spate, 'Changing Agriculture in New Guinea', *Geog. Review*, Apr. 1953.

WEST NEW GUINEA (NETHERLANDS): See Note G, below, and H. G. Verhoeff, *A Bird's Eye View of Netherlands New Guinea*, The Hague, 1958; McArthur, op. cit., Part VIII—*Netherlands New Guinea*; Greenwood and Harper, op. cit., pp. 202–5 and section ix by J. Andrews, particularly pp. 338–40. The Australian Official Publication *Current Notes* contains much information, e.g. Mar. 1957, statement by Sir Percy Spender to the U.N. General Assembly, 25 Feb. 1957. The Indonesians are distributing considerable propaganda literature in Australia.

NOTE G. Material is difficult to obtain on western (Netherlands) New Guinea. For Dutch accounts see report on 'The Netherlands New Guinea' to the United Nations for the year 1954, Ministry of Overseas Territories, The Hague. This is a long document setting out in detail the work and planning in progress. See Shakels, *Netherlands New Guinea*, various articles; Verhoeff, *A Bird's Eye View of Netherlands New Guinea*; *Antiquity and Survival*, New Guinea, no. 5, 1956. A number of South Pacific Commission technical papers deal with western New Guinea, e.g. no. 80, R. H. Black on malaria quoted in the text; no. 81, R. H. Black, *Malaria in the S.W. Pacific*; no. 56, N. R. Sloan, *Leprosy in Netherlands New Guinea*. For Indonesian propaganda see *West New Guinea and Australia's Future*, Indonesian Embassy, Canberra, 1954; *News and Views*, Indonesia, Indonesian Embassy, Canberra—frequent articles on the western New Guinea problem. For political accounts see Greenwood and Harper, *Australia in World Affairs*, particularly pp. 202–5 and 256–62 for contrast between the Australian and Indian attitudes to the New Guinea question. See also *Hand Book of Netherlands New Guinea*, Rotterdam, 1958.

CHAPTER VI

NOTE H. Jacques M. May, *Atlas of the Distribution of Disease*, Amer. Geog. Society, New York. For the commencement and objectives of this great work, see R. J. Light, 'Progress of Medical Geography' and 'Proposed Atlas of Disease',

Geog. Review, New York, Oct. 1944; J. M. May, 'Medical Geography—Its Methods and Objectives', ibid., New York, Jan. 1950; E. Rodenwaldt, *World Atlas of Epidemic Disease*, Part I, Hamburg, 1952. At that time Rodenwaldt had not published a volume dealing with the Pacific, but his Part I gives important information on elephantiasis, typhoid, para-typhoid, cholera, dysentery, and leprosy, in parts of that area which is noted in this chapter under the headings of 'Filaria' and 'Yaws'. The most famous general work is A. Hirsch, *Handbook of Geographical and Historical Pathology*, translated by C. Creighton, London, 1883–6, 3 vols. These remarkable volumes deal with the chief diseases from the historical and geographical viewpoints, using thousands of examples over a vast range of time and space. In spite of the growth of medical knowledge, Hirsch's work is not wholly superseded.

On the Americas one notes: Ashburn, op. cit.; H. R. Carter, *Yellow Fever*, Baltimore, 1931. Part II of this classic gives much information on the diseases which have been confused with yellow fever.

For Australia and Pacific War Zones, 1939–45: A. S. Walker, *Clinical Problems of War*, Canberra, 1952.

For results of some of the many Rockefeller Health Campaigns: Balfour, Evans, Notestein, and Taeuber, *Public Health and Demography in the Far East*; G. C. Shattuck and others, *A Medical Survey of the Republic of Guatemala*, Carnegie, Washington, 1938; S. M. Lambert, *A Yankee Doctor in Paradise*, Boston, 1946. The Technical Papers of the South Pacific Commission, Noumea, New Caledonia, when written by medical scientists such as R. H. Black, often contain important information on historical and geographical medicine.

NOTE I. J. B. Cleland considered this problem in a series of articles covering Australian aboriginal diseases, *Journal of Tropical Medicine*, Mar.–Dec. 1928, particularly 15 Mar. 1928. More recently he referred to it again in the Archibald Watson Memorial Lecture, *Medical Journal of Australia*, 29 Apr. 1950. In Cleland's opinion the Malay trepang fishers brought smallpox to Australia just before the arrival of the first fleet in 1788. The disease travelled gradually, passing from tribe to tribe until it reached Sydney in 1789. Dr. Mair of the 39th Regiment, who reported on a second outbreak in 1830, referred to this attack, as did Collins, who reported on the tragic state of 'the wretched natives of the country'. The second outbreak seems to have appeared in Wellington Valley in 1830 when Mair went out and made a report from which a medical scientist, Dr. George Bennett, fortunately made extracts, as the original disappeared. The disease killed many natives, devastating some tribes. It also attacked a few Europeans. Soon after the epidemic Major Mitchell found pock-marked natives and decimated tribes on the River Darling. Sturt reported a great diminution of aboriginal numbers between his journeys down the Murray in 1829–30 and 1838 (A. Grenfell Price, *Founders and Pioneers of South Australia*, Adelaide, 1928, p. 45). White observers saw pitted aboriginals as far west as Adelaide in 1839, and in 1853 P. Snodgrass of St. Kilda, Victoria, wrote that the natives had been much more numerous when the whites reached the Goulbourn district, but had suffered severely from smallpox of which many still bore the marks (*Letters from Victorian Pioneers*, Melbourne Public Library, 1898, pp. 208–9).

CHAPTER VII

NOTE J. G. P. Marsh, *The Earth as Modified by Human Action*, a new edition of *Man and Nature* (1864); A. I. Woeikof, 'De l'influence de l'homme sur la terre', *Annales de géographie*, 1901, vol. x, pp. 97–114, 193–215. Other references to this aspect of the subject are in W. L. Thomas and other editors, *Man's Role in Changing the Face of the Earth*. Amongst the mass of literature on destruction and conservation of natural resources are: J. de Castro, *Geography of Hunger*, London, 1952; L. D. Stamp, *Land for Tomorrow*, Indiana University Press, 1952; Fairfield Osborn, *Our Plundered Planet*, London, 1947; E. Ayres and C. A. Scarlott, *Energy Sources—The Wealth of the World*, New York, 1952; Food and Agriculture Organization of the United Nations, reports mentioned below. There does not seem to be a very large bibliography on the actual invasions of the Pacific and its continents by flora and fauna, although considering the small size of New Zealand and its comparatively recent settlement, its biologists, as previously noted, have published some valuable research. The following works have been used in this section: E. Anderson, *Plants, Man and Life*, for America; E. D. Merrill, *The Botany of Cook's Voyages*, particularly for the Pacific islands; id., *Plant Life in the Pacific World*, Washington, 1945; V. W. von Hagen, *South America, The Green World of the Naturalists*, New York, 1948; E. V. Wulff, *An Introduction to Historical Plant Geography*, Chronica Botanica, Waltham, Mass., 1943; Thomas, op., cit. Part II, section on 'Modifications of Biotic Communities', pp. 677–804. This contains seven important contributions, but attention is drawn particularly to E. Anderson, 'Man as a Maker of New Plants and New Plant Communities', pp. 763–77, and Marston Bates, 'Man as an Agent in the Spread of Organisms', pp. 788–804. All seven contributions have select bibliographies. *The Australian Environment*, C.S.I.R.O., Melbourne, 1950; J. G. Wood, *The Vegetation of South Australia*, Adelaide, 1937; D. C. Swan, MS. (p. 196, n. 1 above); G. H. Thomson, *The Naturalization of Animals and Plants in N.Z.*, C.U.P., 1922; A. H. Clark, *The Invasion of N.Z. by People, Plants and Animals*, Rutgers University Press, New Brunswick, 1949–50; K. A. Wodzicki, *Introduced Mammals of N.Z.*, Wellington, 1950; F. R. Callaghan, ed., *Science in N.Z.*, Wellington, 1957.

INDEX

Acadia, 77.

Adelaide, 194.

Africa, 4, 6, 22–23, 30–31, 55, 99, 185–7, 193–5, 203, 212; diseases in, 149, 155–6, 158, 163–70.

Ainus, 12.

Alaska, 3, 123, 171, 200, 210; Russian interest in, 80–83; U.S. administration, 83–88.

Alaska Highway, 78, 86.

Alberta, 77–78.

Aleutian Islands, 81, 210.

Aleuts, 65, 82.

Allen, H. H., 197.

Allison, R. S., 152.

Amazon, 17, 157.

Ameda tree, 154.

Amur (river and province), 88–89, 103.

Amurstal, 91.

Anderson, Edgar, 59–60, 183–4, 192.

Angkor Wat, 16.

Anson, George, 154.

Antarctic, 7, 28, 40, 203.

Arabs, 2, 16, 31, 35, 157, 172, 205.

Arctic, 7, 25, 56, 76, 78, 207, 213.

Araucanians, 19.

Argentine, 55, 62–63, 68, 73, 94, 196, 203.

Ashburn, P. M., 145, 147, 157, 159, 161–2, 166.

Asia: physical and human geography, 7–9, 29–31, 51, 58–59, 78, 87, 92, 158, 165, 169–70, 184, 186, 190, 193–4, 212; migrations and invasions, 1, 2, 20, 161, 170; history and civilizations of, 13–17; population problems, 48, 68, 97–98, 100, 102, 114–18, 204; aggressiveness of, 3–4, 57, 124, 135, 138, 142, 210–13, 218; Western influence in, 3–4, 36, 45–48, 54–58, 103–14, 118–20, 151, 172–3, 203, 218–20.

Astoria, 157.

Attlee, Clement, 142.

Australasia, 2, 5, 30, 41, 56, 58, 62, 68, 94, 105, 126, 132, 193, 203, 215.

Australia, 7, 52, 54, 56, 111, 123, 145, 208, 210, 211, 213; physical geography, 8–9; prehistory, 10–12, 16; discovery and early history, 31, 41, 51, 60–61, 95, 187; aboriginals, 21–22, 65–67, 121, 126, 156, 158, population, 67–69, 76, 94, 97–98, 117, 175; migration policy (White Australia), 96, 98–100, 102, 115; tropical northern—, 3, 30, 69, 78–79, 100–2, 124, 167; and New Guinea, 125, 133–42, 168; flora and fauna, 177, 179–80, 184, 189, 191, 193–7, 201.

Australoid peoples, 6 n., 11–12, 19, 94.

Ayamaras, 19.

Ayres, E., 182.

Aztecs, 18–19, 51, 143.

Backer, C. A., 190.

Baldwin, E. R., 162.

Balfour, M. C., 145.

Ball, MacMahon, 44.

Bancroft, 165.

Banks, Sir Joseph, 172, 185.

Baranov, Alexander, 81–82.

Barkley, 97.

Barrineans, 11.

Batavia, 104, 167, 172.

Bates, Marston, 47, 188–9.

Bay of Islands, 160–1.

Beaglehole, J. C., 28.

Belshaw, H., 96–97.

Bering Straits, 11, 81, 91.

Bering, V., 81.

Berkeley Research School, 64.

Birdsell, J. B., 11, 12.

Birobidzhan, 91, 93.

Birth control, 102, 118.

Black, J. M., 193–4.

Black, Robert H., 140, 145, 167.

'Blackbirding', 98, 121, 130.

Blagoveshchensk, 88.
Blaxland, G., 61.
Bligh, Captain, 129.
Blue Mountains, 61.
Boethuk Indians, 77, 94, 177.
Bolivia, 18.
Borah, W., 64.
Borneo, 97, 102, 117, 139.
Borobudur, 16.
Borrie, W. D., 101.
Brazil, 55, 62–63, 68, 73, 97, 123, 155–7, 169, 187–8, 196, 202–3.
Britain, 7, 39, 56, 60, 81–82, 121, 124, 150, 160, 165, 187, 221; early exploration and settlements, 24, 28–30, 108; and sea power, 32, 34, 36–37, 44, 54, 123, 205–6; and India, 45, 105–6, 109, 111–12; and American Indians, 74, 77, 156; and Australia, 53, 95–97, 99–100, 134; and Canada, 79–80; and China, 109–10; and Fiji, 127, 130, 132; and Malaya, 46; and Burma, 57, 142; and New Zealand, 95, 121, 179.
British Columbia, 7, 77–78, 86, 94.
Buck, Sir Peter, 13, 185.
Burke, Robert O'Hara, 61.
Burma, 4, 7, 15, 55, 57, 68, 105, 109, 112, 116, 142, 219.
Burnet, F. M., 165.
Buttfield, Senator, 138, 139.

Cabot, J. and S., 26, 177.
California, 7, 20, 42, 59, 64, 81, 82, 94, 192.
Cambodia, 15–16.
Campbell, E. M. J., 131.
Canada, 39, 52, 54, 62, 85, 86, 183, 200, 204, 213; population of, 67–68, 75–76, 78, 97; and the Indians. 66, 74, 76–77, 94, 121, 146–7, 156; French Canada, 79–80.
Carpentarians, 11.
Carrington, C. E., 221.
Carter, H. R., 145, 149, 163, 166–7.
Cartier, Jacques, 154.
Casey, R. G., 111.
Castiglioni, Arturo, 151, 172.

Caucasian, 12, 125, 128, 129.
Celebes, 12.
Central America, 20–21, 50, 66, 70–71, 145, 164.
Ceylon, 68, 103, 112, 114, 133.
Chandrasekhar, S., 68, 107, 114–16, 132, 173, 212.
Chibchas, 18.
Chile, 18–19, 68, 70, 72, 82, 121, 124, 178, 180.
Chilkoot Pass, 85.
China, 4, 10, 13, 15–16, 21, 26, 49, 60, 98, 102, 104, 106, 149–50, 172–3, 178, 190, 205, 213, 217, 220; and the Pacific, 12, 14, 48, 72, 113, 125, 127–9; and the West, 31, 38, 46, 50–51, 57, 107, 109–11, 189, 202; and Russia, 81–82, 89, 92–94, 119, 211; population, 14, 22, 48, 74, 103, 115–16, 202, 204, 218; communism in, 119–20, 209.
Christmas Island, 188.
Cieza, Pedro de, de León, 143.
Cinchón, Countess d'El, 168.
Cinchóna, 168,
Clark, A. H., 181, 197, 199.
Cleland, J. B., 156.
Clowes, Laird, 33, 35.
Cole, J. P., 92.
Cole, Dr. M. M., 201.
Colombia, 18, 68, 122.
Colombo Plan, 111, 117, 138, 212.
Colongulae, Lake, 11.
Colonialism, 4, 54–55, 104–6, 111–13, 119–20, 122, 133, 137, 141, 212.
Columbia, British, 7, 86.
Columbus, 26, 27, 35, 38, 41–43, 147, 155, 161, 177.
Communism, 4, 55, 104, 106, 111, 117, 119–20, 209–10, 212–14.
Compass, 2, 32, 38–40.
Constaninople, 4, 25.
Cook, Dr. C. E. A., 170.
Cook, James, 34, 39–41, 121, 148, 154–6, 162, 171–2, 178, 185, 187, 191, 198, 201.
Cook, S. F., 21, 64, 70–71.
Cook Islands, 124, 170.

INDEX 231

Cortez, Hernando, 143, 166.
Coral Sea (battle), 206.
Costa Rica, 146, 152.
Cressey, G. B., 115, 189.
Crone, G. R., 38–40.
Cuba, 165.
Cuitlahua, 143.
Cumberland Gap, 61.
Czaplicka, M. A., 64.

'Dalstroy' state enterprise, 90.
Darwin, 15.
Darwin, Charles, 19.
Davenport, Dean, 180.
Dawson Creek, 86.
De Castro, J., 114, 182.
Deficiency diseases, 152–5, 170.
Diaz, Bartholomew, 27, 41.
Dohi, Keizo, 161.
Drew, John, 159–60, 163.
Dyea, 85.

Easter Island, 13, 124.
Ecuador, 18, 178.
Ellet, G. G., 144.
Ellice Island, 164.
Elton, Charles S., 201 n.
Embry, Sir Basil, 208.
Eskimos, 12, 20, 76–78, 84, 163.
Eyre, E. J., 61.
Eyre, Lake, 41.

Fairbanks, 78, 86–87.
Fairchild, W. B., 182.
Fernald, M. L., 192.
Fiji, 12, 99, 117, 121, 125, 133, 135, 191; population problem, 127, 129–32; diseases in, 157–9, 164.
Filariasis, 140, 148, 163–7.
Filipino, see Philippines.
Finnie, Richard, 78.
Fitzgerald, C. P., 15, 106, 119, 120, 124.
Forster, G. and J. R., 185.
Forsyth, W. D., 98, 99.
France, 24, 28, 30, 36, 60, 142, 170, 204; in Canada, 39, 74, 77, 79–80, 154, 177; in Pacific, 7, 45, 108, 112, 121–4, 127, 134, 190; and China, 109–10.
Furnival, J. S., 142.

Gale, Dr. Fay, 67.
Gama, Vasco da, 27, 103, 153, 187.
Gentilli, 97.
Germany, 122–4, 134, 204, 206.
Gilbert Island, 164.
Gill, E. D., 10.
Glavsevmorput, 91.
Gokstad ship, 32.
Golder, F. A., 64.
Gorgas, W. G., 167–8.
Great Australian Divide, 61.
Great Bear Lake, 78.
Green, C., 39.
Greenland, 32, 123, 210.
Gregory, A. C., 61.
Gressitt, J. L., 49, 191.
Gruening, Ernest, 80, 85.
Guam, 59, 122–3, 132, 188, 190, 210.
Guatemala, 155.

Hagendorp, G. K. Van, 112.
Haiti, 43.
Hancock, Sir Keith, 206, 214.
Hanson, Earl P., 88.
Harrison Church, R. J., 43, 44.
Harrison, John, 40.
Hasluck, Paul, 95, 135–7, 158.
Havana, 167.
Hawaii, 13, 49, 59, 121, 126, 156, 164, 191, 210; and the U.S., 122, 124–5; and Russia, 8, 81–82; population, 127–9.
Hawkins, Richard, 154.
Heaton, H., 22, 25, 27, 29, 107.
Henze, Dr., 134.
Heyerdahl, T., 13, 185–6.
Hirsch, A., 145, 155, 156, 157 and n. 1, 158, 167, 169.
Holdsworth, M., 64–65, 93.
Holland, 7, 24, 58, 60, 97, 100, 212; early development, 28–30, 108, 121, 187; in New Guinea, 133–4, 139–42, 212; in Java, 47, 117, 173, 190; achievements in Pacific, 45–46, 57, 109–10, 112, 124–5, 145, 148.
Honduras, 157.
Hooker, J. D., 200.
Hookworm, 126, 148, 154.

Horn, Cape, 56, 69, 186.
Hourani, G. F., 31, 34, 35.
Houtman, Cornelius, 29.
Hrdlicka, Ales, 162.
Huayna Capac, 143.
Hudson Bay, 76–77, 157; — Company, 77, 82.
Humboldt, von, 176.
Hunter, Governor, 187.
Huntington, Ellsworth, 216.

Igarka, 92.
Incas, 18, 19, 21, 51, 72.
India, 12, 16, 23, 25, 55, 60, 66, 107, 132, 141, 149, 155–6, 186, 194, 204, 212; Western contacts, 3, 4, 45–46, 103, 202, 218–19; and Britain, 105–6, 111; population, 68, 100, 115, 118, (Eurasian) 72; Indian emigration, 48, 113, 117, 135, (in Fiji) 127, 131–2.
Indians, American, 6 n., 12, 34, 51, 65, 134, 138, 177, 179, 181, 185, 192, 219; civilization of, 17–21; population, 22, 66–70, 72, 74, 78, 125–6; and disease, 76–77, 143–4, 146–9, 156–7, 162.
Indo-China, 7, 15, 16, 18, 55, 109, 142, 210.
Indonesia, 3, 8, 11–12, 15, 55, 105, 173, 190, 202, 217, 219; and the Dutch, 7, 46, 49, 72, 112, 141; population of, 100, 103, 116–17; and West New Guinea, 133, 139, 142.
Influenza, 155.
Iroquois, 20, 156.

Japan, 12, 15–16, 51, 107, 110, 122, 219–20; and Europe, 4, 31, 46, 49, 60, 103, 105, 112, 189; and the U.S., 109, 111, 123–4, 183, 210–11; military power of, 38, 78, 113, 124 n., 135, 142, 168, 206–7, 217; population, 8, 22, 47, 68, 100, 103, 118, 173–4, (in Hawaii) 125, 127–9.
Jaramillo-Arango, J., 164.
Java, 10, 15, 16, 18, 22, 47, 117, 139, 141, 168, 173, 190.
Jenner, Edward, 150–1.

Jenness, Diamond, 74–77.
Jepson, W. C., 192.
Jones, W. H. S., 144.
Juneau, 84.

Kamchatka, 64, 81, 156.
Kamehameha, King, 82.
Kanakas, 98, 101.
Kazakhstan, 92.
Keesing, F. M., 12, 13, 126 n. 1, 149 n. 1.
Keller, A. G., 43–44, 107.
Kellogg, C. E., 182.
Kerner, R. J., 64, 89.
Khabarovsk, 88, 91–93.
Khetagurova, G. Valentina, 88, 90.
King, Governor, 179.
Klawak, 84.
Klondike, 77, 85.
Kodiak Island, 80, 81, 171.
Kolarz, W., 63–65, 89–93.
Komsomolsk, 90, 91, 93.
Korea, 15, 16, 31, 68, 91, 93, 111, 116, 128, 149, 210.
Krieger, A. D., 10–11.
Kroeber, A. L., 6, 11–13, 20.
Kurangara cult, 67.
Kuzbas, 92.

Lambert, S. M., 126–7, 145, 148, 160, 167.
Lancaster, James, 154.
Lapage, G., 165.
Latin America, 18, 30, 58, 60, 62–63, 73, 132, 164–5, 170, 178, 180, 186–7, 192, 210; Indian populations of, 21, 66, 68, 70, 121; and Spain, 50–52, 54–56, 59, 64, 69, 71, 219.
Latourette, K. S., 15, 111–12, 119.
Lawson, W., 61.
Leeper, G. W., 181.
Legaspi, Miguel Lopez de, 59.
Leprosy, 49, 67, 126, 140, 148, 150, 169–70, 172.
Leroy-Beaulieu, P., 44.
Lind, Dr. James, 154.
Lindsay, Lord, 120.
Lippmann, Walter, 122–3.
Longitude, Board of, 39–40.

McArthur, Norma, 130, 132–3, 157–8.
Mackenzie, river, 77–78.
Mackinder, Halford, 203–5, 207, 209.
MacLaurin, Charles, 143–4.
Madariaga, Salvador de, 24, 69.
Madeira, 26.
Madura, 47, 173.
Maegraith, B. G., 149–50.
Mapellar, F., 41, 121, 153.
Majaphit Empire, 16.
Malacca, 29, 107.
Malaria, 126, 140, 144–7, 149–51, 163–5, 167–9, 172, 182.
Malaya, 12, 15, 16, 46, 55, 109, 112, 116, 156, 167–8, 190.
Mananuska, 86.
Mander, L. A., 130–2.
Manikam, Rajah, 106–7, 219.
Manila, 108, 153, 188.
Manitoba, 78.
Maoris, 65, 125–6, 138, 146, 179, 198; population of, 22, 66, 94–95; susceptibility to Western diseases, 148–9, 152, 155, 157–8, 160–3, 171–2.
Markham, Commander, 130.
Marquesas Islands, 164.
Marsh, G. P., 1, 10, 176–7.
Martin, S. M. D., 155, 161, 163, 171.
Maskelyne, Nevil, 40.
Mauritius, 157.
Maury, M. F., 41, 58.
May, Jacques M., 145, 149, 151, 165–6.
Maya Indians, 18.
Measles, 49, 126, 130, 144, 147–8, 155, 157–8, 171.
Meigs, P., 64, 74.
Meiji Restoration, 47, 174.
Melanesia, 6, 11–12, 22, 125, 127, 133, 159–60.
Mendana, Alvaro de, 187.
Merrill, E. D., 13, 49, 60, 133, 183–5, 188, 190, 192.
Mexico, 18, 51, 59, 143, 187–8, 194; population, 21, 68, 70–73, 150; diseases in, 146, 153, 155, 157, 159, 162.
Micmacs, 77, 177.
Micronesia, 6, 12, 49, 122, 125, 127, 159, 191.

Midway Island, 123, (battle of) 206.
Miller, David, 199.
Milne Bay, 168.
Mao-Tse-tung, 220.
'Moa Hunter', 198.
Mongolia, 92–93, 203.
Mongoloid, 11–13, 15–17.
Montagnais Indians, 77.
Montezuma, 143.
Mook, H. J. Van, 112.
Mooney, J. H., 21, 74, 144, 146, 171.
Moore, R. M., 195.
Murray-Darling rivers, 156–7.
Murrayian-negroid people, 11–12.
Myrdal, Gunnar, 48, 142.

Nauru, 124.
Navarez, 143.
Negroes, 12, 48, 51, 71–72, 99, 128, 156, 166–7, 169, 215,
Nehru, 141.
Nerchinsk, treaty of, 89.
Nevins, Allan, 122.
New Britain, 124, 149.
New Caledonia, 121–2, 128, 134, 149, 159, 191.
New Guinea, 7, 9, 12, 16, 122, 125, 149, 159, 167, 181; (Australian) East —, 124, 133–9, 168; (Dutch) West —, 139–42, 145, 212.
New Hebrides, 42, 121, 122, 135, 159, 167, 187, 191.
New South Wales, 156, 179, 181, 187, 193, 195–6.
New Zealand, 9, 13, 56, 60, 62, 122, 126, 170, 192–3, 210; prehistory and early settlement, 16–17, 51, 121, 179, 198; advances in Pacific, 3, 7, 124, (Samoa) 125, 138; and Maoris, 21–22, 52, 66, 152, 171; population of, 67–68, 94–97; diseases, 155, 157–62, 164, 170; flora and fauna, 197–200; soil erosion, 180–1.
Newfoundland, 77, 80, 94, 177.
Newton, A. P., 42.
Nordenskiöld, A. E., 91.
Northrop, F. S. C., 217.
Nunn, G. E., 41.

Okazaki, A., 118.
Okhotsk, 81, 90.
Okun, S. B., 22, 63–65, 80, 83.
Oliver, D. L., 48, 126–8.
Orr, Sir J. B., 182.
Osborn, Fairfield, 180, 182.
Osborn, T. G. B., 201.
Ostiaks, 156.
Otapo, 158, 181.
Oviedo, 43, 157.

Papete, 179.
Pakistan, 212, 219.
Panama, 21, 47, 59, 146, 163, 167–8, 187; — Canal, 10, 60, 70, 122, 165, 168.
Pannikkar, K. M., 103–10, 114, 172–3, 218.
Papua, 121, 124, 133, 135.
Parry, J. H., 32–33, 35–36.
Parsons, J., 64, 128.
Patagonia, 19, 20, 123, 147.
Pearl, R., 75.
Pellagra, see Deficiency diseases.
Pelzer, K. J., 139.
Penrose, B., 35.
Perry, Commodore, 109.
Peru, 18, 51, 59, 70, 72, 143, 155, 168, 178, 185–7.
Petroff, Ivan, 81, 83, 171.
Phillip, Governor, 196.
Philippines, 109, 110, 149, 190; and the U.S., 7, 111, 122–3, 210; and Spain, 59, 103, 153, 188; population of, 8, 12, 22, 68, 116, 173–4; independence of, 54–55; Filipino population in Hawaii, 127–9.
Phillips, M. O., 87.
Pigafetta, Antonio, 26.
Pizarro, F., 143.
Polo, Marco, 25–26.
Polynesians, 6, 12–13, 22, 72, 125–7, 153, 159, 179, 184–5.
Portugal, 36, 38, 49, 54, 58, 60, 109, 127, 133, 148, 161, 177; early exploration, 24–30, 107–8, 187; shipbuilding, 33–35.
Prescott, Dr. James, 182.

Pribilof Islands, 83, 178, 183.
Price, Charles A., 69, 100.
Pueblo Indians, 19.
Puerto Ricans (in Hawaii), 127–8.
Purcell, Victor, 113, 221.

Quechua, 19.
Queensland, 47, 87, 98, 100–2, 124, 134, 146, 152, 165, 196, 201.
Quiros, Pedro Fernandey de, 42, 121, 187.

Radcliffe, F. N., 181.
Ramsden, E., 160.
Reed, author, 75, 167.
Rennell Island, 160.
Rio de Janeiro, 58, 187, 196.
Rio Grande, 21, 56, 69, 79, 146.
Rivers, W. H. R., 126.
Robequain, C., 44, 117, 190.
Rockefeller Report (1950), 22, 47, 106, 118, 145, 151–2, 173–5.
Rodenwaldt, Ernst, 145.
Roebourne district, 158.
Rose, Holland, 35.
Rosenblat, A., 21, 70–71.
Ross, Sir Ronald, 144.
Ross Colony, 81.
Russell, Lord Bertrand, 5, 205, 209.
Russell, R. J., 32.
Russia, 8, 25, 30, 56, 78, 88–93, 97, 103, 109, 110, 112, 119, 156, 171, 176, 178, 203–5, 208, 210, 211, 213, 220; treatment of indigenous peoples, 22, 64–65; population increase, 68, 74; and Alaska, 80–83, 171. See also Siberia.
Russian American Company, 63 n., 65, 81–83.

Saavedra, Alvaro de, 134.
St. Lawrence, 17, 39, 77.
Sakhalin Island, 88.
Samoa, 7, 122–5, 138, 164, 170, 210.
Samojeds, 156.
Sandwell, B. K., 75–76.
Santiago Agreement, 178.

Saskatchewan, 78.
Sauer, Carl O., 1, 6, 10, 11, 64, 182, 192.
Scarlott, C. A., 182.
Scheffer, Dr., 82.
Schurz, W. L., 24, 64, 69.
Scrofula, see Deficiency diseases.
Scurvy, see Deficiency diseases.
Sealy, K. R., 79.
Seeley, J. R., 204-5.
Sellards, Dr., 10.
Seward, 83, 84, 86.
Shailendras, 16.
Shapiro, H. L., 71.
Sharp, A., 13, 186.
Shattuck, G. C., 143-5, 147, 159, 166.
Shelikov, 81.
Shovel, Sir Cloudsley, 39.
Siam, 15.
Siberia, 3, 5, 7, 16, 30, 56, 62-63, 68, 78, 81-82, 87, 94, 105, 132, 156, 179, 215, 216; Russian colonization and development, 51, 82, 88-92, 189, 203;'White Siberian Policy', 93, 99, 115, 211; indigenous population of, 21-22, 64-66; population figures, 79, 89 n.
Sigaud, J. F. X., 157.
Silow, Dr. R. A., 186.
Simpson, L. B., 21, 64, 70-71.
Sitka, 82, 84.
Skagway, 85.
Sloan, N. R., 170.
Slonaker, J. R., 114.
Smallpox, 49, 76-77, 83, 126, 130, 143, 147-8, 150, 155-7, 170, 172.
Smith, C. M., 199.
Smith, J. Russell, 74-75, 87, 178, 180.
Society Islands, 122.
Solander, 172, 185.
Solomon Islands, 122, 149, 167, 187.
Sorong oil area, 140.
South America, see Latin America.
Southampton Island, 77.
South Pass, 61.
Spain, 22, 24, 27, 28, 30, 60, 81, 95, 122, 127, 143-4, 159, 166, 184, 187, 188, 190, 192, 206; and sea power, 25, 27,

32-35; and the Americas, 42, 50, 53-54, 56, 64, 69-72, 219; and the Pacific, 59, 108-9, 121, 134, 148.
Spate, O. H. K., 181, 212.
Spencer, J. E., 188, 190.
Spice Islands, 107, 134.
Spinden, H. J., 21.
Stamp, L. D., 72-73, 182.
Stanner, W. E. H., 131, 132, 138.
Steers, J. A., 72.
Stefansson, Vilhjalmur, 79, 88.
Stitt, E. R., 66.
Stoll, N. R., 165.
Stone, K. H., 83, 87.
Strehlow, T. G. H., 67.
Sturt, Charles, 157.
Subandrio, H., 219.
Sumatra, 15, 16, 102, 117, 139.
Sumner, B. H., 65.
Susitna valley, 86.
Swan, D. C., 195.
Syphilis, 144, 146-8, 159-62, 170-2.

Taeuber, I. E., 102, 118.
Tahiti, 7, 37, 122, 125, 128, 156, 160, 179, 185, 191.
Taiwan, 68, 114, 149, 173, 210.
Tanana valley, 86.
Tasman, Abel, 41, 121, 129.
Tasmania, 11, 12, 121, 177, 195, 201.
Tasmanoids, 6, 12, 66, 94.
Taylor, Griffith, 76, 97, 98.
Terra del Fuego, 19.
Thailand, 15, 50, 57, 109, 116, 217.
Thiel, Professor Van, 140.
Thompson, W. S., 68, 98, 175.
Thomson, Dr. A. S., 155, 157, 162.
Thomson, G. M., 197, 200.
Tlinkets, 82.
Toltecs, 18.
Tomari, 82.
Tonga, 122.
Torres Strait Islanders, 67, 167.
Toscanelli, 26.
Townsend, Meredith, 45.
Toynbee, A. J., 53.
Trans-Siberian Railway, 90, 92.
Trevelyan, G. M., 36.

Trewartha, G., 47, 115, 189.
Tuberculosis, 49, 77, 140, 162–3.
Tunguses, 156.
Turner, F. J., 1, 61.
Turner, George, 148.
Typhoid, 147–8, 171.
Typhus, 147–8, 155, 158–9.

Unalaska, 81, 171.
United Nations, 124, 137, 139, 140, 142, 180, 202, 211.
United States, 7, 17, 42, 53–56, 62–63, 65, 73, 78–79, 99, 152, 154, 166, 168–9, 180, 183, 192, 202; expansion in Pacific, 3, 8, 45, 109, 111, 119, 122–7, 174; prehistory, 10–11, 17; and the Indians, 19–22, 51–52, 66, 74, 144–8, 181, 192; population (increase), 67–69, 74–75; and Alaska, 80–88; and China, 110–11; and Japan, 112, 211; and Hawaii, 128–9; and geopolitics, 203–9, 210–11, 213.

Vance, R. B., 154.
Veniaminof, 83.
Verdoorn, Franz, 184.
Vespucci, Amerigo, 26.
Victoria, 181, 193, 195.
Vikings, 32, 153.
Vitu Levi Island, 130.
Vivaldi brothers, 26.

Vladivostok, 88–93.
Vlekke, B. H. M., 167.
Vogt, W., 182.

Wadham, S. M., 181.
Wake Island, 123.
Walker, A. S., 145, 149.
Walker, Sir Hovenden, 39.
Walker, R. L., 119–20.
Wallace, A. R., 176.
Wallace and Weber boundaries, 9, 133.
Wallis, Helen M., 37, 41.
Ward, the Hon, E. J., 135–6.
Weigert, H. W., 211.
White Pass, 85.
Wills, W., 61.
Wint, Guy, 105–6, 113, 117.
Wisconsin, 11.
Wissler, Clark, 74, 216.
Wodzicki, K. A., 197, 198, 200.
Woeikof, A. I., 176.
Women, status of, 106, 219.
Wood, J. G., 193–4.

Yakuts, 156.
Yellow fever, 163–5.
Yenisei River, 92.
Yukon, 83, 85.

Zinkin, Maurice, 102, 108–9, 111–14.
Zinsser, Hans, 159.